SCOTTISH COUNTRY LIFE

ALEXANDER FENTON

Country Life Section
National Museum of Antiquities of Scotland

JOHN DONALD PUBLISHERS LTD
EDINBURGH

The publisher acknowledges the
financial assistance of the Scottish
Arts Council in the publication
of this volume.

ISBN 0 85976 011 1

Printed and bound in Great Britain by
Morrison & Gibb Ltd., London and Edinburgh

Preface

To write a single book on Scottish Country Life is an impossible task, unless an extremely selective approach is adopted. Selection is influenced by subjectivity to some extent, though an effort has been made to let the material selected speak for itself, dictating its own patterns as far as possible. No attempt is made to expand on aspects of the subject that are dealt with in existing, easily accessible sources – the droving of cattle, for example, is well covered in J. R. B. Haldane's *Drove Roads of Scotland* – though these are included in the general Bibliography.

Though the emphases are on the preparation of the ground for crops, the harvesting and processing of cereals for food and fodder, the grazing of livestock and the uses of their products, everyday food, the housing of people and animals, and changes in the farming community, this is not a history of the agriculture of Scotland, but a study of some of the major aspects of the changing life of the countryside, especially in the eighteenth and nineteenth centuries when the face of the land as we now know it was being shaped. It is an exercise in the historical interpretation of the rural environment. Nevertheless it seemed reasonable to put an emphasis on agriculture, and on its regional variations and regional interaction, for agriculture remains one of the primary sources of the country's income, and the further back we go in time, the more important is agriculture, arable as well as pastoral, for the history of Scotland.

In presenting the material, apparently minor details may be given as much prominence as major items or events. The sickle for shearing grain crops, and its regional replacement by the scythe, has more to tell about the character and activities of the country population than the invention of Bell's reaper, though this has importance for world agriculture. A knowledge of Scottish country life amounting to accurate historical insight derives in the end not only from studying the broad patterns and trends that come through official statistics, not only from recording the lives and actions of men like Lord Kames or Sir John Sinclair, not only from plotting on a map the diffusion of James Small's plough or Andrew Meikle's threshing mill, but also from learning about the everyday activities in byre and barn, home and workshop, about small-scale equipment and its techniques of use, and about the unspectacular, indigenous changes that took place in these over a period of time in response to local conditions. This is what the book is primarily concerned with.

Such changes have been kept constantly in mind in two ways, firstly in relation to the kinds of regional variation that have given rise to the various types of farming in Scotland – dairying in the South-West, cropping in the East and South-East, stock rearing and feeding in the North-East and stock-rearing in the Highlands and Islands, with specialist types based on pigs, poultry, or horticulture near the industrial areas of the Forth and Clyde valleys, and fruit farms in Perthshire and Angus – and secondly, in relation to the ways in which the regions may interact. In particular, the Highland line is not taken to be a hard and fast boundary, and indeed influences from a South-East direction have been strong and pervasive, perhaps more so than can be easily realised, throughout the country.

A major incentive in writing this book has been the range of questions asked over the years by the public and by those concerned with education at various levels, as well as by colleagues in other countries. This is an attempt to answer them in greater detail than was possible by word of mouth. The need for the provision of comparative data for international projects like the European Ethnological Atlas, and the regional hand-book series proposed by the Ethnologia Europaea group, has also been borne in mind.

The number of dialect terms has been kept low. These have not been included in a Glossary, but are inserted in the Index, with cross-references as required. The Index is also used to bring together scattered references to topics, such as women's work, that deserve to be more constructively treated in the future.

So many people have helped directly or indirectly with the material presented, that no more than a collective word of thanks can be offered. It is certain, however, that without the data in the Country Life Archive of the National Museum of Antiquities of Scotland, and without the ready advice and help of my colleagues, this would be a much poorer production.

The bulk of the photographs come from the Country Life Archive of the National Museum of Antiquities of Scotland. The numerous donors are acknowledged individually. The way in which a casual snap-shot may become the stuff of history cannot be too much emphasised.

The diagrams have been drawn by John Brown (14, 16a, 38b (4 flails), 63), Colin Hendry (38b (East Lothian flail), and Helen Jackson (all others).

The jacket illustration appears by courtesy of D. C. Thomson & Co. Ltd., Dundee.

I am also indebted to the Keeper and staff of the Scottish Record Office for advice and help over estate plans.

1976   ALEXANDER FENTON

Contents

I

The Face of the Land

FROM the earliest beginnings of settlement, the landscape of Scotland has been undergoing a series of modifications. The face of the land has never been static, even though the degree of change may be clear only in retrospect. The zeal of the late eighteenth- and early nineteenth-century improvers blinded them to much of what had gone before. They were farmers who turned aside from the plough to write, ministers and lairds who had theoretical as well as practical skill in agriculture. They praised and encouraged what was new, and stigmatised as stagnant and outmoded what was old. When a time of rapid improvement comes it often happens that the previous period, when the firm basis for an accelerated rate of change was laid, is forgotten, and the roots of growth are thrown aside. This attitude of the improvers has been caught and held by many later writers on social and economic history, especially in relation to the eighteenth century, but it is always worth remembering that the enthusiasm of the sources on which they depend conceals a great deal of previous progress from the time of the Reformation onwards. In the perspective of what is usually called the 'Agricultural Revolution', this seems very little. From the standpoint of the period itself it meant a great deal.

Agriculture on the eve of the Agricultural Revolution cannot really be described as primitive. Rather had it evolved to suit the needs of the communities it served in the different regions of Scotland. It was a system or set of overlapping systems, that varied in sophistication according to local resources and terrain (Fig. 1), to administrative organisation, to access to labour supply and markets, and to earlier historical circumstances. But for as far back as history and archaeology take us, in this and in all countries of Europe, the basic essential was the way in which the arable, producing grain, was integrated with the pasture, producing grass to feed stock, in relation to the general milieu, and to the size of the population.

Such relationships are implied already in the Stone and Bronze Ages when at least three types of grain (hulled and naked barley, *Hordeum hexastichum* and *Hordeum distichum*, and emmer, a kind of wheat, *Triticum dicoccum*) were being grown and harvested with sickles of flint and bronze, and reaping knives of stone, in fields which – at least in Shetland – were dyke-enclosed and cleared of stones, and when sheep and cattle had already been domesticated. These periods together cover over 2,000 years, long enough

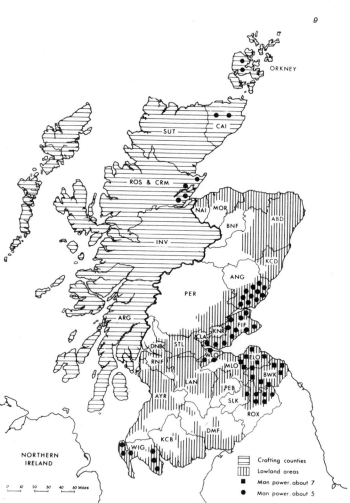

1. Map showing: a. the former counties, b. the farming regions, with farm-sizes graded according to manpower requirements around 1950. The major farming areas, marked by square and round dots, are where the bothy system operated. The vertical hatching shows the family sized farms, with a labour force of about three. Based on A. Geddes, *The Isle of Lewis and Harris*, 1955, 16.

for a basic subsistence economy to have developed quite sophisticated features, as the spread of population brought more and more land into productive use through the clearance of wood and scrub areas.

Subsistence requirements impose their own discipline, and in St. Kilda, for example, it can be seen how the seasonal round of activities relating to the fields, the stock, fowling, and the gathering of fuel, was controlled by the members of the community itself, the main external pressure coming from the need to pay rent in kind. This meant that the natural sequence of operations in the course of the year had to be adjusted to create the necessary surplus, whether of birds' feathers or of webs woven from the wool of the sheep. This kind of pressure has been exerted on communities to a greater or lesser degree for as long as there have been ruling classes, with a considerable tightening up of the organisation under monasticism and feudalism. But even these great institutions could only work within the limits set by the land itself and its resources, and it is likely that by the third or fourth centuries AD the pattern of subsistence agriculture that survived till the eighteenth century in Lowland Scotland and almost till the present days in parts of Highland Scotland had been given its basic shape. By this time too, most of the basic tools were to be found, the iron sickle for grain, the iron-bladed scythe for grass and hay, ploughs with iron shares, rotary hand-mills for grinding grain, as well as the main grain crops, bere and wheat, and rye and oats which were introduced about the time the Romans came, and the basic stock, of sheep, cattle, horses, and goats. The close inter-relationship between tools and methods of land use will be dealt with in the chapters that follow. Here, we shall take a closer look at the way in which the basic farming methods shaped the face of the land in the past, to serve the needs of the rural communities of Scotland.

BEFORE THE IMPROVERS

In many parts of the country, especially on the lower slopes of hills above the present cultivation level, there can be seen a pattern of corrugations, a series of ridges and furrows, marking the cultivating technique of earlier generations. This man-made landscape shows up particularly well in a light covering of snow, with slanting sunlight. There are also areas like the Lammermuirs (Fig. 2) where traces of former cultivation and settlement lie high in the present moorland core,[1] fossilised evidence of early medieval agriculture at a time of better weather conditions in the twelfth and thirteenth centuries, practised probably by farmers attached to the Abbeys of Melrose, Kelso and Drygrange, and of the Priory of Coldingham. These settlements were abandoned about 1400–1600, and never reclaimed, though the time-softened skeleton of the medieval landscape remains. It is likely that some of these settlements mark the sites of seasonally occupied shieling or grazing

2. Abandoned ridge and furrow at about 750 ft. (228·5 m.) in the Lammermuirs, above Ellemford, Cranshaws parish, Berwickshire, map ref. NT76:718614. Taken by Dr. M. Parry for his work on Changes in the Upper Limit of Cultivation in South-East Scotland, 1600–1900 (unpublished Ph.D. thesis, University of Edinburgh, part of which will appear in *Climate, Agriculture and Settlement: Studies in Geographical Change*, David & Charles, forthcoming).

areas that were eroded in the twelfth–thirteenth centuries when the expansion of the wool trade led to the taking over by religious houses of large tracts of hill pasture for hill grazing. Thus, something in the nature of clearances for sheep farming took place in the Borders six or seven hundred years earlier than in the Highlands.

The ridge and furrow pattern was created by the plough, and was standard almost everywhere, whether on lower or higher lying ground (Fig. 3), from the Middle Ages until the first half of the nineteenth century. It involved ploughing the land into a series of raised ridges on which the crops were grown, with furrows between that served as ditches for draining surface water. Since the system of underground tile drainage did not become general till well through the nineteenth century, there was really no earlier alternative to the ridge-and-furrow form of cultivation, except in places where the soil was naturally well-drained. But even there, ridge-and-furrow was used, because the ridges were the basic working units of pre-improvement farming, and their width in particular was adapted to suit the needs of sowing grain by hand (Figs. 4–5b), and to shearing it with hooks or sickles. Ridge-and-furrow is a form of land use suited to the use of hand-tools rather than machinery, and this factor is as important as the drainage function.

Ridges varied in width, however, according to terrain, character of soil, and date. Those of the straight, parallel, relatively low type that can be seen on the slopes around Castle Law hill fort in the Pentland Hills, for example, are unlikely to be much older than about 1800. Such ridges often lie in neat parcels that form individual fields, and are generally 10 to 18 feet (3–5·5 m.) wide.

The older *rigs*, however, are less evenly laid out. They tend to be broad, 18 to 36 feet (5·5–11 m.) or more, and often have a curved shape. Their height at the crowns can be considerable, up to 3 feet (0·9 m.) or more. They became permanent fixtures, on which ploughing went on year after year, and since the slices of earth cut by the plough were always turned towards the crown of the ridge, the height gradually increased over a period. These are the rigs so frequently marked in outline on early estate maps. They had to be levelled and spread – often a task of great difficulty – in the days of improved farming, and once this had been done (or where new land was broken in), it was normal for the new ridges to be split from time to time, so that the positions of ridge and furrow alternated. The ploughing techniques used for this were known as cleaving or splitting, and gathering up (Fig. 4).

In the wet, peaty areas of Highland Scotland, although the main emphasis was on grazing and stock-rearing, nevertheless the people could live no less without bread and ale than their Lowland counterparts, and grain crops also had to be produced. On the sandy machairs, flat stretches of land by the shore, made fertile by the calcareous sand, oat crops and less often rye and bere were sown following cultivation by the plough, but on the peat it was

A

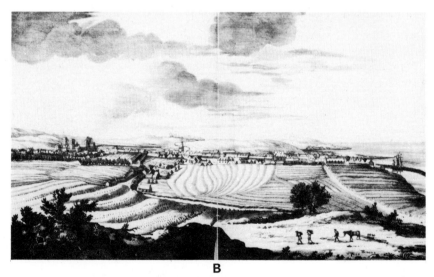

B

3. a–b. Seventeenth-century ridges and furrows at Haddington, East Lothian, and Arbroath, Angus. Some lie in straight, parallel groups, others are curving and unequal in width. From J. Slezer, *Theatrum Scotiae*, 1693.   C408, C3854

necessary to till with the spade and to make use of the lazy-bed techniques. This was in part equivalent to ridge and furrow, since it was formed by raised beds with ditches between (Fig. 5). The word lazy-bed (Gaelic *feannag*) preserves an obsolete sense of the English word 'lazy', untilled, un-cultivated, probably with reference to the strip of ground on which the bed was built. Manure, usually sea-weed carried in creels on horseback or on the human back, was laid in parallel strips of 3 to 4 feet (0·9–1·2 m.) wide, and about the same distance apart, on the untouched ground surface, then turf and earth from each side was dug up and laid on top (Fig. 5a). In some areas, for example in parts of Lewis, quite large beds may be seen on slopes, built up to a considerable height at their downhill ends and held by a retaining wall of stones. These are permanent, but with the narrower lazy-beds, at least from the late eighteenth century, the positions of the beds and of the ditches could be alternated from time to time. In this respect also there is a resemblance to ridge and furrow cultivation. Bere was the usual lazy-bed

4. The structure of ridge and furrow. The furrows provided surface drainage. The ridges were made by turning the plough furrows into the middle from each side. A second ploughing on top of the first increased the height further. C4154

crop. It has been said that bere is a fine gentleman, it likes a fine bed, and lazy-bed cultivation with its almost horticultural intensity suited it. From the mid-eighteenth century, however, potatoes came to be, increasingly, the main lazy-bed crop (Fig. 5), that is within the 'Improvement' period, but lazy-beds for grain crops were known long before then, from the early sixteenth century at least.

The functioning of pre-improvement farming depended on community activity, regardless of whether the farm was run by the laird or a substantial tenant as an independent unit – for example, a 'mains' farm, serving the estate and producing primarily for the maintenance of the laird's household – or whether it was a joint-farm, occupied by a number of tenants who paid their rent jointly, or by co-tenants who paid their rent individually (as in a modern Highland township). The work to be done required many hands and the pooling of resources in man and animal power, and in tools, at all farming levels, by neighbouring, by the provision of services by tenants as part of their rent, or by payment for services rendered. The last method scarcely comes into question until the later part of the seventeenth century, in parts of the eastern Lowlands where an increasingly commercial approach to farming was beginning to make more money available for the payment of employed servants and of bands of shearers who came to these areas annually from the Highlands at harvest time.

For the most part, land was occupied in *run-rig*, that is to say, the ridges and patches of land occupied by different tenants and even by different

MAKING A LAZY BED

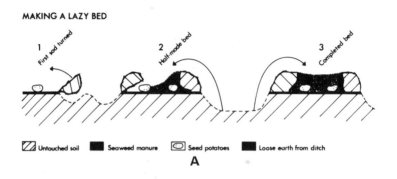

A

B

5. a. Making a lazy bed or *feannag*. Seaweed manure is spread in strips about 3 ft. (1 m.) wide and 3 ft. apart, sods are turned up over the edges of the seaweed with a *caschrom* or other spade, and earth from the spaces between them is then shovelled on top, making raised beds with ditches between.   C1201

b. Potatoes in lazy beds at Lochboisdale, South Uist, in 1934. By courtesy of Göteborgs Historiska Museum.

6. A pre-enclosure plan of Lord Morton's estate at Aberdour, Fife, 1750. RHP1022, from the Morton Muniments, Scottish Record Office. C4132

7. The same estate (Lord Morton's) after enclosure, 1785, surveyed by Robert Mitchell. RHP1023, from the Morton Muniments, Scottish Record Office. The run-rig strips have disappeared and the fields have been blocked out.   C4131

proprietors lay intermingled with each other, and in some areas were re-allocated by lot at regular intervals (Fig. 6). It may be presumed that the system, which was widespread in Europe, was intended originally to provide for an equitable distribution of land of different qualities amongst tenants, but the available historical sources show it at so many stages of evolution and fossilisation that its birth and early growth is not easy to see clearly.

In Lowland farming communities, the arable, divided as it was in run-rig, took two forms technically distinguished by the names *infield* and *outfield*. The method of cultivation was the same in each case, and the differences lay in the closer proximity of the infield to the houses, in its better quality, in the types of crops, in the periodicity of cropping, and in the methods of manuring. The English open-field system with its three-year rotation (which included a fallow year) did not reach Scotland.

The infield, also known as *croft land*, or *mucked land*, or, in Galloway, the *fey*,[2] was cultivated almost like a garden, which goes on producing year after year without being rested. For this the ground had to be well fertilised, and therefore all the available manure from the byres and stables, from earth middens (composed of rotted turf cut with a *flauchter* (Fig. 8) or turf spade) and from compost middens (Fig. 10) (of earth or turf and other kinds of manure), was laid on an area amounting to approximately one-third of the infield each year (Fig. 9). Seaweed was also applied in quantity where it was available along the coasts, and made an important increase to the cropping potential – indeed servants who had to work a good deal with seaweed were paid higher wages than their fellows in the eighteenth century in Banffshire.[3]

Bere was always sown, usually in May, after manuring on the infield, and there followed two crops of oats in the next two years, without manure, in the place where the bere had been. This was not an absolutely fixed sequence, and in some areas, notably Galloway, bere was sown on the same land units year after year. In any one year the infield would have a crop of bere scattered on various ridges throughout its whole area, and oats on the ridges that made up the other two-thirds, or whatever the remaining portion was, of its extent.

In the more favoured parts of the country where wheat was grown, the infield was in four parts and the cropping sequence was, for example, bere, oats, wheat, pease, the wheat also getting manure but less than the bere. Skene of Hallyards, writing c. 1666, noted that the ground was limed before pease in Midlothian. Where evidence for such a fourfold division of the infield appears in the seventeenth century, it can be assumed that a more commercial emphasis was developing, and that basic changes in the joint- or co-farming system had taken or were taking place. Since wheat was sown in November or December, the infield areas could no longer be left open for the common winter grazing of stock, but remained as individual units. The inclusion of pease, sometimes with lime, was important for keeping up the nitrogen in the soil, and was probably as good as if not better than leaving the ridges fallow for a year. Nevertheless, fallowing was not completely unknown, for 'wheat fauche'[4] or fallow was mentioned in the Melrose area in 1673, but such references are rare. The four-part system was a forward-looking farming practice in the seventeenth century and shows that some flexibility was possible within the relatively rigid framework that the infield imposed.

The outfield areas were less well treated, because they were thought of in a

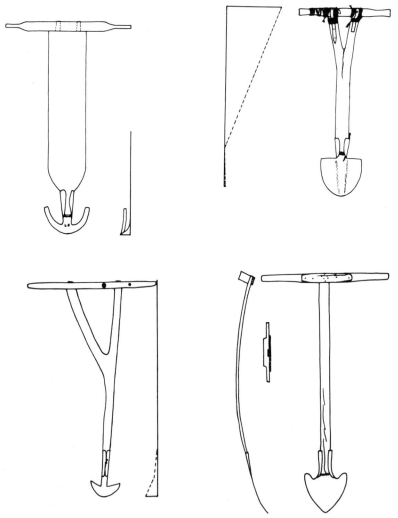

8. Turf or flauchter spades: *top left,* Shetland, 4 ft. (1·2 m.); *top right,* **Glenesk, Angus,** 3 ft. 8 in. (1·1 m.); *bottom left,* Aberdeenshire, 4 ft. 4½ in. (1·3 m.); *bottom right,* Glamis, Angus, 4 ft. 11 in. (1·5 m.).

different kind of way. In the first place, the outfield was a kind of general resources area, supplying turf for manuring the infield, for roofing buildings, for erecting dykes and walls of buildings, and for bedding the beasts in the byres, as well as providing close-at-hand grazing areas. Secondly it provided crops, invariably of oats, on sections that had been manured by the controlled grazing of stock in temporary folds which were moved from time to time. The name *folds* was sometimes given to this part of the farm-unit. In some districts, particularly of the north-east of Scotland, there were also areas called *faughs* which may be considered as part of the outfield (Fig. 9).

There was a kind of fallow on the outfield which involved ploughing or ribploughing. Strips or ribs of turf were ploughed up from the mossy ground, left to dry, then gathered into heaps and burned. The ashes were spread on the ridges as manure, and ploughed in. The surfaces of peat bogs could also

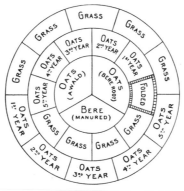

9. Schematic division of an Aberdeenshire farm about 1850. The inner circle is the infield, the middle circle the folds and the outer circle the faughs. The folds and the faughs constitute the outfield. From *T.H.A.S.S.* 1902, XIV, 79.   C3852

be burned to manure a following crop, a practice that has left its mark in the place-name 'Bruntlands', common in north-east Scotland, where techniques of manuring by burning, leading to eventual peat clearance and land reclamation, seem to have been of especial importance.

The outfield, therefore, could consist of various kinds of land of a quality inferior to that of the infield, each requiring treatment of a special kind. Folding was probably most common, and by using the stock to fertilise the soil, the outfield ridges could be subjected to a fairly regular cycle of use, extending over several years. The diagram, Fig. 9, gives a schematic breakdown of the arable in pre-improvement Aberdeenshire farming into infield, and outfield consisting of folds and faughs. It should be understood, however, that these areas were not necessarily blocked out into units, but lay scattered amongst each other, each marked by the characteristic corrugations of ridge and furrow cultivation, and protected from stock only where necessary for growing crops, by means of earthen dykes.

Infield and outfield are not so much parts of a system as means of effecting land utilisation. In many districts of the Highlands, for example, there could be no such division because of the terrain, but this does not mean that the farming system was incomplete there. It was of a different kind, with a primary emphasis on grazing and stock. Since the stock was away from the main settlement at the hill grazings or shielings for three months of each year, there was less opportunity for regular outfield folding. Nor would folding have helped very much where the grain crops were mainly cultivated on lazy-beds.

THE PERIOD OF IMPROVEMENT

Although the main period of widespread agricultural improvement, affecting buildings as well as land, began in the third quarter of the eighteenth century, nevertheless a number of forward-pointing changes can be traced already in the seventeenth century. Liming was practised increasingly from the early 1600s in places where lime and coal to burn it were readily available. In general, liming – which was nearly always on the outfield, on oatland – led to increased rents, and since it improved the grazing as well as the oat crop, it was doubly beneficial to the economy. Furthermore, the resultant more continuous use of outfield meant that such areas were being brought more and more up to infield standards, and the way was therefore prepared for the establishment on them of one of the primary features of improved farming – the single, independent farms that replaced the earlier farm-town clusters.

Enclosing began in the late seventeenth century in southern parts of Scotland, especially the South-West, in connection with stock, not with arable. Enclosed parks or folds appeared early in Galloway, under the stimulus of the cattle trade with England. They were being set up by lairds like Sir David Dunbar of Baldoon already before 1684, and though the spread of such enclosures led to the Levellers' Revolt of 1724, nevertheless Galloway was among the first areas in Scotland where the tenants' lands began to be widely enclosed. There were also grazing enclosures in other parts of southern Scotland, for example, around Edinburgh[5] which itself provided a good market for meat.

Enclosure appears to have taken place in overlapping stages. First there were the lairds' grazing parks, where animals were fattened for the market. Then the mains farms on estates began to be enclosed and taken out of the joint-farming system, so that they became independent units where innovations or experiments in cropping techniques and in stock-breeding could be tried out. And finally tenants' holdings began to be enclosed, and subdivided into fields, though this did not happen as a rule till well through the eighteenth century (Fig. 7). In East Lothian, one of the more advanced farming counties, the main period of enclosing was 1730–90, though it started in the 1690s on some estates.

The early improvers had to learn how best to make their enclosures, and some made mistakes by enclosing without considering the lie of the land for drainage. Some also planted trees with their hedges, which meant that the roots and shade came to spoil the crops as the trees grew. However, the lessons were soon learned.

The type of enclosure wall varied from district to district according to the natural resources. Many were made with thorn or beech hedges and ditches,

10. A midden composted of seaweed and byre-manure, in Papa Stour, Shetland, 1967.

the hedges being planted on the upcast from the ditches. Tenants did not necessarily like hedges, which harboured birds that ate the corn, and often stone dykes were preferred, or sometimes hedges combined with low stone dykes (Fig. 11) that formed one side of the ditch. The building of stone dykes was, in fact, a useful way of clearing the ground of stones. One of the most spectacular examples of such clearance is at Kingswells outside Aberdeen, where the late eighteenth century 'consumption' dykes are broad enough to drive a horse and cart along. The biggest is nearly half a mile long, up to 30 feet (9·1 m.) wide, and 6 to 7 feet (1·8–2·1 m.) high. It is scheduled as an ancient monument under the Aberdeen Regional Town Planning Scheme.

11. Tom Arres's dyking squad at work near Jedburgh, 1973.

Earthen or *fail* dykes were also built in places, following an old tradition, and many stone dykes were topped with turf. The most durable type of dyke, built of stone and lime, was too expensive for use outside estates, and dry-stone dykes, 4 to 5 feet (1·2–1·5 m.) high, were normal on tenants' holdings.

The enclosing of estates, farms and fields completely changed the appearance of the landscape in the course of the eighteenth century, in a manner so general and so sweeping in all parts except the Highlands, that little trace has remained on the ground of what went before, apart from the long unused fields of ridge-and-furrow at higher levels. With enclosing went the mushroom spread of individual, self-contained farms, replacing the old clustered farm-towns and cot-towns which were much more akin to the farming villages of other European countries. Only in the clustered townships of parts of the Highlands and Islands can some conception be got at the present day of what these villages were like, but even in those areas changes have been so great since the early 1800s that any attempt to interpret back must be undertaken with great caution. The net effect, however, of the general creation of farms with enclosed fields and new buildings was to give Lowland Scotland a face lift that was probably more thorough-going than in any other country of Europe in the course of the eighteenth century.

LEGISLATION AND AGRICULTURAL LITERATURE

The period of James VI was one of peace and relative prosperity, during which Parliament could take time to think of matters agricultural. Several acts were passed on aspects of the subject from 1579 onwards, but it was not until well through the seventeenth century that a series of acts, culminating in those of 1696 on lands lying run-rig and on the division of commonties, established a broad legal base for changing the basic structure of agriculture. Their implementation, however, did not come till well through the eighteenth century, yet their effect in the long run was to break down the old community structure with its run-rig infield and outfield, its common grazings, and its clustered farming villages, to create the landscape of estates with individual farms and crofts, each unit with its own houses and fields, which forms the familiar countryside of the present day.

The time lag between legislation and practice did not mean, however, that things were static. It merely shows the relatively small scale of indigenous development, which nevertheless proceeded in its own way, without drastic alteration, until well after the Union of Scotland and England in 1707. The cumulative effect was that of an increasingly commercial approach to farming, as the early writings on agriculture also indicate.

The first of these dates from 1595 and was written by Archibald Napier, son of the inventor of logarithms. It was called 'The New Order of Gooding and Manuring of all Sorts of Field Land with Common Salts', and dealt with salt as a manure, and with an intricate system of folding for the better dunging of land.

Over 60 years later, about 1666, John Skene of Hallyards wrote some notes on the farming system in the parish of Kirkliston in Midlothian. He described the cropping sequence of bere, oats, wheat and pease on the infield, and of oats on the outfield. He noted the marketing system for stock, especially cattle which were important for beef as well as for milk production. He knew that there were regional variations in types of farming and that in Ayrshire cheese was made of cows' milk. The more general practice was to make cheese of ewes' milk, whilst cows' milk was reserved for butter. Though short, Skene's text is a factual and practical piece of observation, of much value for a study of the farming of the period, in his area and beyond.

At the end of the century there appeared two treatises, of which the first was James Donaldson's *Husbandry Anatomiz'd*, 1697. The writer, an Edinburgh printer and journalist, leaned heavily on earlier English agricultural writers who – along with the growing general interest in the land as an improvable resource that the legislation of the period indicates – no doubt inspired his work.

Much more practical, however, was *The Countrey-Man's Rudiments, or An Advice to the Farmers in East Lothian how to Labour and Improve their Ground*, by

ABC, 1699, probably the pseudonym of John Hamilton, the second Lord Belhaven. This was aimed at ordinary farmers as well as lairds, and relates mainly to conditions in East Lothian. The writer proposed the inclusion of a fallow element in the existing four-break East Lothian sequence of wheat, barley, oats and pease. The lack of fallow was one of the ways in which Scottish farming differed from English, and it was very hard to introduce the practice into Scotland. Farmers were used to fallowing on the outfield – that is, after cropping almost to exhaustion the cropped area that was left on its own for some years to recover – but did not feel they could afford to lose the infield which produced their best grain, from which came bread and ale, and food for the stock, and out of which both servants' wages and rents were paid, either in money or in kind.

It is surprising that Belhaven barely considered enclosure, which stresses the small scale on which it existed at that time, at least for arable purposes. It was not until 1729, when William Mackintosh of Borlum wrote his *Essay on Ways and Means of Inclosing, Fallowing, Planting, etc. in Scotland*, that the subject was dealt with at any length.

These early writers were not, for the most part, critical of the farming system. They could see where the need for improvement lay, and much of what they say is forward-looking, but they are still far from the point of revolutionary change. The progress made by Scottish agriculture during the eighteenth century can be gauged by comparing these works with the writings dating from the end of the century, particularly the Old Statistical Account and the County Agricultural Surveys, even allowing for the prejudices of ardent improvers against what was old.

THE DRAINAGE REVOLUTION

The effect of systematic underground drainage on the appearance of the landscape is not easy to realise, now that it has taken place, although where formerly drained arable has reverted to grazing and the drains have become choked, it is possible to get, from the flourishing rows of rushes, some conception of what the land used to be like in wet areas. Rows of rushes often also follow the hollows of fossilised ridge and furrow ploughing.

The importance of surface drainage is made clear by the widespread use of the ridge and furrow technique, but this alone could not lead to the reclamation of wet and marshy areas. For these, ditches had to be cut and maintained. Monastic farmers of the thirteenth century drained an extensive area at Inchaffray in Perthshire by cutting a *pow* or ditch that ran to the River Earn from the west end of a large peat morass. The same ditch was later the subject of two Acts of the Scottish Parliament, in 1641 and 1696,[6] the Pow of Inchaffray Acts, which legislated for collaborative effort between proprietors on the drainage of this flood-prone area. National legislation of this kind underlines oo the one hand the small scale of activity, and also on the other emphasises the new national awareness of the importance of agriculture.

In the eighteenth century, much draining of marshes and lochs was in progress. This, it was often said, reduced or brought to an end the annual agues to which people living in wet areas were subject. It also had an effect on the bird life, for the drainage of low-lying land and the reclamation of moorland was said to be reducing the number of lapwings in Auchtermuchty parish in the 1790s.[7]

Various methods of draining were possible. The simplest was the open ditch, often about 4 or 5 feet (1·2–1·5 m.) wide at the top by 3 to 4 feet (0·9–1·2 m.) deep, narrowing to 2 feet (0·6 m.) wide at the bottom (Fig. 12). Macneill of Carskey in Argyll employed a labourer for summer ditching in 1720 and in 1763 Thomas Wilson, drainer, cut 1,663 falls of drains (nearly 10,000 yards or 9,140 metres) at Cassilis and Culzean in Ayrshire in the course of the year.[8] Open drains were complemented by *gaw-cuts* or *gaw-furs*, shallow drains made to follow the slope of the ground or else cut to slant across the ridges, or to take water across the head-ridge in a ploughed field. Open ditches round enclosures also helped drainage considerably.

Another method was the covered drain, of which there were two types, the box drain (Fig. 12) and the *rumbling syver*. The first was made by laying flat stones in the bottom of the ditch to form a square or triangular drain. A layer of stones, turf, straw, brushwood, heather, rushes, or ferns was laid above the box to keep it clean and to provide a pervious mat through which excess water from the plough-soil above could percolate.

The *rumbling syver* or stone drain was narrow, only 1 foot (0·3 m.) wide at the bottom, and loosely filled for a foot of depth with rounded stones. Draining and clearance of surface stones went hand in hand. Such drains were widespread and were being made for most of the first half of the nineteenth century. Where stones were scarce, woody plants like thorns and broom were used in the ditch bottoms, in which case the bottom was made very narrow, to prevent choking, by means of special draining spades.

In general, stone drains went with sloping, and box drains with level land, or where a great deal of water had to be run off. They could be laid in herring-bone fashion, with side drains running into a main drain or leader, or else were laid along the lines of the furrows between the plough ridges, following each furrow or alternate furrows, often at about 18 or 36 feet (5·5–11 m.) intervals, but the frequency varied according to terrain and moisture content. Later tile drains followed similar patterns.

Drainage was by no means confined to arable fields. It was also carried out on pasture land, to some extent as a complement to liming, from the late eighteenth century, and open sheep drains (Fig. 12) about 2 feet (0·6 m.) wide by 1 to 1½ feet (0·3–0·5 m.) deep, with the upcast forming a low bank on the downhill side, are still a feature of the sheep pastures in the Border Hills and elsewhere. The draining of hill pastures also helped to prevent sheep diseases, especially liver fluke.

In the first draining phase, the emphases lay on drying out lochs, bogs and morasses, and very wet areas, as a means of extending the usable acreage, and on surface drainage on sheep land and cattle pastures. The second phase involved improvement of the fields by systematic underground tile drainage.

The first tile works to be set up in Scotland was on the Duke of Portland's

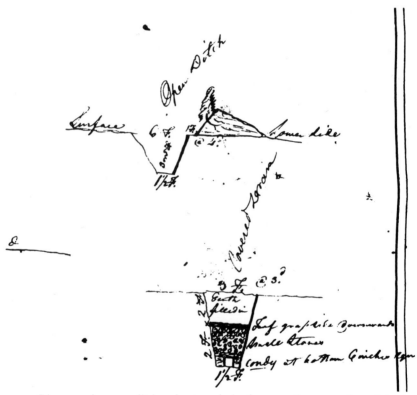

12. a. Diagrams of an open ditch and a stone drain, drawn on the corner of an estate plan of Hatton Lodge, Aberdeenshire, 1769.   C4105

estate at Cessnock in Ayrshire in 1826, but the man who exerted the greatest influence was James Smith of Deanston in Stirlingshire, who also produced a reaping machine for cutting grain corps in 1811. In 1831, Smith published his *Remarks on Thorough Drainage and Deep Ploughing*. Eight years before he had taken over a farm at Deanston from his uncle. He undertook an extensive programme of drainage with stone drains, at the same time doing away with the ridges and furrows and laying his fields flat. This is one of the earliest

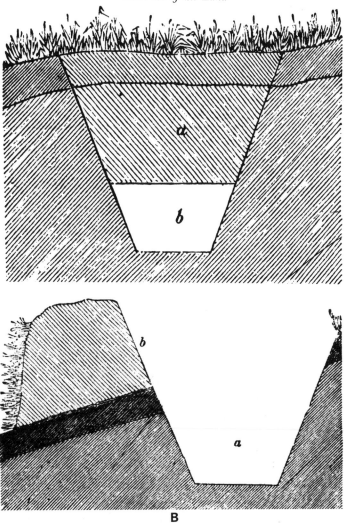

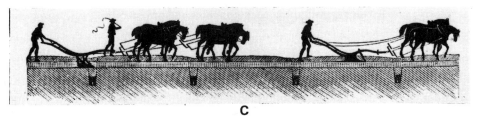

12.   b. Covered and open sheep-drains in grass. From Stephens, 1844, I, 498.   C482
c. Subsoiling, to break up the hard pan and let the water through to the stone drains
below. The subsoil plough is worked in the bottom of a plough furrow. From Stephens, 1844,
I, 654.   C3855

examples of fields being given their present-day form. His drains were not entirely successful, and he realised that this was because the unbroken sub-soil remained impervious to water. To break the subsoil without bringing its infertile content to the surface, he invented a subsoil-plough (Fig. 12c) which penetrated up to 16 inches (0·4 m.) when drawn by a team of four to eight horses. The final result of the combination of draining and subsoil ploughing was to turn sour, waterlogged soil into high quality, productive land, which made both Smith and his system of drainage famous. The change must have seemed nearly miraculous, and it is small wonder that the example of this oasis was quickly imitated by neighbours and fellow-members of the Gargun-nock Farmers' Club, and spread far and wide through the enthusiastic reports in the agricultural papers.

Progress was also speeded up by the wide establishment of tile-works. There were at least seven in Stirlingshire by the 1840s, by which time also there was a foundry in North Berwick making machines for drain-tiles, according to an invention patented by the Marquis of Tweeddale.[9] At Fenton Barns in East Lothian, George Hope set up a kiln in 1836–7 which produced 1,000 tiles a week and served both his own and neighbours' farms. The sale of tiles more or less paid for the cost of drainage of Fenton Barns, £2,500, which Hope, as tenant, carried out almost entirely at his own expense. Tile-making was given up by him in 1843, when the work of drainage was done. In the Agricultural Museum run in the 1830s by W. Drummond and Sons, the seedsmen, in Stirling, drains and draining equipment formed an important part of the display. A drain-tile or pipe machine that could be driven by steam or horse-power, made by William Brodie, Airdrie, was shown at the Great Exhibition in 1851, and such was the international interest in draining methods in Britain generally that tile making machinery, like The Bedford Prize Tile Machine by W. Williams, Bedford, 1857, found its way as far afield as Finland, where an example is now preserved in the Agricultural Museum at Mustiala.

The first drainage tiles were horse-shoe shaped, and known as saddle-back or mug tiles. They were open underneath and, except in very stiff soil, were laid on separate soles of tile or wood, the latter cut in estate sawmills. Mug tiles were made by shaping rectangles of clay in a wooden mould, and pressing these over wooden semi-cylinders of the desired size.

Cylindrical tiles were first made by a Kentish gardener in 1843, though at first the bore was only 1 inch, and too small for continuous service. The size of the bore was gradually increased. Mug tiles, however, continued to be made for some considerable time, and many are still servicing fields on the farms of Scotland, whilst their small-bore successors choked and became weed-grown long ago.

So great was the zeal for this drainage revolution that in 1840 an Act was passed to allow landowners to raise loans for drainage. Peel's Public Money

Drainage Act of 1846 offered a loan of £2,000,000 to be repaid over a 22-year period – an offer eagerly snapped up by Scottish farmers. Following the Private Money Drainage Act of 1849, numerous private companies were formed which further helped to finance drainage and land improvement. It was the cumulative effect of this great surge of activity, in the middle span of the nineteenth century, that effectively created the face of farming Scotland as we know it at the present day – with level fields free from ridge and furrow – though the problem of achieving proper drainage in all parts of the country still remains unsolved.

The obvious effect of systematic underground drainage was the levelling of the fields, but there were also several side effects. The quality and yield of crops improved, and it became possible to use easily types of farming equipment whose spread and development had been inhibited by the ubiquity of ridges and furrows. Rollers, harrows, seed-drills, and above all reaping-machinery could be worked with ease on well-drained, level fields, and this in turn had an encouraging effect on the smithies and agricultural engineering firms that began to proliferate in the course of the nineteenth century. The widespread adoption of underground drainage even before the production of tile-drains, also stimulated the establishment of spade-making works such as James Rigg & Sons, Sanquhar, Dumfries, 1772, T. Black & Sons, Berwick-on-Tweed, 1788, and, later on the Holm Forge Co., Glasgow, the Barblues Forge, Airdrie, the Chieftain Forge, Bathgate, and others. The Chieftain Forge still produces draining and forestry spades in considerable numbers.

THE LANDSCAPE OF THE HIGHLANDS

It is often assumed that the Highlands and Islands are places where the landscape is age-old, that things have been static there from time immemorial. This is not so, however, though it needs an effort of mind to realise that the Highland landscape, in terms of land use and settlement, is more recent than that of the Lowlands. The main changes that shaped it lie within the nineteenth century, though change had already begun earlier.

As in Lowland Scotland at an earlier date, agriculture was based on the run-rig system, with clustered villages or townships. The shieling areas for the summer grazing of stock were essential adjuncts to the proper working of the system, for when the stock was at the hills, the crops got leave to grow and ripen in their unfenced fields, and the grass around the township was rested. In the second half of the eighteenth century, much surveying of Highland estates was undertaken, after which the township lands were in many cases lotted, so that individuals got small, consolidated holdings. The processes of lotting and abolition of run-rig, and with it the ending of the shieling system, took place over a period, and villages have retained their run-rig form to the

13. A nineteenth-century township near Strathy, Sutherland. The houses stretch along the road, and the fields lie in strips above and below them. The major crop is grass and hay. 1960.

C3896

present day in some areas such as Iochdar in South Uist, Valtos and Crow-lista in Uig, Lewis, and Aith in Fetlar, Shetland. Lotting was taking place in Tiree, the outermost of the inner Hebrides, in 1776, in Netherlorn by 1783, on Lochtayside by 1797, and in the islands of Coll, Oronsay, Gigha, parts of Mull, of mainland Argyll, and of West Inverness by 1800. Skye, Lewis and Harris, Sutherland, and Wester Ross remained untouched for another 20 years. By 1850, however, it could be said that run-rig and its accompanying organisation for stock and crop was more or less extinct in the Highlands, as it had been for over a hundred years in Lowland Scotland.

The ending of run-rig in the Highlands and the excision of the shieling areas were effective enough in ending the older system of joint-farming. Much more drastic, however, was the wholesale removal or displacement of entire village communities in the course of the 'Sheep Clearances', when both the arable and the hill grazings were formed into large single-unit farms, which were leased to sheep-men (several of whom came from the Borders of Scotland) in return for much higher rents than the former inhabitants could have paid. Such clearances took place mainly in the nineteenth century, and swept from the landscape – except as archaeological remains – many of the old villages and shieling hut groups, leaving formerly populated areas almost empty. It was these same areas that often became deer forests in the later Victorian period, let at high seasonal rents to sporting gentlemen.[10]

The people who were cleared from the relatively fertile straths suffered a decline not only in living standards but for a time also in equipment and housing. The population of the pre-clearance village of Rosal in Strathnaver, for example, could cultivate by the plough in ridge and furrow before 1820.[11] The crop was oats, and the plough was drawn by four ponies, yoked abreast. At the same time, bere and potatoes were being cultivated with the spade and caschrom on lazy-beds. It was one of the effects of the Clearances that plough-cultivation ceased almost entirely, and the spade and caschrom came into much more general use on the small patches and lots of land near the coast, on which the evicted people were re-settled, mainly on land never before used for either settlement or cultivation. By 1812 in Assynt for example, there were no more than 6 ploughs, and 300 families cultivated 300 acres of arable with the caschrom alone.

This movement of people in relatively recent times was revolutionary rather than evolutionary in character. It resulted in the pattern of small coastal settlement which is characteristic of the present-day Highlands. These villages were not clustered like the old ones, but were scattered, consisting of houses standing each on its own strip of land which ran from the shore to the hill dyke (Fig. 13). The result was a ladder-like or splayed out arrangement of field boundaries along the coasts and around the bays. Each tenant used his inbye strip for cropping and grazing, and beyond the hill dyke was the common grazing area. In this way, the change was more partial than in the Lowlands, for whilst the arable ceased to be held and worked jointly, the grazing continued to be used in common.

The new settlements allowed a maximum number of people to be maintained on a minimum amount of land. The land was not sufficient in extent to keep them fully occupied, but it was the lairds' intention to use the men for fishing, not farming. It therefore came about that more of the farm work came to be done by the women than had been the case in the past, since the men were engaged at sea for a considerable part of the year.

As an alternative to fishing, there was also the work of gathering and burning seaweed to make kelp, especially in the Hebrides and parts of the Western sea board, and this was a further incentive to a concentration of settlement on the coast. This trade, however, did not much survive the 1830s, and with the gradual concentration of the fishing industry on a limited number of ports, the economic basis of these settlements was removed or reduced. The point is, however, that these population movements have left an indelible mark on the landscape which, however archaic it may appear to be, is, even in such a place as St. Kilda, often little more than a hundred years old.

2

Tilling the Soil

FOR over 3,500 years the soil of Scotland has been cultivated to make it bear crops. Archaeological evidence and the use of modern laboratory techniques for radio-carbon dating wood have shown that ploughing implements pulled by animals were being used from the time of the early Bronze Age, perhaps even the late Neolithic period. Though the implements were different from the plough of more recent times, the very fact of plough cultivation argues for a considerable degree of sophistication, not only in tillage techniques, but also in work organisation.

The available evidence shows that crops of hulled and naked barley, and of emmer, were cultivated by wooden ploughs without mould boards (technically called *ards*). In Shetland and Orkney, it appears that stone shares (Fig. 14a) were used, fixed at a shallow angle in the lower end of the beam in the same way as the iron bar socks of the present day. The large number of broken tips of stone-shares that have been found shows that they had a high mortality rate, and also that cultivation with stone-shares must have gone on over a long period of time, perhaps until the Vikings came with their iron plough fittings.

The kind of plough into which the stone shares fitted is a type well known from finds in peat-bogs in several countries of Europe, but especially Denmark. Several finds have also been made in Scotland and Ireland. Of these, the wooden beam from Lochmaben, Dumfriesshire (Fig. 14c) has been radio-carbon dated to 80 BC, and the combined head-and-stilt from Milton Loch crannog to 400 BC. The two Shetland finds, and an unlocalised head-and-stilt in the Hunterian Museum, Glasgow, resemble those from Milton Loch, and are unlikely to be very different in date. Such ploughs or ards were almost certainly drawn by pairs of oxen wearing wooden yokes, as was still the case in much later days when the monks of the Celtic Church were tilling their monastic lands. And no doubt they worked in small, irregularly shaped fields like those at the Scord of Brouster in Shetland, where a group of six prehistoric fields covers an area of 2¾ acres (about 1 ha.).

A major advance came with the introduction of iron ploughshares, of which a small number survives from the Romano-British period, 1st to 3rd century AD. It was at this time too that oats and rye appeared as cultivated crops.[12] Significantly, all the early iron plough-shares so far discovered

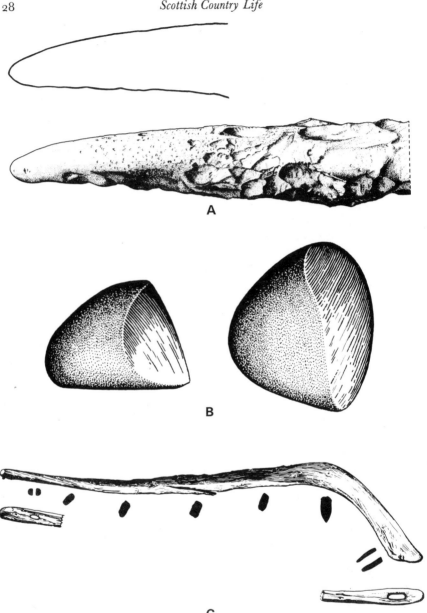

14. Plough parts of stone: a. A stone bar-share from a wooden plough or *ard*, from Shetland. 21 in. (530 mm.). National Museum, AC17.   C3976

b. Examples of plough pebbles, thrust into plough soles to reduce wear, showing the characteristic convex wear on the face.   C3974

c. The wooden beam of an ard, from Lochmaben, Dumfriesshire, of the type into which stone shares could have been fitted. Radio-carbon dated to 80 BC (*Tools and Tillage* 1972. II/1. 64).

belong to the fertile south-east of Scotland, apart from a later one from Bonar Bridge, Sutherland, said to be Viking in date, but possibly a little earlier. The shares are in the shape of wedge-shaped shoes, or flat, socketed blades. This could indicate variations in the types of ploughs used, or may point to different ploughing functions – that is, the wedge-shaped share is more suitable for breaking in, and the flat share for giving subsequent tillings. Either way, further advances in the sophistication of ploughing equipment are evident, and this in turn may be related to field systems around the Early Iron Age hill forts and settlements of south-east Scotland, which have a more geometrical, organised appearance than the earlier Scord of Brouster fields.

It also appears from finds of the same period that the range of equipment included iron bladed spades for digging soil and cutting turf, and there were also peat-spades with a cutting wing at right angles to the blade. One such was found in a hoard of metal-work at Blackburn Mill, Berwickshire (Fig. 15a). Peat, therefore, was undoubtedly being burned as fuel in the hearth, or was being cut for conversion into peat charcoal for the smiths to use in forging tools and weapons.

The ploughs so far discussed were probably all ards, without mould-boards. There is no clear early evidence for coulters, though they were known in the Romano-British period in southern England. Ploughs with mould-boards and coulters, however, were certainly in use in the early medieval period, at first probably on the rich abbey lands of southern Scotland. In this area, small pebbles of quartzite or flint of a type known to have been inserted into the wooden soles of heavy ploughs in parts of France and Denmark in later times, to prevent wear, have been found in considerable numbers. These pebbles have convexly worn faces, with parallel scratches running across the face (Fig. 14b). Another type, flat and highly polished, belongs – on the analogy of Danish evidence – to the wooden axle-ends of plough-forecarriages, of the kind later used with the Kentish plough in Britain, but otherwise unknown in Scotland. These 'plough pebbles'[13] have not been dated, apart from stray examples at Jarlshof in Shetland from a twelfth-thirteenth century context, but must in general be early medieval. Possibly the coulters and shares on fourteenth century grave slabs – the earliest known illustrations of plough parts – from Pennershaughs (Fig. 15b) and Cummertrees in Dumfriesshire, belong to such ploughs.

Ploughs with pebble studded soles and, in some cases, wheeled fore-carriages, represent a totally different tradition from the two-ox ards of earlier times. They represent a much more organised, commercial type of approach to farming, and imply a considerable investment in animal-power and in manpower. This goes with the foundation of the monasteries, largely in the hundred years between 1120–1220. But by the time literary evidence

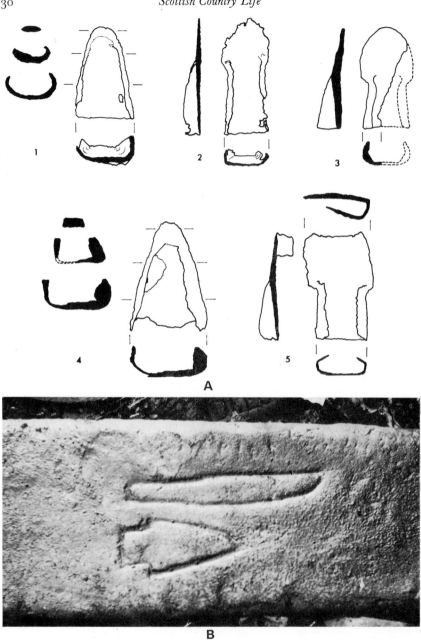

15. a. Romano-British iron shares: 1. Blackburn Mill, Cockburnspath, Berwickshire, DW113; 2. Traprain Law, GUM479; 3. Traprain Law, GUM480; 4. Bonar Bridge, Sutherland; 5. Blackburn Mill, DW108. All in National Museum.   C4153

b. One of the earliest gravestone illustrations of a coulter and symmetrical share, from Pennershaughs, Annandale, c. 1300–c. 1350. By courtesy of Dumfries Burgh Museum.

C2955

becomes available in the fourteenth, and more especially the fifteenth and sixteenth centuries, it is the 'old Scotch plough' with its large team, often of eight oxen or horses, that appears as the main cultivating implement in lowland areas. In the Highlands and Islands, however, plough types derived from the older ards remained in use, and on the Highland fringes the old Scotch plough developed a particular form of its own.

THE OLD SCOTCH PLOUGH

The old Scotch plough had developed, already by the sixteenth century, the form that it kept until it began to be displaced by improved plough types in the course of the eighteenth century. It was a swing-plough, without wheels to support the front of the beam (Fig. 16). It was long and heavy, with two handles or stilts, and a flat, wooden mould-board. The only iron parts were the share or sock, the coulter, a strengthening band around the opening in the beam for the tang of the coulter, and the hook or bridle at the front end of the beam, to which the draught-yoke or chain was fixed. The sole of the plough, that ran on the ground at the base of the cut furrow, was long, and made longer by the iron share fitted to its tip – either a pointed, symmetrical share with an open grid type of construction, used for heavy, stony land, for breaking in and reclamation, or a solid share with a feather at the right-hand side for undercutting the roots of weeds and thick grass.

It was usual for writers of the Improvement period to speak of the old Scotch plough as a clumsy, awkward, inefficient instrument. It is true that the length of the sole combined with its flat mould-board created a lot of friction and made a large team necessary, but criticism should only be made within the framework of the conditions within which it worked, and of the cultivating techniques to which it was suited. In fact, the old Scotch plough was well adapted to the purpose it had to serve, which was to plough the soil into a series of ridges and furrows. The result was that the old Scotch plough always had to turn its furrow up the slope created by the side of the ridge, which in itself created further friction, and this also helps to explain the need for a large team. The plough, therefore, had always to be held tilted to the right, and in this position the sole acted as an anchor in the base of the furrow, whilst the flat mould-board, shaped to slope upwards from front to back, came into its correct position for pushing up and pressing into place the freshly cut furrow-slice. Such work could not have been easily done by light ploughs on the old high-backed ridges.

The size of the team varied according to terrain, soil type, whether it was a first, second or subsequent ploughing, availability of animals, and so on, but the average seems to have been eight oxen, yoked two by two in line ahead. Horses were also used, or a mixture of horses and oxen – as on the mid-eighteenth century tombstone in Liberton Kirkyard, Edinburgh (Fig.

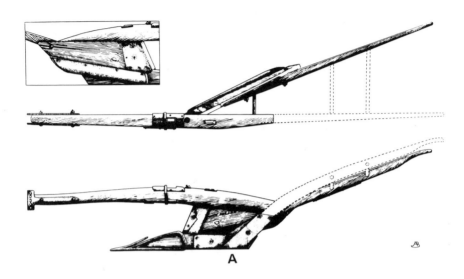

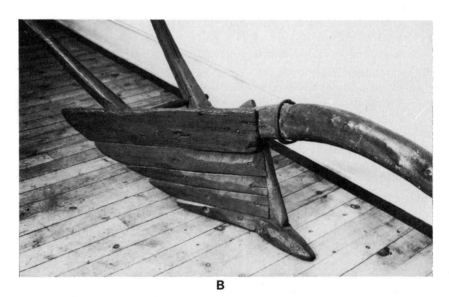

16. The two surviving old Scotch ploughs: a. from Chilcarroch, Wigtownshire, about 1793. County Museum, Stranraer.   C1556
   b. A lighter version, date unknown. Arbuthnot Museum, Peterhead.

17), which shows a team of six animals pulling an old Scotch plough, with a pair of horses preceding two pairs of oxen – but oxen must have been accepted as the norm, for the unit of land extent known as the *ploughgate* was reckoned as the amount that could be worked by eight oxen in a year. The amount one ox could deal with was an *oxgate* (of which the latinised

17. Ploughing and harrowing, on a table-stone in Liberton Kirkyard, Edinburgh, 1753. Two horses precede four oxen in the plough. XIX.16.1.

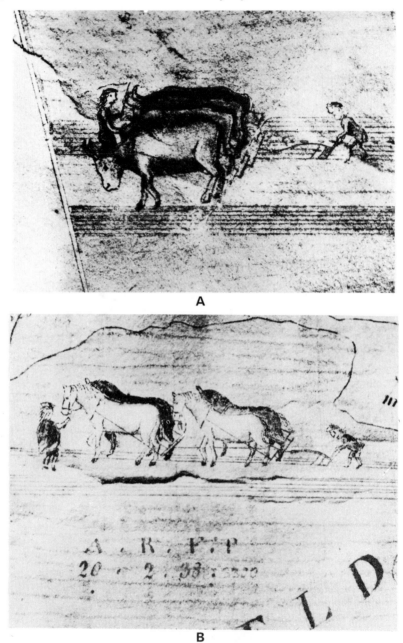

A

B

18. The lightened version of the old Scotch plough, drawn by a. four oxen abreast (old style) and b. four horses yoked two by two (new style). From W. Aberdeen's plan of Castlehill, Caithness, 1772. RHP 1220, Scottish Record Office. See *Scottish Studies* 1962. VI. 318–223.   C2549, C2548

English equivalent was *bovate*). The number of animals in a team could vary in numbers from two to twelve, including odd numbers, but the large teams of twelve were confined to the big farms of North-East Scotland at the turn of the eighteenth century (Fig. 18). The comments of contemporary writers suggest that a certain amount of prestige and rivalry in keeping up the style was involved in this.

The length of the team had in turn an effect on the configuration of the ridges. Ridges that are older than about 1750 are usually not straight, but have a serpentine appearance. This is almost certainly a result of two functional factors – firstly, the fact that the long team had to start turning on the headland before the plough was out of the furrow, and secondly, the need to keep the mould-board pressed firmly against the furrow-slice right up to the end of the furrow.[14] These factors could have had a cumulative effect over the years in giving the ridges a curved shape. There is, therefore, a close and inevitable link between the implement, its draught-power, and the old unenclosed plough-landscape, which had no dykes or hedges to inhibit the turning of the big teams.

A further consequence of the size of the team was that an additional hand was required to control it, using a whip or goad, whilst the ploughman was concerned only with operating the plough. The find of the iron tip of an ox-goad of Romano-British date on Traprain Law in East Lothian shows that the same system prevailed there at that period. It was not until the advent of the lighter, improved two-horse ploughs of the second half of the eighteenth century that the fashion developed of the ploughman himself controlling the team with reins. Before then, ploughing represented a heavy annual investment in animal and manpower, especially when a far greater number of ploughings was undertaken than in later times in the course of a year to prepare a reasonably weed-free seed-bed. In most cases, this investment was too heavy to be carried by individuals. The provision of men and animals for ploughing, and the associated operations of harrowing and sowing, was very much a function of the farm-toun communities.

This point comes out clearly from the late sixteenth or early seventeenth century Pleugh-Sang. This is a three-part, polyphonic song, first published in 1666 by John Forbes, the Aberdeen printer. Not only does it mention the various parts of contemporary ploughs, but it also names 25 *hinds* or farm-workers:

'Higgin and Habken, Hankin and Rankin,
 Nicol and Collin, Hector and Aikin,
 Martin Mawer, Michel and Morice false lips,
 Fergus, Rynaud and Guthra, Orphus and Arthur,
 Morice, Davie, Richard, Philpie Foster and Macky Millar,
 Ruffie Tasker and his marrows all
 Straboots, Tarboyes and Ganzel'

This is well beyond the basic manpower requirement of two people for a plough, and must include hands for harrowing and sowing as well. Not only was their work done on a communal basis, but also the stock and equipment were shared. An Act of James I in 1424 laid down that every man of simple estate who worked as a labourer should have half an ox in the plough, or else should dig, on every work day, an area of 7 square feet (0·58 sq. m.). It was therefore theoretically possible that a plough-team of eight oxen could belong to sixteen owners, each with half a share in an ox. Since further draught-animals were required for the harrow, the large number of people attending the operation is explicable in terms of the kind of community involvement that was the mainspring of the run-rig form of farming organisation.

PLOUGHS OF THE HIGHLANDS AND ISLANDS

Along a broad strip lying roughly along the Highland line, stretching from Orkney in the north to Galloway in the south, a lighter version of the old Scotch plough was in common use (Fig. 18a-b). It was similar in form, but was much shorter and lighter, with a pair of very upright stilts. It differed, however, in the disposition of the team, which consisted of four – or sometimes six – animals, arranged side by side, instead of two by two in line ahead.

This team formation was similar to that for the single-stilted ploughs that have been recorded in the northern and western parts of the country. They survived into the nineteenth century, and even fall within the period of living memory on the West-side of Lewis. Shetland, Orkney and Caithness, and the Hebrides each had a particular variety of single-stilted plough, showing different kinds of adaptation to local conditions. The Hebridean form, for example, called in Gaelic a *crann-nan-gad*, was adapted to rocky conditions and shallow soil (Fig. 19a). The front end of its beam ran like a skid on the ground, making it easy for the ploughman to lift the implement over stones, and the share had a very broad cutting feather that allowed the plough to skim off shallow slices of earth. However primitive and crude in appearance such ploughs may appear in the light of present knowledge, nevertheless they are not so in fact, for their form and function has developed in relation to their environment. This cannot always be said of the implements of the present day, for their form may be conditioned by different sets of factors of a broad economic nature, and they are intended to do their work regardless of local conditions.

In Shetland the plough-team was usually of four oxen yoked abreast (Fig. 19b). This was also true of Orkney and Caithness, but in the course of the eighteenth century horses came to be as common there as oxen, and teams of two or three horses abreast were employed as well as of four. The

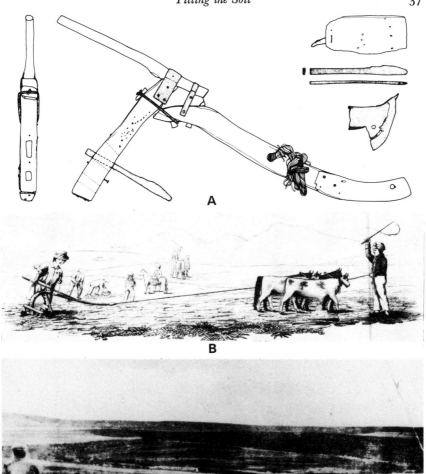

19. a. A Highland *crann-nan-gad*, with its mould board, coulter and broad sock for shallow'
rocky soils.

b. A single stilted plough in Shetland, drawn by four oxen abreast. From S. Hibbert,
Description of the Shetland Islands, 1822. C1594

c. An Orkney *stiltie-ploo* in stubble, drawn by one ox. A man with a pole presses on the
beam to keep the plough in the ground. C1531

Lowland Scottish practice of yoking two by two in line ahead was also penetrating Orkney and Caithness by the late 1700s. In the rest of Highland and Island Scotland, including the high lands of Aberdeen, Angus and Perth, wherever the single-stilted plough or the lighter version of the old Scotch plough was used, the animals were always horses. The presence of horses in Orkney ploughs is explained by the lively trade in horses (for example, from Strathnaver) that went on across the Pentland Firth, and here they can be seen to be spreading into an area where oxen had formerly been used. It appears, therefore, that the country can be divided into lowland areas, where oxen were the main plough animals, and the higher or highland areas, where horses predominated. It is not easy to say how old this division is, but it was so well established that in parts of North Scotland, Perth, Argyll, Angus and Lanark, the term *horsegang* replaced the lowland *oxgang* or *oxgate*. It was equivalent to two *oxgangs*, and as a term dates back to the late seventeenth century. Its area of use coincides closely with that of the lighter version of the old Scotch plough. This in itself may indicate a seventeenth century spread of incipient ideas of Lowland farming improvements into the neighbouring upland areas, for example into old shieling or grazing grounds where the droppings of animals over the centuries had made the ground fertile to bear cereal crops.

THE IMPROVED PLOUGHS

Pre-Improvement ploughs of whatever type, whether in the Highlands or the Lowlands, whether they were light or heavy, required a large team of animals, and a minimum of two men, one to control the plough and the other to control the animals. The Pleugh-Sang and other sources show that the manpower was often greater—a third hand to help to press down the beam and keep the plough in the ground, others to follow with spades to break clods and tidy up badly-turned strips of furrow. This kind of organisation arose out of the economic capabilities and needs of joint- or co-farming communities, and was adequate as long as the economy remained at or only a little above the subsistence level, as long as manpower was plentiful in the countryside, as long as actual money played a relatively small part in the relationships between laird and tenant, tenant and employee, and as long as most members of the community had some stake in the community's land, even if it was no more than grazing for a cow.

Agricultural improvements, however, incipient in the seventeenth century and thereafter rapidly gaining momentum, introduced and were themselves dependent on new sets of factors that required much more of a money-based economy, and different kinds of relationships between employers and employed. In the seventeenth and early eighteenth centuries, the will to improve was strong, and examples can be found, for example in relation to harvesting techniques, of how the indigenous farming methods were capable of adaptation, within the limits of available tools and skills. At the same time, money was becoming more readily available, for example through trade in cattle, grain, and textiles. In addition, the Union of 1707 led to a familiarisation course with English farming methods and equipment for many Scottish lairds, who then set about trying them out at home. It may have been in this way that 'English' ploughs began to be introduced into Scotland in the first half of the eighteenth century by improvers such as Barclay of Urie in Kincardineshire, Grant of Monymusk in Aberdeenshire, and the Earl of Galloway, on whose Orkney estate a number of English ploughs, some of them old, were listed in an inventory of 1747.[15] Barclay of Urie tried out the Norfolk plough but for the most part the ploughs were of the Rotherham make, a swing plough patented in the West Riding of Yorkshire in 1730.

Like the old Scotch plough, the Rotherham plough (Fig. 20a) was made entirely of wood except for the bridle and irons. It was, however, much lighter, and by the 1790s 'English' ploughs drawn by up to ten horses were being used in almost every county in Scotland. It is in this context that the chain-plough patented by James Small (Fig. 20b–c), the Berwickshire ploughwright, must be seen.

James Small, the son of a Berwickshire farmer, served his apprenticeship as a joiner at Hutton. Between 1758–63 he worked at Doncaster, where he saw and studied the Rotherham plough, which may even have been familiar to him before he went south. On returning home, he settled at Blackadder Mount in his native county, set up a manufactory of ploughs and other agricultural equipment, and began to carry out experiments on the construction of ploughs. The knowledge he gained was digested and made available in his *Treatise on Ploughs and Wheeled Carriages*, published in 1784 – a work that shows him as having literary as well as technical expertise.

Like all intelligent craftsmen, he thought deeply about what he did with his hands, and experimented constantly. In his plough experiments, it seems that he took the old Scotch plough and gradually adapted it by combining with it the main features of the Rotherham plough, until, in 1767, he was ready to patent it. Its rapid subsequent spread had a profound influence on Scottish farming. It also spread well beyond the bounds of Scotland, and already in 1803 it was being produced at a plough-making factory at Engeltofta in Sweden, under a group of Scottish ploughwrights – Alexander Hall, Alexander Bonthron, and David Pride.[16]

The old Scotch plough belongs to a class sometimes technically described as 'four-sided'. This is because the beam, left-hand stilt, sole and sheath join together to make a frame of this shape. In the Rotherham plough, however, and following it Small's plough, the sole is very short, and the lower end of the left stilt is attached to it at the point where it is linked to the sheath.

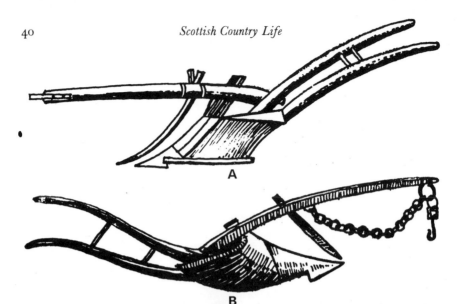

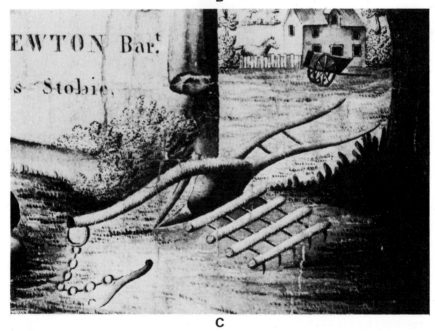

20. a. The Rotherham plough, by which James Small was much influenced. From R. Brown, *Agriculture of the West Riding of Yorkshire*, 1799, 53. The diagram shows a left-sided plough.
C2590

b. James Small's chain plough. From Lord Kames, *The Gentleman Farmer*, 1776.

C2591

c. An improved plough on the estate plan of Smailholm Spittal, Roxburgh, surveyed by James Stobie in 1777. RHP3607, Scottish Record Office.
C2558

By permission of Tods, Murray and Jamieson, WS.

The basic frame, therefore, is triangular. This is one main feature of improved Scottish plough types.

A second is the form of the mould-board, which is curved instead of being flat. At first curved mould-boards were made of wood, which could be plated with iron, but about 1780 Small took his wooden pattern to the Carron Iron Company and had his mould-boards cast in metal. A few years later he also had the sheath and plough-head cast in iron. After that it was not a very big step to the first all-iron plough in Scotland, which appears to have been made about 1803–4 by the firm of Gray of Uddingston, near Hamilton.

21. A ploughing match, with Tom Duncan and Adam Simpson, at St. Martins, Perthshire. Per H. F. Davidson. C2396

The name 'chain-plough' was given because at first Small fixed a chain from the bridle to a hook on the underside of the beam as a means of taking up some of the strain during ploughing. The chain was eventually discarded.

Another feature was Small's careful alignment of the beam, coulter and share with the land-side of the plough, which meant a considerable reduction in friction, and led to the production of a type of plough which stood the test in farming until it was eventually displaced by tractor-drawn equipment in recent times. In both the Rotherham and old Scotch ploughs, the tip of the share was not parallel with the beam but protruded into the land-side. These ploughs were adapted for work on ridges. Small's plough, however, came at a time when ridges were being levelled and straightened out, and the long sole, flat mould-board, and protruding share point were no longer necessary. The occasion and the implement coincided, and as David Low, professor of agriculture in the University of Edinburgh, pointed out, it was capable of being used everywhere in the world.

In spite of the high praise given to Small's plough, it was not by any means the earliest improved plough in Scotland – indeed, various modifications of the old Scotch plough have been recorded, and the 'English' plough was widespread – and though it spread rapidly to all parts of the country, it was not necessarily the only or favourite plough everywhere. Its chief rival – which was nevertheless based on it – was James Wilkie's plough, a type adapted for use in the south-west of Scotland. This was especially popular in Ayrshire and in Annandale, where one farmer was said to have 'run a plough of Wilkie's construction for nine years, without finding a loose pin in it'.[17] It was made at Uddingston, and between 1801–12 Wilkie made about 2,500, at first in wood and then in iron. The stilts were set so as to allow the ploughman to walk comfortably in the bottom of the cut furrow, and the twist of the mould-board was made less hollow, to help to lay the furrow slice more neatly on edge. It was particularly suitable for stony land, and less easily choked than Small's plough in rough stubble.

The plough is a particularly sensitive implement in relation to local conditions, and in the country districts, ploughman and smith would combine in working out the modifications, however small, that improved the plough's performance.

In the nineteenth and twentieth centuries local smiths, agricultural engineering firms, and foundries, like Smail of Lanton in the Borders, Gray of Uddingston in Lanarkshire, Barrowman of Saline in Fife, Sellars of Huntly in Aberdeenshire, Banff Foundry and many others, continued to produce ploughs with local characteristics (Fig. 21), but in general the variations were relatively small. The essential form of Small's swing plough remained until tractor ploughs began to spread during and after the First World War, though by the middle of the nineteenth century, English firms such as Ransome and Howard were looking at the Scottish market, and from the 1870s the Oliver ploughs from America were becoming popular. The original Oliver was of shepherd stock, from the Newcastleton district of Roxburghshire. The firm's ploughs were distributed through Wallace of Glasgow. They were light, relatively cheap, and economical in use since their iron parts were made in easily replaceable sections.

The improved plough types of the eighteenth century onwards should be seen as part of the whole context of agricultural improvement. Enclosing and the creation of individual farms, liming and the improvement of grass and grain crops, better feeding and controlled breeding of livestock, all worked together to create a situation of rapid development within which the evolution of new tools and equipment was both possible and necessary.

The new plough types, capable of being drawn by two good horses, and of being controlled by one man, played a big part here, and can be taken as symbolising one of the most radical changes that ever took place in the Scottish countryside – the change from the community system of joint- or co-farming, to that of individual farming units depending on paid employees.

SPADE, CASCHROM AND RISTLE

Cultivation with the spade is probably very old, but no evidence has been found earlier than the Romano-British iron spade blades from south-east Scotland. It was, however, a widespread and essential substitute for plough cultivation in the rocky and peaty soils of the north and west, where ploughing was difficult or impossible. In some instances, spade cultivation came into increased use in the course of the eighteenth century. In Shetland, where the lairds were then seeking to develop the fishing industry, much reorganisation of settlement took place, which resulted in the fragmenting of units formerly big enough for a plough to work. Township areas were broken up into small crofts, and new crofts were set up on the common grazings, as *outsets*, each only big enough to provide a basic form of sub-sistence to the families whose menfolk were primarily employed in fishing. These small units could no longer maintain the number of oxen needed for the plough, nor were they necessarily big enough to justify plough cultivation. As a result, people had to resort to the spade to till their arable patches, more than ever before, but since the Shetland delving spades were small, they were used by groups of three or four working together as a team (Fig. 22a). The members thrust in their spades and turned a long spit together, and after years of practice worked with the synchronised movements of ballet dancers. Team cultivation was here a response to economic and social circumstances that precluded or did away with the use of the plough.

Team work was also a mark of the spades used in the Highlands and Western Islands, the *cas dhireach* or straight spade, and the *caschrom* or 'crooked' spade (Fig. 22b). The former is similar in shape to equivalent spades from Ireland. The latter is a unique instrument confined in its distribution to the north and west, dating back at least to the seventeenth century. It is particularly well suited to undercutting turfy soil and to levering up stones in rocky terrain. The operator moved backwards as he worked the caschrom, undercutting and turning each sod to the left before stepping back to deal with the next one in line. Whereas Shetland diggers stood side by side, with the caschrom the workers followed each other in echelon. Though it seems to be a large and clumsy instrument, the caschrom nevertheless evolved in response to a particular set of environmental needs, and in the hands of a skilled worker it was four times faster than an ordinary spade. Twelve men using caschroms could till an acre a day, and a season's

A

B

22. a. A delving team using Shetland spades in Foula. Per L. A. A. Holbourn.   C2966
b. Planting potatoes with the caschrom, in the Lochcarron area of Ross-shire. Per Miss A. M. Mackay. C109

work with one from Christmas till late April or mid-May could till enough ground to feed a family of seven or eight with potatoes and meal for a year.

The blades of the Shetland delving spades (being made for the Shetland market by T. Black & Sons, the Berwick-on-Tweed spade makers, as well as locally), and of the *cas dhireach* and *caschrom* are flat, and socketed, like the Romano-British blades. Other spades, however, had wooden blades shod with iron, like the one used for team-cultivation in Dunbartonshire in the late eighteenth century. This probably represents the 'foot-spade' frequently mentioned in documents from the fifteenth century onwards, from Inverness to the Borders.

Another implement confined in its distribution to the north-west is the *ristle*, in Gaelic *crann ruslaidh* (Fig. 23a). The name is Norse in origin, which argues for the antiquity of the ristle. It consisted of an iron blade, like a plough coulter, mounted in a wooden beam. One or two horses were attached at the front, and a handle was fixed at the rear end for control. It was used especially in areas where the soil was full of the matted roots of weeds and grasses, and its function was to cut a long slit through these. The slit prepared the way for the horse-drawn plough to follow, or else it made the work of the caschrom easier.

The ristle can be traced back at least to the seventeenth century, and its distribution covers the islands of Coll, Tiree, Harris, the Uists, and Eriskay. This coincides with the main oat-producing areas of the Western Isles.

Just as the old Scotch plough and the single-stilted ploughs of the Highlands and Islands were implements whose proper functioning depended on communal activity, so also were the hand and foot operated spades, and the ristle, which could serve both the plough and the caschrom. A ristle with two horses and two people working it, followed by a single-stilted plough with four horses and two more people, gives a minimum requirement of six horses and four individuals. Others would follow with spades, and if the caschrom followed the ristle, a number of men would normally work together in a team. These smaller implements, therefore, required the same kind of community involvement as the bigger implements of the more favoured farming districts.

HARROWING AND SOWING

When the ground had been ploughed, the final preparation of the seed-bed was by harrowing to break down the clods of earth before sowing the seed, which was also harrowed in afterwards. In earlier days it was usual for seed to be sown immediately the ground had been prepared, so that the field would contain, as on the farm of Straiton in Midlothian in 1753 (Fig. 17), the plough and the harrow with separate teams, and the sower, with someone to fill his hopper, all at the same time.

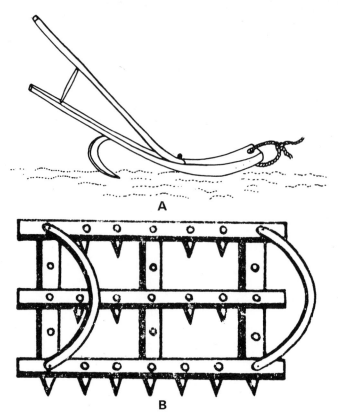

A

B

C

23. a. A *ristle* for cutting a slit in weedy soil in front of a plough or caschrom. From J. Blackadder's Report on a Survey of Skye and North Uist, 1799–1800. By permission of Sir Ian Macdonald of Sleat, Bart. See *Tools and Tillage* 1969. I/2. 119.   C4156

b. A 'Highland harrow' used by women in Dunbartonshire in the late eighteenth century. From D. Ure, *Agriculture of Dunbartonshire*, 1794.

c. Back-harrows in use in Lewis about 1912.   C1234

Harrows are first referred to in Scotland in 1375.[18] They were pulled by horses or sometimes oxen on Lowland farms, and in the crofting districts smaller harrows for covering the seed were dragged by human beings. In Lewis in the 1690s, back-harrows had wooden teeth in the first two rows, to break up the lumps, and rough heather was fixed on the third row, like a brush, to smooth the soil.[19] Back-harrows were frequently pulled by women in the Highlands and Islands, especially after the efforts of the lairds to develop the fishing industry had taken the men away from agricultural tasks. But even as far south as Dumbarton, a so-called 'Highland harrow' was in use in 1794 (Fig. 23b). It was 2 feet 3 inches long by 1 foot 2 inches wide, and had twenty-seven wooden teeth. There was a hoop-shaped handle at each end, by which a woman dragged it, starting at the highest part of the ground and going backwards, harrowing in the seed as she went. This followed delving with the spade. It was said that a single operator with such a harrow could do as much work as two or three men with rakes.

A method of traction which may be of some antiquity was by attachment to the tail of a horse. This was common in Ireland,[20] and is referred to in Skye in 1790, in Gigha in 1794, in Badenoch in 1795, in Argyll in 1798, and in Ross and Cromarty in 1813. Ropes of twisted birch twigs, heather or hair served to fix them to the horse's tail. Though condemned by contemporary writers as barbarous and 'abominably inhuman',[21] nevertheless the practice was widespread, and was considered the best means of breaking in young horses.

Harrows dragged by the tail or by people (Fig. 23c) had wooden teeth, but otherwise the teeth were of iron. The size varied according to region, though the common type had four bars. These could be drawn as single harrows by one horse, or might be worked in pairs (Fig. 24a), or in greater numbers, the draught being always from one corner of the harrow. Break-harrows, used to tear up fallows after ploughing, were heavier, and required more animals to pull them. They were sometimes in two or more parts jointed together, as on Mr. Keir's farm of Fintalich, Muthill, in 1733,[22] and the tines were up to 8 or 10 inches long, sharpened in front like the coulter of a plough.

Harrows were used after the plough, and in areas like Shetland and in late eighteenth-century Dunbartonshire, after the spade. Where cultivation was on a small scale, however, a different set of implements was required – the caschrom for the primary breaking in, often on the lazy-bed principle, and a rake or *racan*, with a stout wooden head that acted as a combined rake and clod-breaker. Social and environmental conditions, therefore, produced correlations between the lazy-bed, spade or caschrom, and the rake-cum-clod-breaker on the one hand, and the field, plough, harrow and roller on the other, the one set marking subsistence agriculture, and the other, commercial farming.

A

B

24. a. Robert Thomson and his wife harrowing with a horse and ox at Claymires'
Ordiquhill, Banffshire, in 1896. Per Mrs. I. McWhirr.   C294
b. Sowing and harrowing on rigs. From Stephens 1844, II, 509.   C273

The reason for sowing directly after the preparation of the seed-bed and for harrowing or raking immediately (Fig. 24b), was the same as that for the use of the seed-drill – that is, to get the grain buried, out of the reach of birds, as quickly as possible. The original method of sowing was one-handed, using a linen sheet (Fig. 17). One side was brought under the left armpit and knotted on the left shoulder. With the left arm, it was collected into a bag containing about half a bushel. If the ridge was long, the bag was replenished by a helper carrying seed in a blind sieve. In Moray in 1811, four harrows were given steady work in covering the seed for a yoking of about four hours.[23] Though the linen sheet was widespread, containers of basketry were also used, for example in Orkney where it was reported that four casts were made of each handful of seed taken out of the basket. Here, as in other parts of the crofting counties, two-handed sowing came in only in the late nineteenth century, though a two-handed sowing sheet on view in Drummond's Agricultural Museum in Stirling in 1835 had been used by John McFarlane, Cardona, near Doune, for seventeen years before that.

Experiments with seed drills were stimulated, *inter alia*, by the publication of Jethro Tull's *Horse Hoeing Husbandry* in 1733, following his experiments with drills from about 1700 onwards. In Galloway, Mr. Craik of Arbigland invented a machine that sowed grain in rows 6 inches apart by about 1760, and a number of these were in use by 1794.[24] S. Morton, Agricultural Implement Maker, Leith Walk, was producing an improved grain drill in 1829, for three drills at a time.[25]

In the 1830s, Drummond's Agricultural Museum exhibited drills and also broadcast sowing machines. One made by Mr. Morrison, factor at Clangregor Castle, had been in use for two years. It could be regulated to sow 1 peck to 2 bolls an acre, and could cover 24 acres a day. It was drawn by one horse. Another from Major Graham of Meiklewood had the same capacity. At the Great Exhibition of 1851 in London, James Watt of Biggar displayed a broadcast sowing machine with jointed seed-chests for passing through gates, and amongst the drill-machines on view were examples by Thomas Sherriff, West Barns, near Dunbar, and W. & J. Hunter, Samuelston, Haddington.

Scottish farmers, therefore, played their part in this area of agriculture as well, though the use of the seed-hopper on the chest continued on crofts and small holdings, supplemented by the mechanical seed-sowing fiddle that came in during the second half of the nineteenth century.

3

Harvesting the Grain

IN 1827, it was related that one of the wickednesses to be encountered in
Argyll was the sight of bands of natives walking to or returning from the
Lothian harvest, carrying large bundles on their backs, on the Sabbath
day.[26] The evangelical ministers of the time greatly opposed such pro-
fanation, not only because of secular activities on Sunday, but also because
most of those who went from the islands and the Highland mainland to
shear the Lowland farmers' grain were young unmarried females, who spent
their wages on 'superfluous finery'. Sometimes the shearers moved in family
groups, and one crofter from Vaternish in Skye worked for six months each
year for the twenty years before 1850 at the farm of Mr. Dudgeon, East
Broomhouse, Dunbar.[27] It was said that the Highland girls liked to sing at
their work, and if a fair-sized group of thirty, forty or fifty was hired, the
farmer might also employ a piper. But things were not always so cheerful
for them. If the season was bad, they would spend many days looking for
employment, with little food and no wages to buy more – a situation that
must underlie an announcement in the *Caledonian Mercury* for 23 September
1766, that the 'Rev. G. Whitefield preached in the Orphan Hospital Park,
for *The Benefit* of the poor Highland Shearers and collected upwards of 60 l.
sterling'.

The summer earnings of these seasonal migrants made an important contribution to the rents they had to pay at home. No one has yet tried to
estimate the numbers of people involved. It amounted to many thousands,
whose wages bolstered the domestic economy over wide areas. If the money
from the Lowland farmers was needed to keep things going in the Highlands,
equally the people from the Highlands were essential to the Lowland
farmers, mainly those in the major producing districts, for before the days
of machinery to cut grain, they had to have a large extra labour supply at
the harvest season, which more than any other is the focal point of the
farming year. This explains why farms like those of Coates and Hairlaw
in the parish of Gladsmuir, East Lothian, still kept labour forces of 76 and 87
respectively, most of them living in cot-towns, in the 1840s, even though the
days of communal run-rig farming were over. Irish seasonal labour (Fig 26a)
replaced that from the Highlands (Fig. 26b) in the course of the nineteenth
century, but until then, this mutual link between Highlands and Lowlands
was an important one.

It is not certain how old the tradition of seasonal migration for harvest

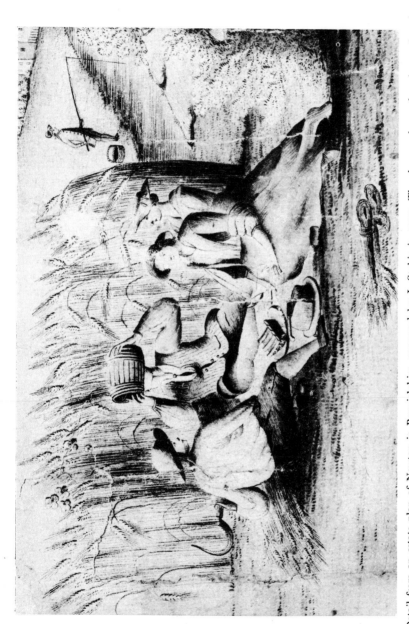

25. Detail from an estate plan of Newton in Berwickshire, surveyed by J. Stobie in 1777. The shearers have ale, wheaten bread, and mutton. One has a toothed *heuk*. There are poppies growing in the crop. RHP3553, Scottish Record Office. By permission of Tods, Murray & Jamieson, W.S.

C4135

work is, but it is likely to go back at least to the seventeenth century, when
there was a series of Acts of the Scottish Parliament that dealt with the local
regulation of shearers' wages by Justices of the Peace, and sought to prevent
the hiring of shearers on Sunday morning. An Act of William[28] established
a shearers' market in Airdrie in 1695. By the eighteenth century, weekly
markets for shearers had been long established in East Lothian and in the
1790s were spreading to neighbouring districts. At the West Port in Edinburgh, Highland shearers were being hired, sometimes in their thousands,
in the eighteenth and early nineteenth centuries.

There was, therefore, an actual market organisation for hiring shearers,
whether from the Highlands or the local towns, or from Ireland, that seems
to have developed its form in the course of the seventeenth century. The fact
that this happened in the main cropping districts suggests in turn that
farming was there beginning to be better organised, capable of producing
a money surplus, for the shearers had to be paid in money and not in kind.
Areas that could afford to hire shearers, therefore, were areas of early
improvements, other indications of which were the use of lime as a fertiliser,
and the expansion of the cattle trade and of the coastal grain trade. The
market organisation was also paralleled by a form of field organisation of
shearers – the *bandwin* – which had already come into being in the first half
of the sixteenth century. This further implies improved organisation on the
farms themselves. But this was based on the capabilities of nothing more
elaborate than the sickle.

THE SICKLE

In one form or another, sickles are as old as cultivation itself. They are not
strictly necessary for harvesting crops, since grain can be plucked by hand – a
practice that was carried out in several parts of north and west Scotland as
long as bere-straw was required for thatching the roofs of houses – but
prehistoric sickles of flint, bronze and then, from the Romano-British period,
of iron, show that some kind of cutting tool was preferred.

Throughout the centuries, the sickle was the tool for cutting cereal crops.
The most general form in the Lowlands appears to have been the type with
a toothed cutting edge (Fig. 25). The teeth were set so as to saw against the
stalks that were being severed, as the sickle was pulled back towards the user.
During the late eighteenth and early nineteenth centuries the toothed sickle
was replaced by a smooth-bladed type which was bigger, and faster in
operation. In the Northern Isles, a small, half-round sickle with a rather
broad, smooth blade is known to have been in use from the seventeenth to
the nineteenth century, though it is likely to be older and to have been more
widespread in the north and west. This, like the toothed sickle, was chiefly,
but not exclusively, used by women.

A

B

26. a. An Irish shearer, Nannie Egan, who lived in Corstorphine in the 1890s. Photo by
S. Salmon. Per Miss R. S. Cowper.   C1755
    b. Shearing barley at Ness, Lewis. Photo: J. MacGeoch.   C2989

Sickles were not only made by local smiths, but were also imported. In 1593–4, the Customs Accounts of Dumfries and Kirkcudbright recorded the import of 178 dozen, in 1593–4 of 168 dozen, and imports continued through the following century.[29] These came from England, and were probably toothed. In the 1760s, however, the smooth bladed type, called the *scythe-hook* or *sharpin' hook* (since a stone was used to sharpen it), appeared in Galloway. It may have been introduced from Ireland. By the 1830s it had spread over most of the Lowlands, and was no doubt being made locally in quantities, in the sickle-making workshops in the Ayrshire villages of Ochiltree, Banton and Auchinmully. Sickles continued to be imported from England as well, to be sold by ironmongers, joiners and smiths. The importance of this small tool only little over a century ago is emphasised by the amount of experimenting that went on with sickles. In the 1830s Drummond's Agricultural Museum in Stirling had on view several improved sickles, as well as English, American and Russian types – and this at a time when the reaping machine was already several years old.

No doubt the spread of the scythe-hook was due to the fact that it could do a quarter to a third more work than the toothed sickle, a factor which would appeal both to seasonal workers on piece rates, and to farmers who wanted to secure the crop as quickly as possible. Another factor that hastened its adoption was the technique of using it. The toothed sickle cut only small bunches at a time, and because of its rasping action, it was easier to cut the stalks low down where they were firmer. For this reason it was especially used by women, who are said to be physiologically better adapted to bending than men. The scythe-hook, however, was a man's tool, used with a slicing motion over a breadth measured by the strength of the arm, or else with a swinging motion called *dingin' in*, more in the manner of a scythe, which gave 50% more speed.

The coming of the scythe-hook marked a watershed in seasonal migration. From the seventeenth century or before until the early 1800s, the Lowland harvests were reaped by blue-bonneted Highland shearers, many of them women, using the toothed sickle; but after the Napoleonic Wars brought about a great increase in corn cultivation in England as well as Scotland, seasonal migrants, most of them male, began to come across from Ireland in increasingly large numbers, carrying their sickles sheathed in straw for safety. In the 1820s, they have been estimated at 6,000–8,000 a year, rising in the mid-1840s, with the development of steam ships and cut-throat fares by rival companies, to 40,000. From the 1850s the number of grey-coated Irishmen gradually declined, partly as a result of the spread of agricultural machinery such as the reaper.[30]

The line of spread of the Irish reapers (Fig. 27b) was first towards the Lothians and south-east, where the harvest was usually early, then north-west to Stirlingshire, along the Forth valley, touching the southern borders

A

B

27. a. A *bandwin* team of seven. Six people shear with the sickle on two rigs, and one man binds and stooks. From Stephens, 1855, II. 332. C280

b. Shearers near Lamington in Lanarkshire. The smooth-bladed sickles are strapped to their wrists. By courtesy of B. Lambie, Gladstone Court Museum, Biggar.

of Fife and even the Carse of Gowrie in Perthshire, and finishing at the end of the season with the crops around Glasgow. The *Glasgow Chronicle* for 17 August 1824 noted that the Irish had ousted the Highlanders from their usual market stance at the Cross of Glasgow, though 2,500 Highland shearers arrived later in the month. Gradually the Highland emigration became more and more confined to Hebrideans and west-coast crofters, whilst the mainland Highlanders gradually gave up the practice.

The watershed was marked not only by a change in the main source of origin of the seasonal migrants, but also by changes in harvesting techniques and the organisation of labour.

Teams and Techniques

The field organisation of shearers is first indicated by the term *bandwin*, used in the Aberdeen Sheriff Court records in 1642. This indicates knowledge of the system in the north-east of Scotland, an area from which people also went – especially in the nineteenth century – to help with the Lothian harvest, but the bandwin team was found mainly in the major grain-growing areas of southern and east central Scotland. It was a method of organisation chiefly related to seasonal workers, people not otherwise connected with the farm, who had to be paid and fed. It was not a question of farm-workers, tenants or sub-tenants carrying out duties or services as part of their employment or conditions of lease, but of outright money payments, for which capital had to be available. The bandwin system is a true indicator of a new shaping of farming attitudes in the seventeenth century, with more emphasis on a cash economy.

The bandwin varied in size according to the width of the plough ridge, but usually seven – or less often nine – people were involved (Fig. 27a). They worked along two ridges at a time with three – or four – shearers on each ridge. One man bound and stooked the sheaves for both ridges. The average width of a ridge, which was related to sowing and reaping requirements, was 15 to 18 feet (4·6–5·5 m.), so that each shearer cleared a width of 5 to 6 feet (1·5–1·8 m.) as he proceeded. The worker, usually a man, on the crown of the ridge, had the job of making straw bands for the sheaves, since this was where the stalks grew longest, and the shearers filled the bands as they cut the grain, leaving them for the bandster to tie.

A bandwin could cut 2 to 2½ acres a day. As a rule, several bandwins worked together in a field, and on big farms up to seventy or a hundred people could be seen at work together in the height of the harvest season. Competition or *kemping* between rival groups was common, though it was not entirely approved of by the farmers since it could lead to hasty work and loss of grain. There could also be competition between the members of a bandwin group, though this did not necessarily lead to uneven work,

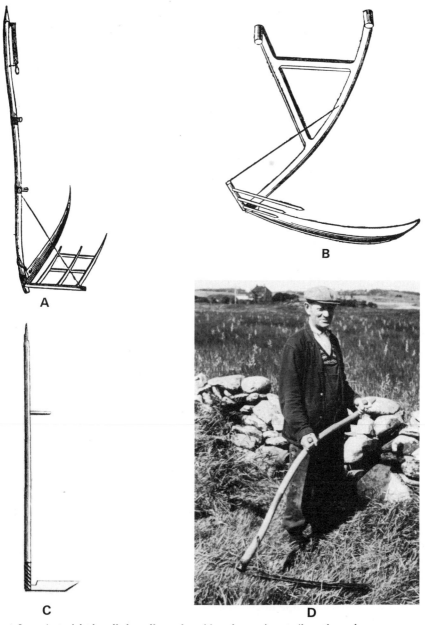

28. a. A straight-handled cradle-scythe with a sharpening *straik* on the end.
b. A Y-shaped cradle-scythe of the North-East type. From Low, 1840, 216–217.

C4004, C4009

c. A short-bladed, short-handled scythe from Shetland. From S. Hibbert, *Description of the Shetland Islands*, 1822.

C1597

d. An S-shaped scythe, used by a Wigtownshire roadman, July 1963.

C3194

since the farmer or his foreman would try to ensure that those in the team were of evenly matched strength. Since a bandwin was paid as a unit, it could not afford to have a weak member.

Such large labour forces required a lot of organising and stewarding, and it is easy to sympathise with George Hope of Fenton Barns in East Lothian, who wrote in 1834 that 'managing thirty-four and thirty-six rigs of shearers is, I assure you, a pretty tiresome job'.[31]

Outside the areas where farming was advanced enough to use and pay for the bandwin system, there was a much looser organisation of shearers who worked by the piece according to a system known as *threaving*, a threave being 24 sheaves of oats or barley, or 28 of wheat – i.e. two stooks. The choice of the bandwin or threaving system depended on social and economic factors and threaving, later called the *gang* system, was certainly well adapted to the abilities of a farm-town community of mixed age and varied degrees of strength. An individual could work on a ridge by himself, or a whole family, or group of friends could collaborate. Younger folk could be trained in the work of shearing, and since there was no specific pressure to keep up with team mates, the weaker and more infirm could work at their own speed. Payment was simply according to the amount they were able to cut. A bandster employed by the farmer tied and stooked the sheaves on the individual ridges, and then at the end of the day the farmer or his steward came along and checked the numbers of stooks for each shearer. The diameter of the sheaves could also be checked by a sheaf-gauge (Fig. 29a).

Threaving was especially common on farms near towns with a reservoir of seasonal manpower. This partly explains why threaving, with the sickle as the cutting tool, survived in the parish of Dundee in the 1840s, when the parishes further from the town had already been largely converted to using the scythe for cutting grain.

In general, on small farms and estates where extra seasonal manpower was less readily available, and therefore more expensive to hire, shearing was done with existing farm labour, plus extra help from the wives and families of farm workers and local tradesmen, and domestic servants. This comes out clearly, for example, from the mid-eighteenth century records of the estate of Grant of Monymusk in Aberdeenshire, where people of all those categories were employed, some working regularly for the full harvest period, some coming for a third or a half or even two-thirds of a day. This was no doubt the normal community method of shearing the crop, out of which the more developed threaving system evolved in the region of big towns.

Where the toothed sickle was used, shearers always moved along the ridge. The smooth sickle or scythe-hook, however, brought a new technique in its train. Instead of cutting along the ridge, it was often worked *across* a set of ridges. This was only practicable if the ridges were blocked out into indiv- idually held groups, rather than lying in intermingled occupancy in the way that is considered to be characteristic of run-rig farming. The presence of the scythe-hook therefore accompanies the tendency to block out ridges into separate holdings, on which the crops could be harvested as units. The new tool and the new technique help to pin-point areas of improving farming. Furthermore, since the scythe-hook could not readily be used in the same field as the toothed hook, one going across and one along the ridges, its adoption had to be total in terms of the unit of land on which it operated.

THE SCYTHE

The iron-bladed scythe with a straight handle or *sned* has been known in Scotland at least from Roman times, but until the late eighteenth century its primary function was to mow grass and hay. The reference in the Acts of the Scottish Parliament for 1643[32] to '2000 hwickis and 100 scythes for sheiring and mowing' distinguishes the function of the scythe in mowing grass and the sickle in shearing grain. There was undoubtedly a demand for scythes, big enough to have to be filled from outside, for the Dumfries Customs Accounts mention the import from England of 17 dozen in 1592–3, and more later.[29]

In the sixteenth and seventeenth centuries, there are only a very few references to cutting cereal crops with a scythe. In the late eighteenth century, the possibility was being much discussed. Lord Kames recommended it – provided the ground had first been made smooth – because of its greater speed, which gave a quicker harvest, but farmers in general were uneasy about it and several trials were made with the scythe in Dumfries, Berwick, the Lothians, Fife, Angus and elsewhere, between the late 1700s and early 1800s and the scythe was discarded in favour of the sickle again. This was partly because some farmers thought the scythe shook out too much grain, especially from wheat, but it was due more to the fact that the strong, often tangled and twisted crops of the Lothians and Carse of Gowrie were less suitable for the scythe than the lighter oat crops of North-East Scotland. The suitability of the tool to the regional type and character of crop is therefore a factor relevant to its adoption.

In Moray, Nairn, Aberdeen and Banff, there was a steady increase in the use of the scythe for cutting grain from about 1805 onwards. It was in this area that a particular type of scythe with a Y-shaped handle appears to have developed in the first quarter of the nineteenth century (Fig. 28b). At first it had a wooden 'cradle' attachment, with three or more wooden teeth (Fig. 29b), that helped to lay the grain more evenly in the swathe, but this was not particularly popular in the North-East, and was quickly given up there. It was found until recent times, however, in districts such as Orkney. In the North-East, this cold shoulder of Scotland, the scythe was used mainly for oats at first, though barley or bere, and wheat, continued to be reaped with the sickle for some time.

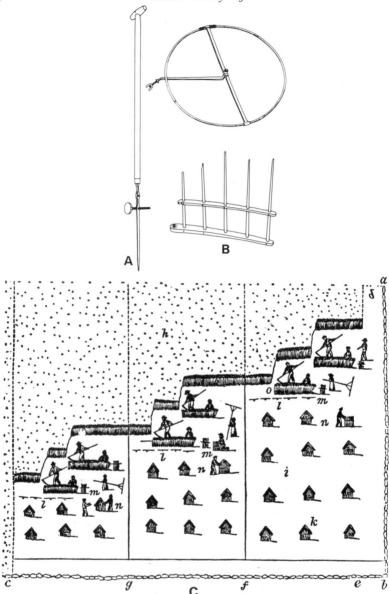

29. a. A sheaf-gauge from Atholl, for measuring sheaf-sizes (the pin was put in the upper hole for wheat) when shearing was being done on the *threaving* system. National Museum, PC5.

b. Round and rake-shaped cradles, fixed between the blade and sned of a scythe, for laying short corn neatly in a swathe. National Museum, PC20, PC21.　　　　　　　　　C4146

c. Scythe teams working across the rigs. Men scythe, women gather and rake, men bind and stook the sheaves, which are hooded. From the *Quarterly Journal of Agriculture*, 1834, IV, 364.　　　　　　　　　　　　　　　　　　　　　　　　　　　　　C1165

By the 1850s the scything pattern in the North-East had thickened almost to the exclusion of the sickle, and the use of the scythe was spreading, not only into the north and west where it was rudely referred to as the 'Aberdeenshire slasher', but also south into Kincardineshire, where shearers were hard to get and therefore costly, and into Angus.

Further south, a type of scythe with an S-shaped handle was the rule (Fig. 28d), probably introduced from England along with the scythe-blades that were made there in places like the late eighteenth-century Abbeydale Industrial Hamlet near Sheffield. The old, indigenous, straight-handled scythe (Fig. 28a) also survived longest in the Borders and in Galloway. The late blacksmith at Lochhead of Elrig, Wigtownshire, T. Thomson, used such a scythe. The lower hand-grip was fixed at the height of the user's hip-bone, and the upper grip the length of the forearm and outstretched fingers above that. Above that again near the top of the long straight handle was the 16-inch (40 cm.) long wooden sharpening *straik* which was left in position to give the scythe its proper balance. One side of the straik was coated with grease and fine scythe-sand from Loch Enoch when the blade needed sharpening. The handle of Mr. Thomson's scythe was 9 feet (2·7 m) long and the blade 5 feet (1·5 m.) long. With it, he could mow a swathe of hay 10 feet (3 m.) wide by 1 foot (0·3 m.) deep. In Shetland there was a variety with a short, broad blade, adapted for mowing hay on steep banks (Fig. 28c). The North-East type, however, still appears to be spreading into those areas, though the day of the scythe is almost over.

In North-East and East-Central Scotland, the adoption of the scythe for cutting grain led to fundamental changes in the work-team. Men and women more or less reversed their original roles, for the scythe, like the scythe-hook in the south, was almost exclusively a man's tool. It also made it possible to reduce the size of the team, though this varied according to the size of the farm. Scythers had to be strong men, capable of undergoing great fatigue. Behind them came women or *lifters* who gathered the sheaves into bands previously made by the *strapmakers*, and a male *bandster* followed the women, tying and stooking the sheaves. In the south of Scotland the women gatherers sometimes used a *lifting pin* in the form of an iron hook or small wooden rake, to help the reach of their arms (Fig. 30b). A man or woman came behind the groups, with a large rake to take up loose heads of corn. An economical arrangement was for three scythesmen and their followers, working together, to be served by one raker.

Like the scythe-hook, the scythe was generally worked across the ridges, the men cutting in echelon, one behind the other (Fig. 29c). It was hard to use if the ground was stony and bumpy, so not only was stone-clearance and rolling desirable but also a smoothing and levelling of ridges would have eased its path. From the late 1700s, therefore, whether in relation to the scythe-hook or scythe, farmers were being forced into paying closer attention to the

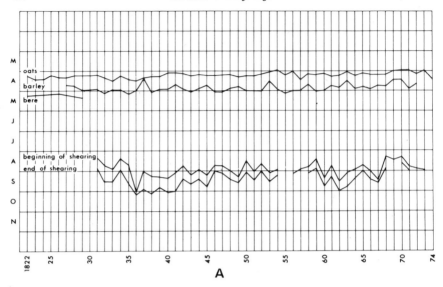

A

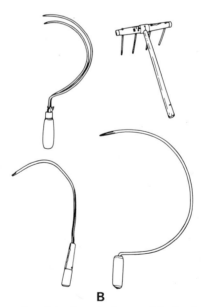

B

30. a. Sowing and harvesting dates for oats, bere and barley in the Camserney area of Perthshire, 1822–1874. Barley replaced bere after 1829. Calculated from Alexander MacGregor's Account Book of Camserney Farm, Perthshire, lent by A. Prior, per Dr. M. Stewart.

C3853

b. Lifting pins from South-East Scotland, used to increase the gatherer's reach in making sheaves. National Museum.

C4147

quality and appearance of the ground surface than ever before. They also had to think in terms of the suitability of crops in relation to the tools used to cut them, and vice-versa; and had to consider crop-acreages in relation to man-power and tools and the time needed to cut the crops, which could become far too ripe and might be badly shaken if the harvest was protracted.

With the sickle, a shearer was expected to cut a quarter to a third of an acre a day, i.e. about $2\frac{1}{2}$ acres a day for a bandwin team working from 6 a.m. to 6 p.m. On a big farm, the number of people required for shearing was cal-culated at 8 to 10 acres a head over a period of sixteen to twenty days. If shearing was done by the piece, as commonly happened near big towns, this cost 4/6 to 5/– an acre in Berwickshire and 7/– to 8/– an acre in Angus in 1794,[33] a difference in cost that reflects the scarcity of seasonal labour north of the Tay, and helps to explain the adoption of the scythe as the main grain cutting tool there. The shearing period was longer there as well, and might stretch from mid-August to early October, depending on the season (Fig. 30a).

A good day's shearing produced an average of 8 to 12 threaves, i.e. 192 to 288 sheaves of oats or bere, or 224 to 346 sheaves of wheat. This gives the number of sheaves in approximately a third of an acre, which is not too far off the figure of 960 sheaves of barley or 768 of oats per acre, given in Morton's *Cyclopedia of Agriculture* in 1871.

A scythesman could cut 2 acres of oats, nearly 2 acres of barley, and something over 1 acre of wheat in a day of 10 hours. It was variously esti-mated that 5 scythes were equal to 9 sickles, or 8 scythes to 12 sickles. There were not only savings in time and manpower, but also in drying time, for scythe-cut sheaves were more open, and also in straw, for the scythe cut lower than the sickle. These were advantages enough in areas of family farms, where relatively few workers were available. But where scythesmen had to be employed, the saving was still considerable, even though men earned more than women. It was estimated by Henry Stephens in 1844 that the food and wages of a bandwin team of seven came to $9/5\frac{1}{4}$ an acre; for a scythe team of ten, the cost was $5/2\frac{1}{2}$ an acre for oats, 6/3 for barley, and $7/9\frac{3}{4}$ for wheat.

Since on this basis there were both direct and indirect advantages in using the scythe rather than the sickle, the long retention of the sickle in the most advanced farming areas of Scotland must be due to other than primarily economic factors. The paradox in South and South-East Scotland is due largely to the nature of the labour supply. Until the third decade of the nineteenth century, the labour was supplied by seasonal migrants from the Highlands, the majority of whom were female, and for them the sickle was not only the traditional tool, but also the one that could be most easily carried on their long, often rough journeys. The scythe, in any case, was a man's tool. Even when Irish labour replaced that from the Highlands, the easily portable sickle still remained the reaping tool.

Because these southern farmers were so dependent on outside labour at harvest time, they were hardly in a position to risk making experiments with an innovating tool such as the scythe, except amongst their regular farm workers. The adoption of the scythe would have involved new deployments in the organisation of work groups in the harvest field, as well as a considerable alteration in the allocation of work roles to male and female labour. It was easier to take the line of least resistance by conforming to the customary methods of the incoming seasonal labour supply on which the quick harvesting of the crop depended, even though the farmers could not have failed to know that this was economically less favourable. It is ironical that the sheer size of the acreage in the best farming regions of Scotland forced the farmers to retain a system suited to the needs and equipment of the seasonal labour supply. Nevertheless, it seems certain that the development of the bandwin and to a lesser extent the threaving systems in the seventeenth century is a sign that farmers were seeking to optimise the usefulness of the available labour force even then, but having reached an optimum (in terms of balance between tools, labour supply, and acreage), they could under existing circumstances do no more. It is little wonder that Scottish farmers were so eager to experiment with reaping machines, and that Bell's reaper ultimately supplied a pattern to the world that led to a revolution in harvesting technology.

MACHINE REAPING

Experiments with reaping machinery started as early as 1805, following the offer of a prize by the Highland and Agricultural Society of Scotland in 1803. The first machine was made in 1805 by Mr. Gladstone, Millwright in Castle Douglas (Fig. 31a). It had a rotary cutter equipped with a small number of toothed sickles. In 1812 Smith of Deanston (Fig. 31b) in Stirlingshire entered a machine for a £500 prize offered by the Dalkeith Farming Club. It worked well on level ground, but did not win the prize. It may not be an accident that it was this same man who later worked out the system of thorough drainage with underground tile drains that finally led to the creation of level fields, free from ridge-and-furrow, on which reaping machinery could work easily. Smith's machine, like those of Alexander Kerr of Edinburgh and Mr. Scott of Ormiston, also had a rotary cutter. Modern tractor-operated hay-cutting equipment shows that rotary cutters were feasible, but at this early date horsepower could not produce enough speed, nor was the ground surface level enough for easy operation.

If the 'first great achievement of the nineteenth century was the invention of the reaper',[34] then the credit for the first real breakthrough in producing a practical machine must go to the divinity student, Patrick Bell, son of a farmer in the parish of Auchterhouse, Angus, and later minister of Carmyllie in the same county. He had seen an illustration of Smith's machine, and he

A

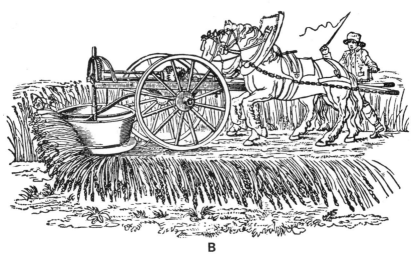

B

31. a. A model of a reaping machine by Gladstone of Castle Douglas, about 1805.

C4093

b. Smith of Deanston's reaper, 1812. From J. C. Loudon, *Encyclopedia of Agriculture*, 1831,

422.   C4038

said himself that the sight of a pair of garden shears sticking in a hedge gave him the idea of using mechanised scissors as a basis for the cutting blade. The principle he evolved was so fundamental that it has remained the basis for cutting blades, whether on reapers, binders or combine harvesters, to the present day.

Bell's model was made in 1827, and his first machine was produced in 1828 (Fig. 32). By 1832, ten machines made by him or made on the same principle were at work, mainly in East-Central Scotland, and examples had been exported to America, Australia, and Poland. But locally and in general the reaper was before its time, however great the need for it in principle. Neither the land surface nor the farm-folk were ready for it. The fields of ridge-and-furrow were not suitable for such a long, heavy machine. It was awkward to turn. The cutting mechanism was relatively complicated, and there was as yet an almost total lack of supporting technical services for the repair and maintenance of machinery. This was something smiths and joiners still had to learn. In those early days, therefore, although it was one of the fundamental inventions in the farming world, it remained as a relatively isolated phenomenon in East-Central Scotland.

Meantime in America, a young Virginian farmer, Cyrus McCormick, was experimenting with his own machine. It was tried in public in 1831, and patented in 1834. The credit for producing the first practical mechanical reaper must go to Bell, but it was McCormick who was able to incorporate and combine the whole range of elements required to make a reaper efficient in all respects, including manoeuvrability. These elements were: the cutting blade that worked with a to-and-fro motion between fixed fingers that gripped the grain stalks as they were cut; the revolving reel that guided the grain on to the machine and helped to control it during and just after cutting; the platform on which the cut grain was gathered; the straw divider on the outer side of the platform separating the cut from the standing grain; the driving wheel, placed directly behind the horses, which carried most of the machine's weight and drove the mechanism; the offset draught, which allowed the horses to walk in front of the machine and at the side of the grain to be cut, as opposed to the system of pushing from behind that applied to Bell's and some other reapers.

McCormick's reaper first came on the market about 1840, and 50 had been sold by 1844. In 1847 the family moved to Chicago, near the great corn-growing prairies of the West, and established there the works that developed into The International Harvester Company, which by 1871 was turning out 10,000 reapers a year.

In 1851, a McCormick reaper was shown before a very wide audience at the Great International Exhibition in London, along with another much simpler American reaper, the Hussey. Bell's reaper was also shown there, and for a period there was a great increase of interest in it. It was realised that the

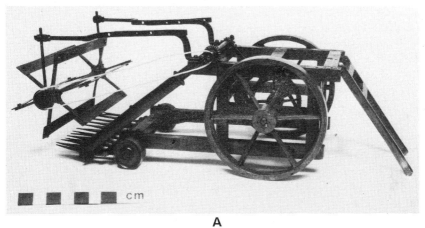

A

B

C

32. a. Bell's original model, made in 1827.   C4092
  b. Bell's reaper in action, pushed from behind. From J. C. Loudon, *Encyclopedia of Agriculture*, 1831, 423.   C4037
  c. Crosskill of Beverley's version of Bell's reaper, from a poster dated 1853.   C3936

country had had an efficient reaper, almost unsung outside East-Central Scotland, for 20 years. In the next year or two various reaping competitions were held. Bell's reaper, nicknamed the 'Lass o' Gowrie', defeated a Hussey at Perth in 1852. A version of Bell's reaper, improved by the English firm, Crosskill of Beverley (Fig. 32c), defeated a McCormick in 1853. George Hope of Fenton Barns extolled Bell's reaper in an address to the Haddington Farmers' Club, and Crosskill's improved reaper had some popularity for a time. In the end, however, the lighter American reapers won the day, on the grounds both of economy and manoeuvrability.

It is evident that the farmers in the main grain-producing areas of Scotland let Bell's reaper lie fallow for a quarter of a century, in spite of considerable discussion in newspapers and farming circles about it and other types, for the same reasons that they did not adopt the scythe, and because of servicing difficulties, as well as the need for high investment in drainage to level out ridges and furrows. The import of American types came at a time when systematic underground drainage was beginning to be well advanced, and when the seasonal labour supply was beginning to tail off as a result, amongst other things, of the Irish potato famine. The Hussey and McCormick reapers, therefore, were able to make very rapid headway.

At first, however, the purchase of a reaping machine did not substantially reduce the labour requirements. George Hope calculated, for example, that to work and keep up with a machine cutting an acre an hour, sixteen people would be required. This meant that the smaller farm areas could not readily adopt the reaper, and the scythe remained the standard means of cutting the crops in North-East Scotland, for example, till the 1870s and later. The adoption of the Hussey is itself to some extent to be related to areas where the seasonal availability of manpower had not decreased too seriously, for its very simple construction meant that it deposited its cut swathe in the path of its next run. There had to be enough hands to gather and sheaf the cut grain in order to let the machine work continuously. Though the Hussey was cheaper to buy and easier to service and maintain, it may not have been any cheaper in the end, because of this manpower requirement, than the technically more complicated Bell or McCormick reapers, which could deposit the swathe clear of the next run.

As improvement were made (Figs. 33a–c), like mechanical rear or side delivery of cut grain instead of manual delivery by a man with a rake, the manpower requirements gradually became less. They were further reduced after the string-tying self-binder produced by McCormick in 1878 began to spread in the 1890s, and local firms like Bisset of Blairgowrie began to make their own versions. Finally, the combine-harvester, designed to cut, thresh and dress grain at the same time, reached Scotland in 1932. It was a Clayton combine, used by Lord Balfour at Whittingehame Mains in East Lothian.[35] Because it performed three functions at a time, it represented an ultimate in labour saving.

A

B

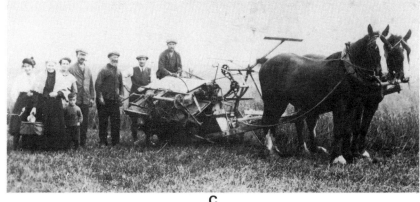

C

33. a. Piece-time in East Lothian. The man on the reaper has a side-rake, and the tilting board is raised to gather the grain as it is cut. Per Dr. J. Richardson.　　　　C295

b. A reaper with a reel to replace a man with a side-rake, and a back-rake attached at the rear. Near Portsoy, Banffshire. Per D. M. Cruickshank.　　　　C2183

c. A pair of horse pulling a Hornsby binder at Howe o' Pitfour, Aberdeenshire. Per Mrs. Simpson.　　　　C4024

HARVEST HOME

Much of the effort of the farmer's year goes into preparing the ground for the crop and then into harvesting it. Quite apart from any original considerations of fertility rites, the sheer relief of getting the last sheaf cut and then of getting it safely into the stackyard was enough to inspire a sense of rejoicing. When George Gall, Oldtown, Atherb, Aberdeenshire, finished on 27 August 1868 he wrote in his diary:

> 'We finished the cutting of the corn this morning——. As we are to have our Meal and Ale tonight my Father went down to the Brewery of Boffa and brought up a little anchor of whisky, so that we are making preparations for the blow up.'

The last stalks of grain to be cut were bound into a sheaf, or sometimes made into a human or geometrical shape, sometimes a cross, and hung in the kitchen or laid on the rafters of the byre.[36] In Argyll, this was often given to the horses when they first began to harrow or plough, and in the North-East the *maiden* or *clyack-sheaf* was given to the best milker in the byre, the first calved cow, or a mare in foal, or was shared out among the beasts at Christmas or the New Year. It might also be set on top of the last stack to be put up in the corn-yard (Fig. 36a). In the Lowlands the last sheaf was treated with honour, but in the North and West the last handful cut might be thrown into the field of a neighbour who had not yet finished, as a kind of insult, in which case it was called in Gaelic the *cailleach*, old woman, or *gobhar bhacach*, lame goat. In some districts, for example Galloway, the last *rip* of standing corn was cut by workers who threw hooks at it until one was successful. The girl who cut the last *rip*, according to the *Galloway Gazette* for 21 October 1961, was regarded as queen at the harvest *kirn* that followed, and was in great demand as a partner.

The *meal-an'-ale* or *kirn* was held at the end of cutting or when the crop had been carted home. The term 'meal-an'-ale' was applied in the North-East to both the celebration and the dish itself, which was made of oatmeal, ale, and sugar, with whisky. Another element in such a feast, as at Corgarff, Aberdeenshire, was a cheese, the *clyack kebbock*, cut by the farmer. The first piece cut, and the biggest, was given to the herd-boy. These customs, of which there are several local variations, gradually died out in the course of the nineteenth century as machines replaced man-power.

STOOKING AND STACKING

When farming became more of a business, and seasonal labour was paid to cut the crops according to the threaving system, the farmer or his steward checked the diameter of the sheaves with a sheaf-gauge (Fig. 29a). The diameter varied according to area, and whereas 12 inches (30 cm.) was normal in the Lothians, in Angus 10 inches (25 cm.) was more usual, in Banffshire the 'muckle threave' was of 10 inches (25 cm.), and the 'little threave' of $7\frac{1}{2}$ inch (19 cm.) sheaves, and in the Hebrides, where the annual rainfall is high, 5 or 6 inches (13–15 cm.) was and remains the standard. The difference in size led to different techniques of tying the band, for in the Lowlands this was done on the ground, and in the Highlands against the workers' thigh. Another effect of larger sheaves was the adoption of a special tool, the *lifting-pin*, in the form of a hook or small hand-rake, used by gatherers in South-East Scotland to extend their reach.

The tying bands were made of straw until the advent of the string-tying binder, of which the first example was exhibited by Walter A. Wood at Birmingham in 1876. American firms in particular worked at developing an efficient knotter, and by the 1880s several were on the market. T. S. Bisset and Son of Blairgowrie (established 1862) produced their own self-tying binder in 1890. By this stage, knotters could be set to regulate the size of sheaves according to the condition of the crop. Tying with a straw band also had its own techniques. For small sheaves a single bunch of stalks was adequate, but bigger ones required a double length twisted near the ear-end. Not only was there a skill to be learned in tying bands, which seems to have been always a man's job, but in the pre-enclosure days of joint-farming, individuals had each their special way of tying bands as an ownership mark to prevent theft. Cases of stealing sheaves 'of uther menis bind'[37] can be found in Orkney as well as Ayrshire in the late sixteenth–early seventeenth century. As recently as the 1920s in North Ronaldsay, Orkney, identification of sheaves was possible after a gale because 'Verracott had the knot and crook, and North Manse the scythe band and soo's tail'.[38] It is possible that such ownership marking points to a period when not only the grazing, but also the patches of arable, were held in common by the members of the community.

An old form of setting-up oat-sheaves, which remained in use in wet conditions, was to stand them singly, with the band tied near the top and the tail well spread out. This was also a good method if oats were cut rather green. The use of such *gaits* was widespread, though where sheaves were small, it was necessary to put three or four sheaves together, bound individually but also with an extra band round their tops. This system, also known in Ireland and Northern England, may well indicate a method of setting up sheaves of oats that was more the norm till the eighteenth century than the more familiar arrangement of six, eight, ten, twelve (Fig. 34a) or fourteen sheaves leaned against each other in a line, with or without one or two hood-sheaves on top to run the rain off. Stooks of wheat usually contained fourteen sheaves and in Midlothian conditions in the late eighteenth century this long-strawed crop could dry in eight days, whereas oats required two weeks and barley three.

When the period of drying in the stook had ended, the sheaves were taken

A

B

34. a. Leading hooded stooks at Killiecrankie Farm. From *Scotland Illustrated*, 1850, Plate LXVIII.   C4088

b. Building *screws* in Shetland. The sheaves are being carried in loops of rope on the back.
                                                                                                                          C1641

home to the stackyard beside the barn, though in wet weather, and if the butts of the sheaves were full of grass, then small temporary stacks were built in the field. In Skye, such a *gurracag* had about sixty sheaves in it, built to overlap like slates; the Orkney *scroo*, holding twenty-four to twenty-eight sheaves, was slightly smaller than its bigger equivalent, the *diss*; *rickles* in Ayrshire and elsewhere in South-West and Central Scotland could consist of ten to twelve sheaves laid with their heads together and a single sheaf spread on top, or of forty to sixty sheaves built as a small stack, again with a hood sheaf. These temporary stacks were taken home later to be built into full-sized stacks, which were thatched and roped to preserve them through the winter.

The building of temporary stacks meant extra handling and a consequent risk of losing grain. For this reason, farmers preferred to get their sheaves straight into the stackyard, and in case of wet weather, precautions of two kinds could be taken, alone or in combination. The stack could be built around a wooden tripod so that it had an air-space in the centre, and in conjunction with this a vent leading out to the windward side was common. Such openings provided access and lodging for mice and rats, however, and in the eighteenth century it became common to set stacks on raised stone foundations, consisting of a circle of upright stone or sometimes wooden pillars and one in the centre, each topped with an overlapping coping stone shaped like the head of a mushroom. so that rodents could not climb up easily. The earliest reference noted specifies nine pillars and nine bonnets, for Angus in 1768.[39] The stones were linked by planks, over which the sheaves were built (Fig. 35a–b). Cast-iron stack foundations of similar shape were being made from the early 1800s by engineering firms like C. D. Young & Co., Edinburgh, Gibson & Son, Edinburgh, and others. Where, as often happened, the foundation was no more than a pile of old straw, brushwood or broom, spread on the ground, or over a paving of small stones, then a single fencing post was often knocked into the centre so that it would help to keep up the heart of the stack and prevent it from drawing water. If this did happen, the stack would heat up and the straw and grain would become mildewed and useless. The builder of it would suffer loss of face, and the farm-lads might well rub salt in the wound by putting an old chimney can or bottomless bucket on top of the stack at dead of night.

Throughout the country, stacks varied considerably in shape and size. The temporary field stacks are very similar in shape to the small barnyard stacks of the Northern and Western Isles, which average about 5 feet (1·5 m.) in diameter by little more than 7 feet (2·1 m.) high (Fig. 34b). These are built as cones that start narrowing almost from the very bottom, up to the tip, and this is the shape that no doubt represents the way in which stacks were formerly built. Early representations, dating from 1693, show stackyards at Linlithgow, St. Andrews, Ross and Dunfermline, in which the stacks are neatly

A

B

C

D

35. a. A Midlothian stack on a raised foundation, with diamond roping. From G. Robertson, *Agriculture of Midlothian*, 1795.   C3921

b. A rick stand by C. D. Young & Co., Edinburgh, for ricks 10 to 15 feet in diameter, with a wooden frame over the pillars.   C3934

c. Stack shapes and roping methods: 1. Net-work roping, or *edderin'*. From Stephens 1844, III, 1096; 2. Lozenge roping, or swappin'. From *ib*, 1094; 3. Half net-work, half lozenge, From a sketch by A. Anderson, Aberdeenshire; 4. A Border method. From Stephens, 1844. III, 1096; 5. An Orkney method, using many ropes and little thatch. From a sketch by W. S. Moar. Previously published in *Gwerin* 1961. III, 3/4, 19.   C3972

d. On the large sheaves of the South-East, a woman or boy, the *striddler*, passed the sheaves to the builder on the stack. From Stephens, 1844, III, 1086.

A

B

36. a. Stacks in Fife, one with a straw cross on top.   C3909
   b. Stack-building at Currie, Midlothian. There is a *striddler* on the stack to help the builder. The man on the ground wears sacking to protect his trousers during building, and holds a stack beater for knocking in protruding ends of sheaves. Per J. Watt, Currie.   C2597

built, with round shanks topped by conical hats.[40] This was the most wide-spread form, though the size varied greatly. Slightly more sophisticated was the type Slezer showed at Stirling, in which the foundation was relatively narrow, and the shank swelled out to the eaves. This type was once fairly widespread, and made a fine-looking stack, even though the amount of the overhang was not strictly necessary.

In the South-East of Scotland, stacks were very large by the standards of most other parts of the country. In the mid-nineteenth century stacks of oats and barley were about 15 feet (4·6 m.) in diameter, and those of wheat up to 18 feet (5·5 m.) or more. The size made it awkward both for the man who forked the sheaves, and for the builder, and the custom, therefore, was for a female field-worker, a *striddler*, to stand on the stack (Fig. 35d), taking the sheaves from the forker and placing them for the builder as he moved round the rising stack (Fig. 36b). The relatively good climate of this area, and one or two others, also made it possible for very large rectangular stacks of grain to be built, a method that was followed for wheat as far north as Easter Ross in the early nineteenth century.[41] On a much smaller scale, at the same date, temporary stacks of a rectangular shape, called *dashes*, were to be found. They were 10 to 12 feet (3–3·7 m.) long by 6 feet (1·8 m.) high and 4 feet (1·2 m.) broad, finished on top like the roof of a house, often thatched with straw or hay. After two or three weeks, they were rebuilt into cylindrical stacks of the usual form.

THATCHING AND ROPING

Once the crop was safely in the stackyard and the farmer had 'got winter' – in the eloquent phrase of the North-East – the stacks were thatched and roped. Little or no thatch was used in some parts of the Northern and Western Isles, because the small heads were thought to make it unnecessary, though the stacks were nevertheless well tied down with ropes of heather or straw, or latterly of coir-yarn or binder-twine. Here, as elsewhere in the country, the seasonal roping of stacks required a lot of rope, and much time was spent beforehand in the evenings and on rainy days, twisting ropes by hand or by means of a rope-twister.

Rope-twisting was one of the several crafts carried on on the crofts and farms without ever becoming a specialist job. The technique of twisting heather or bent-grass or the like by hand is an old one, still occasionally done in the islands, but most twisting was by means of a special implement, the *thrawcrook* (Fig. 37), which had various different shapes and a variety of different names throughout the country. It required two workers, one to turn the twister, and the other to 'let-out' or feed the straw into the rope as it formed. The completed ropes were coiled into round balls which could be quite large, or smaller oval balls, to be stored on the couples of the barn till

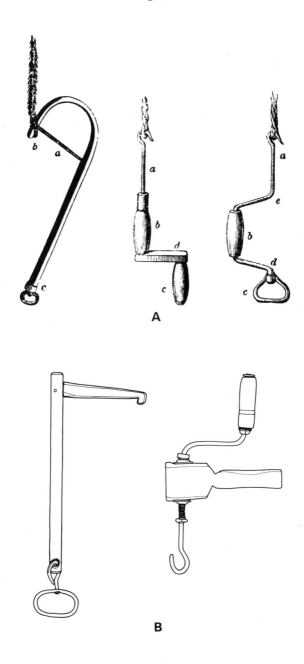

37. Rope twister types: a. From Stephens 1844, III, 1102; 1855, II, 360. C264, C266.
b. In the Angus Folk Museum.   C4148

37. c. Twisting a straw-rope with a *thrawcrook* in the Borders. By courtesy of the School of Scottish Studies.   C3004

required. Round balls were used when roping thatch across the shoulders of round-headed stacks, to form a lozenge pattern. The oval ones were used, like shuttles in net-making, to take horizontal ropes under and round previously placed verticals, the result being a network pattern of squarish meshes. These techniques were used in roping thatch on the roofs of houses as well as on grain stacks. When, in the mid-nineteenth century, there was an influx into Orkney of farmers from the North-East of Scotland, they took this kind of oval ball and the name for it, *edderin*, with them, and introduced the net-work style of roping thatch to an area previously accustomed to a large number of vertical ropes only. The widespread adoption of coir yarn for roping in the early years of this century has led to the loss of the considerable skill needed to make such oval balls, which at one time were the subject of competitions at agricultural shows.

In some cases, especially in the North-East, the net work and lozenge pattern techniques were combined on one stack, and in the Borders, a style was used rather like that found in Orkney. The head of the stack was roped by a large number of verticals, about thirty, the lower ends of which were fixed to or taken round a stout rope that encircled the stack at the eaves. This method, which survived in the Borders and in Orkney, may reflect the older style (Fig. 35c).[42]

The finishing touch was given to stacks in some areas by making a little tuft on the crown, known as a *peerie* in Central Scotland, or a cross, or something more elaborate.

4

Threshing the Grain

AMONGST the important members of the farm labour force before the days of threshing machinery was the *barnman*, also known as the *tasker* or *lotman*, whose main duty was to thresh the grain with the flail. On smaller farms the family saw to the threshing, and on bigger farms a barnman might be employed for a few weeks every year in winter, in which case he got as his wages a twenty-fifth part of the grain he threshed, or he might be a full-time employee, doing outside work chiefly during the hay and grain harvests, when not threshing. He was amongst the first to be ousted from the hierarchy of farm workers as technological advance brought threshing machinery into being.

The fact that grain was threshed by hand limited the amount that could be handled at one time, which meant that not only the stacks, but also the barns in which grain was threshed and straw stored, were smaller. The large stacks of the Lothians and other fertile areas result from the introduction of threshing machinery that could handle them, and the size of barns increased at the same time.

An average to good barnman could thresh 1 to $1\frac{1}{2}$ bolls (6 to 9 bushels) a day. Depending on the kind of grain, the number of sheaves to the boll in the mid-nineteenth century varied between 48 for wheat and up to 72 for barley or oats. On this basis, about 100 sheaves could be threshed daily. At an estimated yield of 37 bushels of wheat, 40 of barley, and 60 of oats to the ton, the barnman therefore threshed a ton of wheat in about six days and a ton of barley in about ten. In practice the work went faster since barnmen rarely worked alone. There was always a temptation for a thresher who was being paid by the piece to go in for quantity rather than quality, but he could always make the excuse that the grain left on the stalks was good for the animals – in the words of an Aberdeenshire writer, they were 'nane the waur o' a wisp wi' a fyou o' the berries on't'.[43] Later on, payment came to be in money rather than in kind.

PROOFCASTING

Grain was threshed for sale, as well as for internal consumption, as food for men and animals. When the question of sale arose, the amount of grain in the stacks had to be worked out by a method called *proof-casting*. A *proofman* was appointed, satisfactory to both buyer and seller, to cast down the stack, selecting one sheaf out of every twenty-four as a rule, which was set aside to be threshed. A stack of a hundred stooks would give sixty proof sheaves. Two men worked with flails, one for the buyer and one for the seller, and the proofman winnowed, cleaned and measured the corn threshed from the proof sheaves. In late eighteenth century Moray, the sixty proof sheaves would produce about three bushels, which was multiplied by 20 to ascertain the amount in the stack, for which the buyer should pay. The buyer also got what was threshed from the proof sheaves as part of his bargain.[44]

FLAIL THRESHING

Even a tool as simple as the flail had an effect on the form and layout of the barn. The couples had to be high, so that the beater or *souple* of the flail would not strike them as it swung over, and a special threshing floor had to be incorporated. The simplest form was of clay, spread over the threshing area of the barn. In 1766 an Orkney farmer in Sanday recorded in his diary the transport of 28 horse-loads of clay to lay his threshing floor. Such floors were laid across the barn, alongside the space between the doors, between which winnowing was done (Fig. 72, Ch. 10). In some areas, square wooden threshing platforms, called *chaps* in the North-East, with joists resting on the earthen floor, or sunk into the floor, were used.

In threshing with the flail, there was always a sheaf or a bunch of straw under the head of the one that was being threshed (Fig. 38a). If several men were working together, the sheaves were laid side by side in a row with the bands on, and heads together. Opposite this, a second row was laid so that the heads overlapped those of the first row. Threshing was carried on along the heads in the centre of the row, then the sheaves got a half turn, and a further beating. Turning was done by a helper, or by the thresher's flail, or by the toe of his boot. Sheaves could also be laid in a circle, ears inward.

Flails are in two parts (Fig. 38b), a handstaff about 5 feet (1·5 m.) long and a souple averaging 2½ to 3 feet (0·8–0·9 m.) long. Ash or larch were commonly used for the handstaff, and ash, hazel, thorn or any kind of wood that did not split easily for the souple. A length of tarred rope or old hawser tightly bound with cord could also serve, or a thick round piece of tangle from the beach, on occasion. Seal-hide was also used, cured and rolled in a tight cylinder 2 inches in diameter (Fig. 38a). These softer materials were suitable for threshing oats, which bruised more easily than bere.

The two parts were joined by means of a rope, thong, leather caps, or even willow bands. Eel-, sheep- and goat-skin made strong durable thongs, attached to holes or grooves at the ends of the handstaff and souple. A special fastening, consisting of a cross pin of wood or metal instead of a hole or groove, is found only in Orkney, though it must have been more widespread once since it is mentioned by Henry Stephens in 1844.[45] In nearly every case the souple is shorter than the handstaff though two flails from East Lothian have handstaffs 49 inches (1·24 m.) long, and souples of rope that are 61 inches (1·54 m.) long (Fig. 38b). This, however, is exceptional.

Most flails were worked by men, but in parts of the Hebrides there were smaller, lighter flails generally used by women till well into the nineteenth century (Fig. 38b). They were swung round the right arm, not over the head, and the women were said not to stand upright at this work.[46]

Though the profession of barnman died out with the coming of the threshing machine, nevertheless the flail went on being regularly used till about

38. a. Two men threshing with flails in a Shetland barn. The souples appear to be of seal-hide.   C1117

1850–60 in the Lowlands, and there are plenty of people still alive in the Highlands and Islands who can use it. In Ayrshire, as in Ulster, it was retained till the early 1900s for a special purpose – the threshing of rye-grass seed, the bulk of which was grown here for the British Isles. The flail was a major feature of the everyday life of the past for many centuries. The atmosphere of flail threshing in a dark barn, lit by the flickering light of a crusie-lamp that cast indeterminate shadows, the rustle and smell of straw and flying dust, and the rhythmic beat of the souple echoing round the farm-town in the small hours of the morning, are now part of a farming tradition that has gone, and can only be interpreted through books and

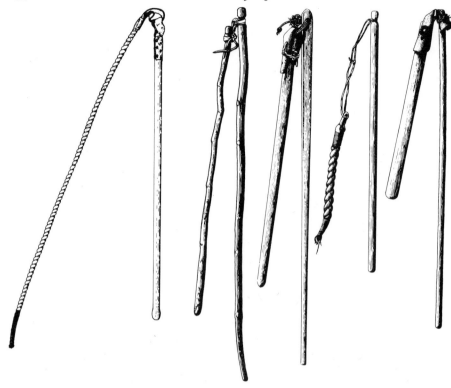

38. b. Flail types (l. to r.): East Lothian, with a rope souple which is longer than the hand-staff. PD48; Colonsay, Argyll. PD8; Harlaw, Inverurie, Aberdeenshire. PD28; Hebrides, PD6. Used by women; Orkney. PD37. All National Museum.

papers, and objects in museums. And the Galloway barnman's jig has also vanished, though in 1824 it was quite a spectacle:

'This is a dance which those persons have who thresh with the flail. The *souple* on the end of the hand-staff being whirled round on the barn-floor by the barnman; every wheel he gives it, he leaps over it, and so produces a very singular dance, worth walking a mile to see, yet few of the *barriers* (barnmen) who do this dance in style, are willing to perform before spectators. The girl who *kaves* (cleans) *the corn* is the only one for common who is gratified with the sight.'[47]

THRESHING WITHOUT A FLAIL

Though the flail was the most widespread method of threshing, a number of alternatives were used, especially when the straw was needed for thatching the roofs of buildings, and had to be kept as long and unbroken as possible.

One Hebridean method was *suathadh* or rubbing, which involved standing barefoot on a barley sheaf at the band, inserting one foot under the ears, and rubbing these until the grain had been removed. As the bunches of stalks were cleaned, they were bent back to let others be got at. Rubbing was preferred for bere or barley because the ears were more tenacious, but for oats, which can shake easily, the grain was sometimes struck out by means of a notched stick, *maide froisidh*, the sheaf being held upsides down in the left hand.

A third way was to lash the sheaf against a suitable object. In the crofting counties many barns have protruding from the wall a stone called in the Northern Isles a *gloy-stone*, that was specially built in for this purpose, as an architectural feature. Freestanding devices included a block of wood mounted on a trestle, with nails in staggered rows, or the rungs of a ladder, studded with nails at a suitable height, or a special frame, with iron cross-bars.

However primitive these threshing-methods may appear to be, they nevertheless had a specific function in providing good thatching straw, which neither the flail nor the thrashing machine could do, so that their long survival was not simply an example of the past in the present, but resulted from the fulfilment of a particular functional need in the remoter rural areas.

THRESHING BY MACHINE

The history of threshing machines goes back more than two hundred years in this country. The early experimenters found it hard to think in terms of anything other than the hand equipment in current use. Just as the men who sought to develop reaping machinery first tried out sets of rotating sickles, so the early threshing machines were based on arrangements of flails fixed to a rotating beam. The principle worked, but the flails or beaters soon broke down. The first man to try it was a Michael Menzies, about the year 1732, and by 1740 three had been made, though their life was short; and they were dangerous to approach. The motive power was water.

Another inventor, Mr. Craw of Netherbyres in Berwickshire, made a machine with 10 or more flails on similar principles, around 1750.[48]

A more promising line began to be explored in 1758, when Mr. Stirling of Dunblane, Perthshire, made a water-driven machine on the principle of the flax-mill. Mr. Moir of Leckie is said to have tried a similar principle about 1764. The mill had four horizontally turning scutchers enclosed in a cylinder $3\frac{1}{2}$ feet (1·1 m.) high by 8 feet (2·4 m.) in diameter, into the top of which the sheaves were fed by hand. The grain and straw were separated by riddles and fanners. It worked well enough for oats, which have easily detachable ears, but not for other grains. The flax-mill types were not isolated occurrences, for a number were in use in Kinross-shire in 1814, and this experiment in one of the stronghold areas of the linen industry was clearly not entirely unsatisfactory, for similar machines were common in Northumberland about 1800, said to have been introduced by Edward Gregson, of Wark, about 1768, after a servant of his, William Menzies, got the idea from a small flax-mill being carried by a Scotsman in a cart.[49]

The next important stage in the evolution of the threshing mill was initiated by a Mr. Oxley, who erected a machine at Flodden, driven by horses. In effect, he turned the cylinder of the flax-mill on its side, so that it lay horizontally, and the grain was fed into hinge-hung switchers through two fluted rollers. About 1778, Mr. Ilderton of Alnwick and Mr. Smart or Mr. Gregson of Wark made a mill with a fluted threshing drum about 6 feet (1·8 m.) in diameter, with small fluted rollers round it, pressed inwards by springs. The weakness of the drum was that it bruised the grain as it was pressed or rubbed out.

At this stage the initiative went back to Scotland. Sir Francis Gilmerton of Kinloch, who saw Ilderton's mill, tried to improve the drum, unsuccessfully. He sent his version to a millwright called Meikle, of Know Mill, in East Lothian, giving him the idea that led to the world's first fully successful thresher in 1786.

Andrew Meikle was one of a notable family. His father, James, built the first barley mill in Scotland and the first winnowing machine, and Andrew's son George later erected the huge water-wheel that was instrumental in the draining and reclamation of Blairdrummond Moss. He died in 1811 at Houston Mill, East Lothian, at the age of 92, having given to the world of agriculture one of its most essential pieces of machinery.

Meikle's mill (Fig. 39) was fed by putting sheaves through a pair of rollers into a revolving drum that knocked out the grain by velocity rather than by rubbing or pressing. The first mill was set up for Mr. Stein, a distiller at Kilbagie in Clackmannanshire. It is not definitely known when the large wooden straw drum equipped with spikes (Fig. 40a) was added, but it was probably not long after. Fanners to separate the corn from the chaff were included in Meikle's original Patent Specification.[50] The mill at Kilbagie was so successful that Meikle quickly got orders for others, and he set up about a dozen in the same district.

Once the correct principle had been evolved, mills mushroomed all over the country. The speed of their adoption testifies strongly to the urgent need that was felt for them, in part because of the increased acreages of cereal crops resulting from improvements in agriculture. The first threshing mill in Midlothian was erected about 1786 by Francis Trells, a Hungarian.[51] In Angus, George Patterson had one by 1787 at Castle Huntly in the Carse of Gowrie, and in the far north, the first in Caithness was erected in 1790 at Castle-hill, by Mr. Traill of Hobbister. By the 1790s, they were numerous

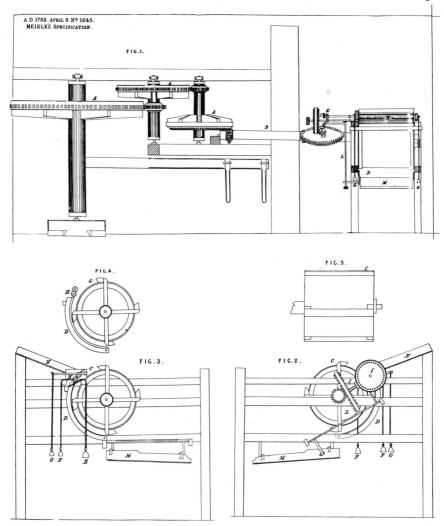

39. The Patent Specification for Meikle's Mill, 9 April 1788.　　　　C4012,-3,-4

on the farms in the main cropping districts and with them the new rural trade of millwright came into existence – people like John Nichol, of Stonehaven, who made about eight mills in six months in 1795, and John Gladstone, of Castle Douglas, who built 200 mills between 1794–1810, at prices varying between £40–£130. One he made for the Earl of Selkirk in 1809 was 'on a plan so complete, that the grain is separated from the straw, cleaned, measured, weighed, and deposited in the granary, and the straw, at the same time, conveyed into the straw-yard by the machinery alone.

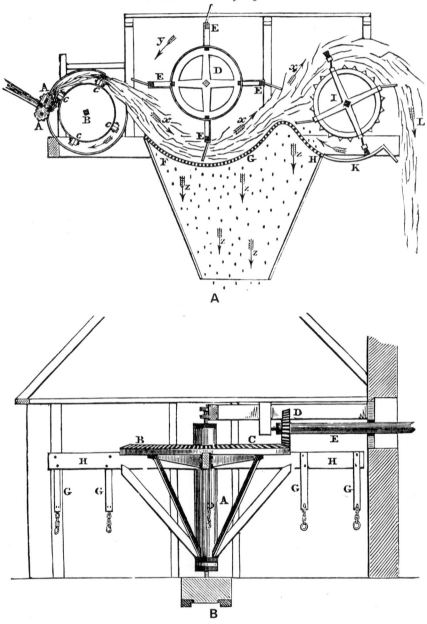

A

B

40. a. Flow diagram for a threshing mill. The grain passes through two fluted rollers, A, into the thrashing drum, D, where the ears are knocked off, and the straw is cleared through the straw drum, I. The ears fall into a fanner below. From Low 1840, 119.   C3998

b. The gearing of a horse-gang. The horses (four to six in number) are yoked to the driving beam at G. As they walked round, their power was transmitted to the mill in the barn through the driving shaft, E. From 2b., 123.

The whole work is carried on at the rate of one bushel per minute, by four persons only.'[52]

In general, mills took a little longer to reach the more northerly parts of the country. Sutherland had only one in 1807, though by 1811 it had ten. By 1811 too, mills had found their way to the larger farms on the Hebridean islands of Colonsay, Islay, Gigha, Skye, and others.

Not only did they spread within the country, but also abroad. There is an account from the Isle of Man of a farmer who went to Scotland to examine threshing machines, and set one up, driven by 4 horses, in the 1790s.[53] The estate of Dowspuda in Poland had two mills on the Scottish model by 1817. They worked there for at least 45 years.[54] In Sweden too, Meikle's principle of threshing was quickly adopted and worked on, and was widely used on the bigger farms by the end of the eighteenth century.[55] Meikle's mill, in fact, was one of the major items in making British agriculture a model for all the countries of Europe.

MOTIVE POWER

In the early days, mills were driven by water, horse-power, or, less often, by wind. Different areas had their own preferences, and where water was preferred to horse-power, mill-dams and mill-lades made their appearance in the layout of farms, with water-wheels alongside the barn-walls. Horse-power, on the other hand, brought into being round horse-walks built against the barn (Fig. 41). These attractive architectural features were set up on pillars with open spaces between, and were roofed with slates or pantiles over an intricate structure of rafters. The gearing was overhead, and was turned by shafts into which up to six horses were yoked, depending on the size of the mill (Fig. 40b). The first mills were clearly stiff to drive, since for some time two horses was usually the minimum number, and a good deal of effort went into the development of lighter mills suitable for one horse, and less expensive, which smaller farmers could afford to install. On such farms the horse-walk was not enclosed, and consisted of a circular raised platform, with underground gearing driven by one or more horses. Enclosed horse-walks, however, are found as far north as Orkney.

In the 1830s, steam-power began to be applied to threshing mills on the big farms. By 1845, there were two at Ratho in Midlothian, and a farmer called James Verner had erected a steam engine for threshing at Inveresk in Midlothian. The spread of steam-engines meant that on the farms where they were adopted, the horse-walks lost their original function and were dismantled or turned into storage sheds. Alongside them, tall chimney stacks were built, marking the coal-fired boiler whose steam-power was made to turn the mill.

Steam was in turn replaced by the oil engine, such as those made by

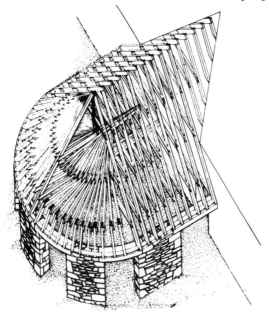

41. Round and half-round horse-gangs attached to barns at Little Powgavie, Perthshire,
and Cossans, Angus. Surveyed and drawn by Bruce Walker, 1975.

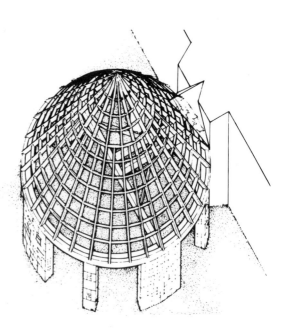

Allan of Aberdeen, in the early 1900s. These involved the addition of an engine-shed alongside the barn, adding another feature to the layout of farm-buildings, but when the tractor came into widespread use during and after the First World War the engine shed itself became redundant, for the tractor pulley could do all that was required for driving the mill. Finally, the combine harvester, of which the first example in Scotland, a Clayton, came to the farm of Whittingehame Mains in East Lothian in 1932, has done away with the need for barn mills altogether, for it threshes as it cuts. In place of the barn mill, drying floors and storage bins for grain have often been installed.

In spite of this sequence of change and adaptation as new types of motive power came into being, the smaller farms nevertheless often stuck to the old ways that could serve them without great expenditure, and it is only within the last two decades that the horse-driven mill has finally disappeared from the country scene.

Another kind of development that took place was the use of travelling mills. It is one of the curious points of agricultural history that in the South of England, travelling mills that could be hired were more popular from the beginning, whereas in the North of England and in Scotland farmers were far more likely to own their own stationary barn-mills.[56] These, however, were often designed to provide straw for bedding and feeding the animals on the basis of a weekly thresh, but could not easily cope with a full stackyard. Barn-mills were therefore supplemented by travelling mills supplied by local contractors, such as James Smith of Dalkeith who was advertising his portable mill in 1864. This may well have been driven by steam, though at this period steam engines did not move on the road under their own power, but had to be towed by horses, like the mills they worked, from farm to farm. The annual or twice-yearly coming of the steam-mill, and later on of the tractor-driven mill (Fig. 42), was one of the main occasions in the farming year when neighbours had an opportunity of coming together in communal activity.

On the very small crofts, flail-threshing went on into the twentieth century, though it was gradually ousted by the hand- or pedal-operated thresher, which agricultural engineering firms like Shearer of Turriff in Aberdeenshire, and Banff Foundry, began to develop after about 1830. These were not only sold in quantities in the Highlands and Islands and on small-holdings in the farming counties, but were also exported to countries like Portugal about the First World War period. There is a Shearer of Turriff hand-thresher in the museum at Seurasaari in Finland, bearing Portuguese or Spanish lettering on its side – so that even at this level, Scotland continued to play a part in the wider world.

A

B

42. a. A Marshall mill driven by a steam engine at Redstables, Glencarse, Perthshire. On engine, James Adamson; beside engine, Alexander Adamson. Per H. Davidson. C2869

b. A Ruston Tractor Thrasher driven by a Case tractor at Gifford, East Lothian. Per A. Hamilton. C1442

FANNERS AND HUMMELERS

When Lord Fletcher of Saltoun sent James Meikle to Holland in 1710 to learn about pearl-barley machines, he got a useful bonus in the shape of the winnowing machine, which Meikle observed there, and of which he built an example at Saltoun. This was a simple device with four vanes of thin wood or metal revolving in a hollow drum and blowing a strong stream of air through an opening. The grain to be cleaned was allowed to trickle through this jet, which blew away the chaff and roughly separated the heavy and light grains of corn. Though the grain had to be put through two or three times, this was still a great saving in time. It is surprising that it was not widely adopted immediately. There is said to have been some opposition by the clergy to the use of the 'de'il's wind' for cleaning corn, though the sources for this suggestion mostly appear to go back to Walter Scott's *Old Mortality*. At any rate, fanners did not begin to spread until a Roxburghshire farmer, Andrew Rodger, started to make and sell them at home and in the North of England in 1737.[57] The tenant in Flemington Mill had a pair of mill-fanners in 1746, and by 1757 fanners had reached Cromarty, for a letter written by Joseph Forsyth, Cromarty, dated 8 April, to Lady Pitcalnie at Arboll, stated that 'John Urquhart has a Corn Fanner, but says it would not be convenient to send it your Length – But that any person you send here may view it at pleasure'.[58] Their use in mills appears to have spread a little more quickly than on farms.

By the time the threshing mill came along they were widely established throughout the country, and quickly began to be built as part of the mill itself, though separate barn fanners to dress grain for seed and for sale remained in the barns. They required four or sometimes five people to work them before riddles were added – a man to turn the handle of the blower, a woman to fill the hopper, and another to take up the good grain and divide it between two others who stood with riddles beside the heap of freshly-cleaned grain (Fig. 43b). This was in the South-East of Scotland, where women workers were plentiful. It was said in Midlothian in 1793 that farmers could run 12 bolls (96 bushels) an hour, and could completely clean the grain in two operations, or three at most.[59]

Winnowing is done before corn goes to the kiln to be dried and to the mill to be ground, to get rid of the *sheelings*, broken bits of straw and loose chaff, as well as seeds. In the days before mechanical fanners, winnowing was carried out in the open air (Fig. 43a) or in barns. The slope or low hill on which the work was carried on was the *sheeling hill*, – *hillock*, or – *law*, terms that sometimes survive as place-names, especially in the neighbourhood of mills. If there was no wind to clean the corn, the mill would have to stop work. For winnowing in the barn, the doors were built opposite each other, and the work was carried on in the through-draught. The opening

A

a Fanner.	*e e* Women riddlers.	*h* Besom.
b Driver.	*f* Corn-basket.	*i* Light corn.
c Woman feeding the hopper.	*g* Wooden shovel.	*k* Chaff.
d Woman taking up corn.		

B

43. a. Open air winnowing in Shetland, using a straw mat or *flackie* to keep the corn clean.

C1118

　b. Winnowing with barn fanners. From Stephens 1871, I, 316.

C1626

of the doors could be adjusted to regulate the draught. In some of the smaller barns of the Highlands and Islands, where there was only one door, a low wall-opening or winnowing-hole was made opposite it.

If the wind or draught was reasonably strong, the grain was allowed to trickle through the fingers on to a sheet below. The heavy grains fell straight down, and the lighter stuff blew further along, forming a tail of second quality corn. On a quiet day, an alternative method was to separate the grain in a *blind sieve* or *wecht*, a shallow, circular tray made of a sheep- or calf-skin stretched over a wooden rim, held in the hands and shaken with a circular, centrifugal motion that swirled out the heavy grains.

Bere or barley is harder to deal with than oats, because of the long awns, which are very tenacious, and well known to anyone who has forked barley sheaves and felt them creeping uncomfortably down the back of his shirt. In order to remove the awns completely, barley has to be *hummelled*, and here too a range of methods could be used. On the small farms and townships, treading with the feet in a tub was often done by women, or else the barley was beaten by a wooden plunger to the bottom of which metal blades were fixed. On the farms of the Lowlands, iron barley hummelers had wooden cross-bar handles, and gridded heads. Rough hummeling was also done at one time by beating the barley with flails on the barn-floor.

About 1812 the threshing mill was further improved by the addition of a hummeling machine, a cylinder with beaters inside. This was invented, as the first in Britain, by George Mitchell, millwright at Bishopmill near Elgin. One attached to the mill at Skelbo in Sutherland worked well, and it was widely adopted in the barley districts.[60] Thereafter hummelers were made and adapted by other firms, such as Messrs Grant Brothers, Wheelwrights, Granton, Aberdeenshire.

5

Drying and Grinding the Grain

GRADDANING AND CORN-KILNS

In the moist climate of Scotland, grain must be dried before it is ground, otherwise the kernels will not granulate easily. This was especially true of oats. Drying was less necessary for the harder grains of bere or barley, but on the other hand, if it was being malted to make ale, bere had to be kiln-dried to stop the growth of the shoots.

A number of drying methods are known, some of them presumably very old, though of such a nature that they leave no trace in the archaeological record. Of these, the simplest, and also the most wasteful, was the process of *graddaning*, by which the ears of oats were set on fire and burned off their stalks. No threshing was required. In the eighteenth century, graddaning was a technique known in Galloway, the Western Islands and Highlands, and North and North-East Scotland, exactly in the areas most affected by the climate. It is documented as far back as the sixteenth century, and in seventeenth-century Ireland it was the subject of legislation because it wasted straw. In 1578 Bishop Leslie described how the Highlanders ground the oatmeal after graddaning, and then made it into a kind of thick oat-cake, baked on a girdle above the fire or against a baking-stone set at the side of the glowing peats.[61]

Graddaning was a picturesque process, always carried out by women. A manuscript description of 1768 related how two women worked together in the open air, beside a fire of chaff. One set fire to the ears of a handful of corn, watched carefully to see when the chaff had been burned off, lit another bunch, and then dashed the first against the ground to extinguish it. The other spread the ears with a stick to make sure they were all properly burned and parched, then raked them away from the fire into a heap alongside. When enough had been done, the heap was put into a tub, in which the women trod it with their feet, and rubbed it in their hands. It was then winnowed four or five times till all the chaff had been separated, when it was ready for grinding in the hand-mill or water-mill.[62] It appears from this description, that graddaning was done to prepare grain for grinding in the water-mill, as well as to serve a more short-term purpose of providing the daily bread quickly. It survived into the nineteenth century in places like Skye, Uist, and St. Kilda, as a means of making fresh bread from the first grain cut during the new harvest season.[63]

Drying methods varied according to the crop. Oats were graddaned on the straw, or if already threshed the corn could be parched in a pot. From the mid-eighteenth century, the three-legged round-bottomed type of pot made by the Carron Iron Works was favoured. Earlier, other kinds of containers were used, such as a flat stone with a rim of clay round it. This was called a *hellio* in Orkney, from Old Norse *hella*, a flat stone. Hot stones could also be dropped into a straw tub full of corn, as in nineteenth-century St. Kilda. In Raasay, James Boswell saw a small 'kiln' of a related type inside a dwelling house. It was about the size of a hogshead, and was made of wattles plastered with clay inside and out. [64]

Bere, on the other hand, could be dried in the unthreshed ear in a net called in Gaelic a *tarran*, formed of a rectangular wooden frame across which was stretched a criss-cross of yellow bedstraw or quicken roots. This was hung above a slow, smokeless peat fire, like similar nets, round or square, once used in the Faroe Islands. [65] In the Records of Old Aberdeen for 1699, there is reference to a big iron girdle being used to dry bere.

The relatively small quantities of grain that were pot-dried or net-dried were roughly ground in the handmill and eaten with milk, or baked with sour-milk or butter-milk into bannocks half to three-quarters of an inch (1·3–1·9 cm.) thick. No doubt they had a tang of peat-smoke in the taste, but scarcely as strong as that of graddaned oats.

Such drying methods continued to serve a temporary purpose, long after drying kilns had come into use.

STONE-BUILT CORN KILNS

In Scotland, there are two basic types of small-scale corn-drying kiln in the north and west. The smaller one is rectangular in shape (Fig. 44), and though its main area of survival into the twentieth century was Shetland, it was originally more widely distributed, for one was found in the corner of a late thirteenth-century barn in the Viking settlement of Freswick in Caithness. [66] The Shetland kiln or *sinnie* was about 2 feet (0·6 m.) high, 4 to 6 feet (1·2–1.8 m.) long, and 3 to 4 feet (0·9–1·2 m.) wide. At one end was an opening measuring about a foot (0·3 m.) square, in which was lit the fire of hard, dry peat. The heat travelled into the chamber, and up through the drying floor, which consisted of cross-spars of wood laid about 2 inches (5 cm.) apart from each other, with a 1-inch (2·5 cm.) layer of straw above serving as a bed for the grain. Such kilns were always built inside the barn, and most had no chimney.

The second type was round or half-round (Fig. 44), and was much bigger, up to about 15 feet (4·7 m.) high with an 8 foot (2·4 m.) diameter drying floor, which could hold about four sacks of oats spread to a depth of 3 inches (8 cm.). It was characterised by a round bowl-shaped drying chamber into

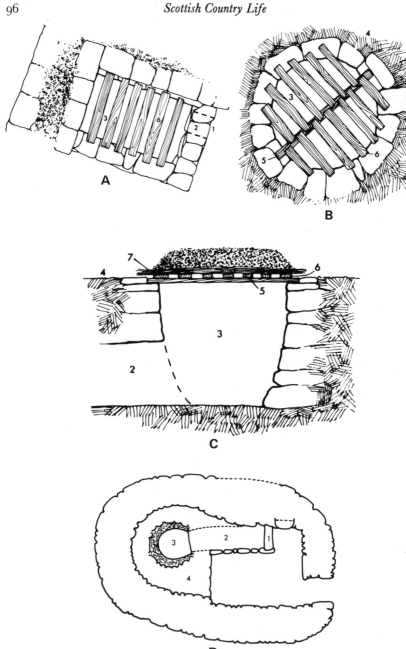

44. a, b, c. Plan of a Shetland *sinnie*, and plan and section of a kiln with a round bowl:
1. Position of fire; 2. Flue; 3. Bowl or chamber; 4. Kiln platform; 5. Kiln-beam; 6. Kiln-sticks; 7. Straw bed.   C1190–1192
    d. Plan of a kiln barn at South Galson, Lewis. Key as above.   C1188

which the heat from the peat fire was carried by a straight or curving flue. The drying floor was also of wood or straw. In Orkney, Caithness (Fig. 45) and the more fertile south mainland of Shetland the kilns are built on to the ends of the barns, where they appear as round towers, forming very attractive architectural features. In other parts of Scotland, north and west of the Highland line, kilns were either free-standing structures, built half into a slope,[66] or else formed part of small kiln barns built separately from the other houses.

Oats were always laid on a straw bed, but in the Hebrides in the eighteenth century, bere was often dried in the ear, being spread over the bare wooden ribs of the kiln floor.

Such kilns, serving single families or groups of families, survived in parts of the Highlands and Islands through the nineteenth and sometimes into the twentieth century, especially in Orkney where they were much used for drying the malt required for home-brewed ale. Their origins, however, remain uncertain. The Romans undoubtedly used kilns, and King David's legislation in the twelfth century showed that they were then widespread also in Lowland Scotland. It is possible that the Vikings learned something about corn-drying from this country, for they borrowed the Gaelic word *sòrn*, the flue or platform of a kiln, which in one form or another has survived in West Norway, the Faroe Islands, and Iceland, and a circular kiln, rather similar to the Scottish examples, was excavated at the farm of Gröf i Oræfum in South-East Iceland. It can be dated to AD 1362, when the farm was over-whelmed by a volcanic eruption.[67] This kiln, therefore, is equivalent in date to a fourteenth century one of similar shape, but built like a corner turret, in the barn at the medieval farm of Jarlshof in south Shetland. This was replaced by another in the fifteenth century.[68]

In Lowland Scotland, agricultural improvement was accompanied by the development in the eighteenth century of new commercial meal-mills to which relatively capacious corn-drying kilns were attached. This happened first in the better farming areas such as the Lothians, but elsewhere farmers went on using their individual or communal kilns. In the highland areas these remained relatively unchanged, though on the highland fringes improvements in farm kilns were also taking place. In parts of Angus in 1794, kilns were being erected with three window openings instead of one, two of them opposite each other, and one opposite the door where the fire was lit, to aid ventilation and to draw off the smoke.[69] But even so they were beginning to be rare except near a corn mill.

The ubiquitous drying floor of wood and straw was also changing. In-evitably, there was a considerable fire risk, and less inflammable alternatives were sought. At Baloch in Perthshire in 1774, the tenant, W. Lawson, had built a new kiln without straw;[70] in Midlothian, a practice that was develop-ing by 1781 was the placing of ¾-inch (1·9 cm.) iron bars on the kiln joists, in

A

B

45. a. A large, round kiln on the end of a barn on a Caithness farm, north of Wick. VI/53/17.

b. A kiln rising above the barn at Ancum, North Ronaldsay, Orkney. The wooden chimney was formerly thatched round with straw ropes.

place of wooden slats;[71] in several counties, perforated tiles were being used, and in Angus strong wire-cloth laid on bars of iron was common by 1813.[72]

A change also took place in the kind of fuel used. Where formerly vast quantities of peat (or more rarely brushwood) were needed – requiring much time to cut and transport – now the chaff from winnowed corn came to be the standard fuel, so that the flavour of peat reek became less evident.

It was during the three decades or so following 1770, therefore, that mills as we know them now, with kilns close by, as at Preston Mill in East Lothian, or joined on to the rest of the building, began to appear in the landscape. In the crofting counties the old types continued in use, surviving well into the twentieth century in an area like Orkney, where they were much used for drying malt. Some of the small kilns built in Orkney and Shetland in the late nineteenth and early twentieth centuries were influenced by the square commercial kilns, for they were like small-scale imitations of them in shape (Fig. 45b). On the other hand, some of the older kilns attached to mills, as at Preston Mill and Samuelston in East Lothian, and on one or two Angus and Caithness farms (Fig. 45a), are bigger versions of the small circular kilns.

GRINDING THE CORN

Knocking stones and barley. The processing of grain for human consumption can be done by beating or grinding. An old device that goes back to pre-historic times is the *knocking-stone* (Fig. 46a), a kind of large mortar in which bere was dehusked by being beaten with a stone pounder or a wooden mallet. Wooden troughs were also used for the same purpose. In some places, hollows were cut in the living rock for knocking barley.[73]

Bere which was 'knocked' in this way was used in making barley broth, a very common dish. The need for knocked-barley as an element in the people's everyday food was recognised by the fact that in Perthshire in 1622, cottars had permission to knock two pecks of bere, free of multure, each year.[74] Normally all grain had to be ground in the mill to which the tenants were astricted by the lairds, and to which they had to pay their dues, but here a special dispensation was given. Malt for making ale was also prepared by being knocked. To aid the process, a little water was put into the bowl, to help to slacken the husks. The knocking of bere was generally a woman's job and sometimes the knocking stone was shared by several families in a community.

Bere was everywhere prepared in this way until 1710, when James Meikle was sent to Holland by Andrew Fletcher of Saltoun to study Dutch barley mills (Fig. 48). Meikle subsequently erected a barley mill at Saltoun, and there pot barley was made and became famous. 'Salton barley', it was said, 'was wrote upon the sign of every slop seller, in almost every town in Scotland.'[75] Pearl – or pot-barley wheels consisting of a stone mill-wheel turning

A

B

46. a. A knocking stone being demonstrated in Foula, 1902. Photo, H. B. Curwen.

OE136

b. A hand-mill or quern at Lungar, North Ronaldsay, Orkney, in 1964. The stones are 19 inches in diameter, and are set on a flagstone platform.   C870 vertically within a metal frame eventually became part of the machinery of meal-mills generally, but the Fletcher family kept the secret of how the barley was processed for some time before it became public knowledge. Two more barley mills were built in East Lothian in 1753-4, and between 1756-63 something like 20,000 bolls of pot-barley were exported each year. The demand for pot-barley led to an increase in the number of barley mills, particularly in the Lothians and Fife, and for a time Scotland must have had something of a monopoly in pot-barley, until barley mills started to be built in England, Ireland, and America. Mills for barley and for wheat, the latter a mark of the increasing demand for bread made of wheat flour, were being built in Banffshire in the 1770s, in Berwickshire in the 1780s, in Fife about 1780, when four barley mills had been added to the twelve corn mills and two flour mills in the Water of Leven, in Moray in 1811 when the first wheat mill was erected at Linkwood in the parish of Lhanbryde, and so on. On the other hand, there are signs of a decrease in the numbers of corn-mills in some areas, in the course of the nineteenth century. By 1845, three corn-mills in Aberlady parish, East Lothian, had already gone, and in the Upper Ward of Lanarkshire, where there had been two millers in 1791, by 1864 none were left. Instead, the oatmeal was brought in from outside.[76]

GRINDING BY HAND

Barley was knocked in a trough in preparation for making broth, but it was also ground into meal. The saddle querns and trough querns, at one end of which a woman knelt, making meal by rubbing the grain with a rubbing stone, are as old as human settlement itself, and were used to grind barley and wheat, at first, and then rye, and above all oats, from the period of the Romans, when the latter two crops first appeared. It was at this same period, probably a little before the Romans, that the rotary quern began to be used, with a fixed bottom stone on top of which an upper stone could be rotated by a handle, the grain being fed in by hand through an eye in the middle. Not only did it speed up the work of grinding, but it must also have been a fascinating novelty, for people even made toy rotary querns for themselves, of which examples have been found in Shetland and western Inverness-shire.[77]

Such hand-mills survived in use almost till the present day (Fig. 46b), in spite of opposition from the feudal authorities who wished to ensure that grain was ground in the official mills and dues paid accordingly. Where water-mills were few, however, there was little alternative to hand-mills and knocking-stones, and the prohibition of their use was not common to all estates. There was also a factor of social differentiation, so that in some areas, such as Harris in the 1790s, querns had become confined in use to the 'lower orders'.[78] In areas where barley meal remained popular in the nineteenth century, people often retained querns to grind it, whilst sending their oats to the water-mill.

In general, however, the quern had reached the end of its life, except for small-scale use, by the mid-nineteenth century in the Highlands and Islands, and a good century earlier in the Lowlands, and although in 1767 Gordon's Hand-mill for Grinding Corn was made by the Duke of Argyll's cabinet-maker for a prize offered by the Society for the Encouragement of Arts, Manufactures and Commerce for the most effectual handmill for grinding grain into meal to make bread for the poor, this does not appear to have had much influence.[79]

THE HORIZONTAL WATER-MILL

Sometime in the first century BC, perhaps many years before the hand-operated rotary quern reached Scotland, a water-driven mill was invented or at least became known in the Mediterranean area. From there it spread rapidly, and was established in Ireland before the Vikings came, possibly as early as the third century AD.[80]

The horizontal water-mill is so-called because the water-wheel revolves horizontally underneath it. This is linked directly to the top-stone of the mill by an iron shaft, with no intermediate gearing, so that mill-stone and wheel turn at exactly the same speed. It is a simple adaptation of the hand-mill to water power.

In Britain, the known distribution of the horizontal mill is Shetland (Fig. 47a), Orkney, Caithness and Sutherland, the Outer Hebrides (Fig. 47b), Mull, the Kintyre peninsula, Ireland and the Isle of Man. Finds of mill paddles in Galloway suggest early use there. The distribution is very much influenced by climate and geography. These mills always lie on lades taken off small streams in hilly or sloping terrain, with dams where necessary to build up a head of water. Many were workable only in winter when rain filled the dams.

The quantitative distribution in relation to periods of time is significant. When Sir Walter Scott visited Shetland in 1814 he estimated the number of mills at around 500, and though this figure has never been checked, there are at least a great many mills. The island of Papa Stour, for example, contains twenty-four mills and mill-sites within its six square miles. One or two survive in Shetland in working order, like the mill at Troswick in the south mainland, restored by Gilbert Goudie the antiquarian around 1900. Another at Smith-field in Fetlar was completely rebuilt and restored during the First World War, when supplies of flour and meal were difficult to get from outside. The tradition of their use has remained strong.

In Orkney quite another picture presents itself. Horizontal mills are and always were relatively few, though one has been preserved at Dounby by the Department of the Environment.

Their scarcity is in part due to the feudal mill system introduced by Lord

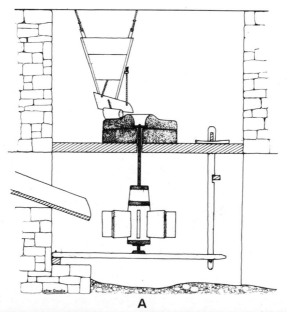

A

B

47. a. Diagram of a horizontal water-mill in Shetland. Grain from the hopper passes into the eye of the stone via the wooden shoe. The wheel is turned by water from the chute on the bottom left, and is linked directly with the top-stone, without intermediate gearing. After G. Goudie, *The Celtic and Scandinavian Antiquities of Shetland*, 1904, 260.　　C1199

b. The interior of a horizontal mill at Bragar, Lewis. Instead of being hung by ropes from the rafters, the hopper is held loosely in a wooden frame. Per M. Morrison 1948.　　C2136

Articles of Agreement between HENRY FLETCHER *and* JAMES MEIKLE.

IT is agreed betwixt Henry Fletcher, brother to the Laird of Salton, on the one part, in the name of his said brother, and taking burden upon him for the said Laird of Salton, and James Meikle, wright in Wester Keith, on the other part, that they shall keep and perform to one another, according to the tenor of the following articles, viz.

1. That the said James Meikle shall go to Holland with the first fleet that sails thither, after the date of thir presents, and learn there the perfect art of sheeling barley; both that which is called French barley, and that which is called Pearl barley; and how to accommodate, order, and erect mills for that purpose, in so far as he can, with his uttermost industry, and recommendations given him.

2. That as soon as the said James Meikle shall find himself sufficiently instructed in said art, he shall return with the first fleet or man of war he can have safe passage in, for Scotland or Newcastle. That, in the mean time, if he shall be forced to wait, he shall endeavour to instruct himself in any other useful trade or manufactory.

3. That when he returns to Scotland, he shall be obliged to communicate the arts he has learned, to *Salton*, or any whom he shall appoint, and shall communicate them to no other person, but by *Salton*'s permission.

4. That *Salton* shall pay all the said James Meikle's expences in going and coming, and in learning said arts.

8. That the said James Meikle, from the time he parts from his own house to go to the ships, till he return, shall be allowed every day two shillings Sterling, to wit, one shilling for his entertainment, and one shilling for his work; and shall give a receipt for any money he gets with him, or any letter of credit he gets, and account for them accordingly, when he comes back.

Both parties oblige themselves to keep the foresaid articles, under the penalty of 500 merks, by and attour performance. In witness whereof, they have subscribed thir presents, written by the said Henry Fletcher at Salton, this 17th of April 1710.

(Signed)   H. FLETCHER.
           JA. MEIKLE.

48. The agreement regarding the barley mill at Saltoun.

Robert Stewart, which eventually resulted in the erection of vertical mills in almost every region of Orkney. At the same time, hand mills were prohibited, in 1625, and again in 1664, 1694, and 1695. Nevertheless several survived almost till the present day. It is not certain whether the mills mentioned in fifteenth and sixteenth century sources were horizontal or vertical mills, but since some appear to have served districts of considerable extent, it is thought that these, at least, must have been too big to be horizontal mills. Orkney has in any case the natural disadvantage of slow-flowing water, which is not suitable for horizontal mills. They can never have been very common, and in earlier days there must have been much dependence on hand-mills – to such an extent, indeed, that one of the architectural features of older houses is the stone shelf in one corner, on which the quern sat. Scarcity of water also led to the use of windmills, one of which was built on the Outer Holm of Stromness in 1763, two in South Ronaldsay in 1785, one in Papa Westray and one in North Ronaldsay (Fig. 49b) in the nineteenth century.

The fewness of horizontal mills in Orkney is paralleled in the other areas of northern and western Scotland where they were used, and this seems to have been true of Shetland also before the late eighteenth century. In the Western Islands, the number of mills is said to have been increasing in the late seventeenth century.[81] It is known that an increase also took place in the Faroe Islands between about 1780 and 1800,[82] by which period there had already been a considerable growth in the number in Shetland. Orkney, therefore, provides a marked contrast with these other areas, where the little horizontal mills were built by individual families or small groups of families, and not necessarily by or on behalf of lairds anxious to exercise their feudal prerogatives.

THE VERTICAL WATER-MILL

Though vertical mills are to be found in the north and west, their main distribution is in Lowland Scotland. They have a special value for study, not only because they processed cereals as well as pease and beans into meal and flour for sale and for consumption, but also because the form of their organisation provides a long surviving picture of an important part of the feudal organisation of estates, showing how a kind of functional self-sufficiency could be achieved. In towns and on country estates there were common mills, serving districts in which the tenants were bound by the terms of their lease to have their grain ground there. This obligation was known in Scots law as *thirlage*, and the astricted tenants paid a proportion of the grain or meal ground, known as the *multure*, to the proprietor or tenant of the mill, as well as undertaking various services to keep the mill, dam, and mill-lade in good order. They also helped with the transport of new mill-stones, if necessary. The district, normally a baronial estate or part of it,

SCOTTISH
WIRE-WORK AND MILLSTONE MANUFACTORY.
ESTABLISHED 1823.

J. SMITH & SON,
WIRE-WORKERS AND WEAVERS, MILLSTONE BUILDERS,
AND IMPORTERS OF FRENCH BURR BLOCKS,
219 HIGH STREET, EDINBURGH.

A

B

49. a. Segmented millstones being assembled. From the Edinburgh and Leith Post Office Directory, 1854–5. XLIV.

b. A windmill in North Ronaldsay, Orkney. There is a water-driven vertical mill nearby. Both now out of use.

which the mill served, was the *sucken*, and all tenants paid dues to the mill to which they were thirled, whether they had their grain ground there or not. The extensive litigation shows that 'out-grinding' in another mill, presumably surreptitiously to avoid dues, was of frequent occurrence.

The characteristic range of dues and duties on both sides can be seen from a 1790 Aberdeenshire contract between the mill superior and the suckeners. The miller was bound to provide a proper service at all times, and to carry the clean winnowed grain from the 'shilling hill' to the mill. The suckeners were bound to grind all their corn, including pease, at the mill, and to pay every 25th peck to the *tacksman* or tenant of the mill, and one peck out of every 6 bolls of winnowed grain as *knaveship*, for the miller's servant; all malt was to be ground at the mill, the 25th peck being paid for multure and knaveship; the same amount was to be paid on all grain sold by a tenant outside the bounds of the sucken; all grain purchased outside the sucken should be ground at the mill and dues paid on it, amounting to the 48th peck, plus knaveship; the dust or fine particles of meal and chaff, and the *shilling seeds* or chaff from winnowing (from which the dish called *sowens* could be made) were at the disposal of the suckeners. The suckeners were also bound to build and uphold their proportions of the mill house and mill dams, to cast the mill-lade, to carry stone, earth, and timber for upholding the mill, mill-house, and mill-water whenever necessary. The tenant of the mill was to furnish the timber at his own expense, and to cart and dry the earth required on the nearest convenient spot outside the arable ground. If the miller failed in his duty, he was liable to be fined, and to be replaced by another, after trial.[83]

The system of thirlage to a mill, perhaps one of the oldest adjuncts of a barony, continued, often almost intact, until an Act of George III in 1777[84] authorised the conversion of multures into money payments. Throughout the period of existence of thirlage, there were constant efforts to keep tenants on the straight and narrow path, starting with national legislation in an Act of the Scottish Parliament for 1284 which laid it down that hand mills were not to be used except through stress of weather or where mills were lacking. Any contravention meant loss of the hand mill, and no one was allowed to have more than two. For the next five hundred years prohibitions on the use of querns were frequently repeated, both by estates and by town councils, but they seem never to have been effective for long. The records of Baron Courts, such as that of Urie in Kincardineshire, are full of complaints and repetition of regulations regarding the milling of grain, in which the miller's deficiencies appear as well as those of the suckeners, for millers had a reputation for seeing to it that they never came off worst, and the mill swine were generally better fed than those of the ordinary tenants. As the proverb put it, 'the miller's soo's aye best fed'. In Stitchill the regulations were taken so far that in 1661 it was decreed that because the buying of bread in the markets for penny bridals was leading to loss for the miller, all wheat for such bread should thereafter be ground in the barony mill, and no bride was to have her wedding outside the barony, so that the mill would get its normal malt duties. Wheaten bread, therefore, and ale, were the things for festival occasions.

The mill was a nodal point in estate administration, and in the everyday life of the community, a large proportion of whose working year was concerned with tilling, manuring, sowing, reaping, stacking and threshing the crops that reached their final stage of processing between the rumbling mill-stones. The maintenance of the mill was a communal activity, and probably no other activity survived as a community function into the period of the improvements as well as this. By the nineteenth century, however, the letting of a mill by an estate had become no different from the letting of an ordinary farm.

One of the big problems was the getting and transporting of the mill-stones themselves. Mill-stone quarries were found in various parts of the country. The coarse sandstone of the Pennan rocks in Aberdeenshire, of a grey colour inclining to red, was much used in the North-East. The stones were shaped in the quarry and were transported by being rolled on edge, with a stout spar of wood thrust through the central eye, and a wooden frame built over the stone. Four to six horses were yoked to it and the various suckeners steered and controlled the stone as best they could. It was not a safe job, hence the North-East saying, 'mony ane's gotten an amshach (mishap) at the spar'.[85] In 1670, each ploughgate in the Barony of Urie in Kincardine was ordered to send two sufficient men and two horses for taking home mill-stones from Cowie, presumably in the same way. It seems, however, that wheeled transport was also possible in some areas, for the records of the Tulliallan Coal Works refer in 1645 to two mill wains for fetching home the mill-stones.[86] There were four 'miller-quarriers' making mill-stones in Dunbar – a centre for the export of grain – in 1497.[87] 'Murray' mill-stones were being imported into Banff in the seventeenth century, as well as Pennan mill-stones, presumably by sea, at a cost of 4/- each.[86] There were good freestone quarries for mill-stones near Glamis in Angus, and in Ayrshire stones were got from Kaim Hill, Fairlie.[88] There was a good mill-stone quarry in the parish of Killearn, Stirlingshire, which began to be regularly worked about 1750–60 as mills increased in number. By 1796 this quarry had been cut down to a depth of 24 feet.[89] In the early nineteenth century, however, the use of native mill-stones began to decline as French burr blocks began to be imported by firms such as J. Smith & Co., 219 High Street, Edinburgh, established 1823 (Fig. 49a), and mill-stones began to be built up of keyed segments instead of being in single pieces.

MOTIVE POWER

Mills were driven by wind or water. Windmills were fairly widely distributed in areas where water was scarce, from North Ronaldsay (Fig. 49b) in Orkney down to the Lothians. In a few places on the coast there were tide mills, for example at Petty in Inverness and at Munlochy in Cromarty. The former was abandoned in 1825. The latter could do 8 hours' grinding with each tide, and had a bigger water wheel than usual.[90]

The great majority of mills, however, were driven by water from a mill-lade opening off a dam or river, and striking the mill-wheel at the top (overshot), middle (breast-shot) or below (undershot). Older wheels were turned by means of flat boards or *starts* that protruded from the circumference, and were breast-shot or undershot. It was only with the development of the more efficient bucket-wheel that the overshot system began to be adopted, as on some of the mills on the Leader Water in Berwickshire in 1809, where large quantities of meal were produced for supplying Edinburgh and its environs through the weekly market at Dalkeith.[91]

6

Root Crops

THE range of effects of the new root crops, turnips and potatoes, after they had begun to be grown as field crops in the eighteenth century and not just as novelties for domestic consumption in the gardens of proprietors, is hard to assess. Both crops became completely integrated into the everyday economy. They provided food and in part wages for the people, helped to improve animal breeds and allowed the overwintering of stock in good condition, stimulated trade in fat cattle, helped to clean the land they grew on, led to new kinds of rotations that could keep the land in good heart, sparked off the development of a whole new range of horse-drawn equipment for making and cleaning drills, and led to adaptations in farm buildings through the addition of turnip sheds (Fig. 50). Their influence was very pervasive not only in terms of farm functioning, of trade in livestock, and improvements in breeds, but also of diet either directly, or by allowing the provision of fresh meat in winter, as against the old style of using salt meat from a cattle-beast or sheep slaughtered at Martinmas.

THE TURNIP

Turnips were known as garden crops from the late seventeenth century, even as far north as Orkney.[92] The Baron Court Book of Urie records the breaking of orchard dykes and stealing of turnips in 1672. Amongst the surviving accounts of the Laird of Mayen is an order for seed from Patrick Lawson, merchant in Banff, in 1693.[93] It was not until half a century later that they became regular field crops, however. At first they were sown broadcast. East Lothian was one of the earliest counties to grow turnips in fields, and at Yester an English land steward called Wade, introduced by John, Marquis of Tweeddale, was using them to feed wedders around 1740. Lord Kames, from about 1746 in Berwickshire, and Sir George Suttie of Balgone, from about 1750 in East Lothian, and William Dawson at Frogden in Roxburgh-shire were growing turnips as regular crops.

Drill rather than broadcast sowing began to come in about then though broadcasting continued in some areas for a long time, especially on poorer soils. The earliest drills were made up to 6 feet (1·8 m.) apart to let horses work easily between them, though the width soon settled down at 22 to 30 inches (0·6–0·8 m.) apart, wide enough for a single horse to walk along, and near enough for seed barrows to sow two drills at a time.

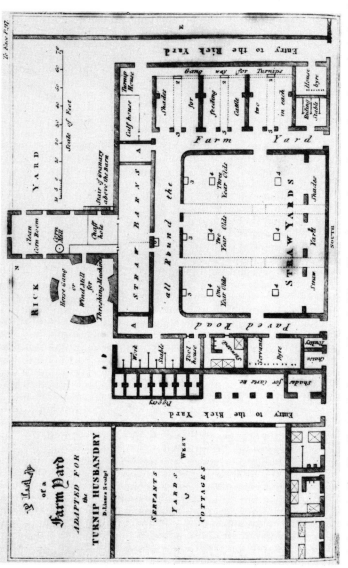

50. The turnip had a considerable effect on the layout of farm-buildings. Here, the easy internal access from the turnip shed to the feeders' byre is shown. In later farms, the house byre or cow byre was made more easily accessible than here. From R. Kerr, *Agriculture of Berwick*, 1809, facing 97.

Drills were originally made with light ploughs that cut a furrow slice
one-way, then came back alongside setting a slice against the first one. When
the drills had been made, muck was carted to the field and spread along the
drill bottoms. The next stage was to split or cleave the original drills, again
with the plough, so as to make new drills immediately over the manure.
On these drills the seed was sown. Although ploughs with adjustable double

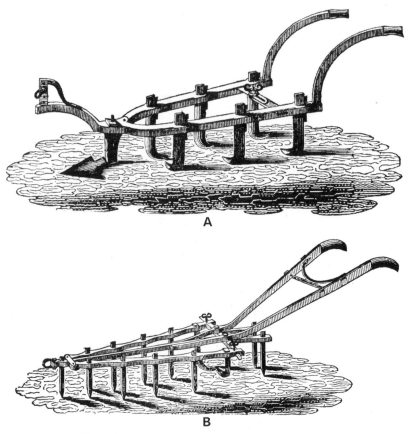

A

B

51. Examples of horse hoes, for cleaning between drills: a, b, from *Prize Essays of the
Highland and Agricultural Society of Scotland*, 1832, IX, 80–81.   C4030–4031

mould-boards were already in use at least from the 1790s in Berwickshire
and elsewhere, these were not at first used for making the drills, as in later
times, but for laying earth back on the drills after cleaning had been done
with an ordinary plough, and hand-hoeing had been completed.

Turnip husbandry is extremely labour-intensive, which explains why it
has been going out of favour at the present time. Turnip land was ploughed

about November, and cross-ploughed in March or April, when it was also harrowed and cleared of weeds; it was twice ploughed in May to June, and again harrowed and weeded.

Sowing was begun in early June using various seeders according to the period and the status of the user. The *bobbin' John*, a white-metal cylinder about 1 foot (30·5 cm) in diameter by 9 inches (23 cm) deep, with a long wooden handle, that was shaken along the drill, is said to have been invented by Mr. Udny of Udny in Aberdeenshire around 1730.[94] This simple device was later made to roll along the drill, and survived until recent times as a *patcher*, to fill gaps left where the fly had eaten the first sowing of turnips.

51. c. A drawing by F. Noël-Paton of a horse-hoe at Lamlash, Arran, Sept. 1882. It is made from an old wooden harrow in imitation of the iron horse-hoes of Lowland farms.

Hand-operated seed-barrows with hoppers and rollers for one drill remained common in the north, though horse-drawn machines for sowing two or more drills at a time were also being used on bigger farms from the early 1880s. A one-drill hand barrow cost £1.6 in 1812, whereas a 2-drill horse drawn one might cost £8.8 or more,[95] so that not only the quantity sown but also the price affected the selection and distribution of seed-barrows of different capacities.

For cleaning between the drills, the earliest implements used were the ordinary light plough for scraping off soil and weeds, and the double mould-board plough for laying the earth back. There soon developed a whole range of drill harrows and horse hoes (Fig. 51), often with three or

more triangular blades that cut the roots of the weeds, produced commercially or made by local smiths out of old cart wheel rings. The young
turnip plants themselves were formerly sown much thicker than in later
days, and often required two or three hand hoeings (Fig. 52). The blade
of an old scythe mounted on a handle made a good hoe.

In autumn and early winter the plucking and storing of turnips was a
regular task, and if not enough had been stored to keep the byre going,

52. Singling turnips in East Lothian.   C2091

they might have to be howked out of the hard-frozen drills with special iron hooks or *cleeks*, and then sledged or carted home.

Some areas took to turnip husbandry much more readily than others. The North-East became a great turnip district, and in this respect greatly influenced Orkney farming, where most of the terms connected with the working of turnips are of North-East origin. Similarly, Berwickshire methods were used in the islands of Islay, Gigha and Colonsay.[96] The diffusion of techniques to the north and west, therefore, had more than one point of origin, but because turnips were so vulnerable to the depredations of animals, the rate of diffusion of the crop was conditioned by the presence or absence of enclosed fields.

Where sheep were commonly reared, especially in the Borders, crops of turnips were used to feed them for up to five months in winter, being eaten directly off the ground. Cattle were stall fed, as a rule, however (Fig. 50). In the early days, turnips were much used for fattening cattle for the market, but by the 1790s, due to poor prices for fat stock, farmers were concentrating more on feeding young stock and milk cattle. From the 1820s, however, there was an upsurge of interest in fat stock, for example in Aberdeenshire, where yearly sea shipments increased as follows: 1828-32, 150 to 800; 1833-6, 1,250 to 8,049; 1836-41, 5,843-8,049; 1842-9, 9,543-15,858. The turnip crop was one of the main bases for this trade.[97]

Another kind of trade developed in Orkney, in the 1860s, when the introduction of Peruvian guano was beginning to make big changes in the nature of fertilisers. This was the production of turnip seed for export, on places like the Graemeshall estate. The plants were allowed to seed, and were then cut, and shaken on to a large canvas sheet.[98]

THE POTATO

Whereas the turnip had its main effect on Lowland Scotland, the potato, at first, made its greatest mark in the Highlands and Islands, very much as it did in Ireland.

Potatoes of two kinds, red knotty and white, were mentioned in 1697,[99] and by 1728 they were being grown as a field crop around Kilsyth,[100] but until about 1750, they were largely confined to gardens in the Lowlands, and were just beginning to become a general article of diet in the Highlands. There was even some opposition to them, as when Clanranald brought back a cargo of potatoes from Antrim to South Uist and Benbecula in 1743 and could not easily persuade his tenants to plant them.[101] It was not until the 1770s that it had spread to every part, and though by that date it was already being grown even by the smallest householders, nevertheless the rate of diffusion had been fairly gradual: South Uist and Benbecula (Inverness) 1743, Lochalsh (Ross) 1750, Clyne (Sutherland) 1756, Lewis (Ross) 1756,

Dornoch (Ross) 1758, Edderachyllis (Sutherland) 1760, Urray (Ross), Kilmalie, and Boleskine and Abertarff (Inverness) 1764, Assynt (Sutherland) 1766.[102] There was an acclimatisation period of a quarter of a century and the original costs of introduction were borne by the lairds and the gentlemen tenants.

From 1770 onwards, coinciding with the period of the Clearances, the breakdown of the shieling system, and a rapid growth in population, the potato became the basis of subsistence in the Highlands and Islands, in many cases taking the place of bread for up to two-thirds of the year. Fish, and milk and milk products, were the main supplements, but the amounts of oatmeal and bere meal declined, for the lazy-beds were turned over more and more to the growing of potatoes, and less and less to the growing of cereals. At the same time there was a great spread in the area covered by lazy-beds which, though at first developed in wet, peaty areas, now spread up the hills amongst the rocks, wherever patches of soil could be scraped together to grow the all-important root. Coast dwellers were on the whole better off than those in the inland parts.

At this period, the settlement pattern came to have a predominantly coastal emphasis. Such a pattern was practical, from the point of view of the lairds, in two ways. It left the hills clear for the development of sheep farms, and it brought the men close to the sea, where the lairds were seeking to develop the fishing industry, It also provided a reservoir of labour for the gathering of seaweed to burn in kilns to make kelp, which for a time was a very profitable source of income. As the men became more and more absorbed in alternative activities, the women took on more of their farming functions, and though as a rule the men dug the lazy-beds with caschroms, it was the women who carried seaweed manure in creels from the shore, who saw to the planting of the tubers, and who, along with older and younger folk, later lifted the potatoes, using small scale hand tools like the *croman* or *crocan* (Figs. 53c and d) to do so. With the mattock-like *croman*, they worked along the drills, as in Lewis, but with the *crocan* or hook, team work *across* the drills, as in Uist, was the common method. Since the cultivation of the potato may well have had an effect on the development of the *caschrom* from earlier types of digging spades, and since the *croman* and *crocan* are particular to the culture of potatoes, it can be seen that in the Highland areas, no less than in a different way in the Lowlands, the potato brought with it its own new complex of equipment.

Extreme dependence on the potato in the outer edges of Scotland led to an inevitable imbalance in the domestic economy. If the fishing or kelp failed, cash returns that helped to pay debts and buy meal disappeared; if the potato failed, the basis of subsistence vanished. And these failures did in fact take place, at a time when the population of the Highlands was at the highest ever recorded, and when the Famine Relief Committee of 1846 found that potatoes constituted 75–88% of the diet of Highland families, as opposed to a Lowland ratio of 25%. There was a recession in the kelp industry. Fishing was becoming more and more centralised on a limited number of ports. In 1835, but worst of all in 1845 and 1846, potato blight decimated the crops, and real famine ensued. In 1851 and 1856 came other years of potato failure, and by the end of the century the pattern had become one of increasing Government

A

B

53. a. Earthing up potatoes with a drill plough drawn by two cattle in Orkney.   C875
b. Planting potatoes. The drills are opened, muck is spread along the bottom, the potatoes planted, and the drills closed. From Stephens, 1844, II, 660.   C1634

intervention, with a great deal of emigration to other countries and to the towns of Britain. The potato ceased to be the staple of the diet, though continuing as an important part of the crofting economy.

In the Highlands, the potato had a fundamental part to play in the social situation between about 1750 and 1880. It played a similar role for poorer folk in the Lowlands, but in general became integrated into the general diet as one element in it. It also came to be part of the married servants' wages either as a direct allowance, or as a certain quantity planted, in the course of the nineteenth century. In the Lowlands, therefore, the effects of its introduction, though pervasive, were of a different kind and degree.

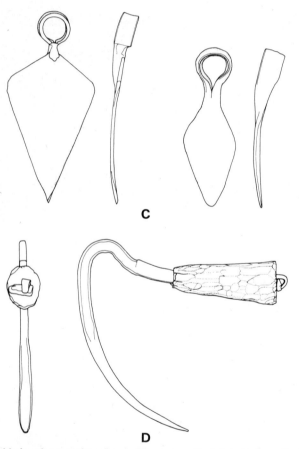

C

D

53. c. The blades of *cromans* from Lewis. The one on the left is modern, the blade having been cut and the socket ring welded on by John McLeod, blacksmith, Einaclete Road, Stornoway; the one on the right was made from an old cart-wheel ring. The *croman* has a wooden handle about 30 inches (76 cm.) long and is worked like an adze.   C791

d. A *crocan* or hook from Uist, for lifting potatoes across the drills. Usually worked by people in teams.   C1187

In Lowland Scotland, potatoes were cultivated in drills very much as for turnips (Figs. 53a–b), though fewer ploughings were necessary. They became a field crop about the same time as turnips. At first, they were used as an element in the reclamation of rough land, old pasture, or wet soils, using the lazy-bed system. Already by the 1770s, even in Assynt, the poor tenants 'are daily enlarging their Corn Lands by potatoe improvements so that the greatest part of the Grounds within the Dykes will soon be brought into tillage, which will be a great addition to the Corn Land',[103] and the same process was going on in several counties in Scotland. Frequently, this kind of reclamation

54. a. A spinner digger by Jack of Maybole drawn by an early steam tractor, in Ayrshire.
C881

through the potato was carried on by herds and cottagers on the moorland edges, leading to an increase in the extent of cultivable land in Lowland Scotland as well. Around the larger towns from which plentiful supplies of dung could be got, there was an intensive development of potato cropping, and farmers around the villages were letting patches of land to tradesmen and other village folk from the early 1780s. This was particularly common around Alloa, Clackmannan, Dollar, Tillicoultry, and Menstrie.[104] Entrepreneurs like Mr. Graham of Kilsyth were already growing potatoes for the Glasgow market by 1796,[105] and there is no doubt that the demand for potatoes by the towns stimulated the increase in this crop almost as much as its value for feeding animals.

In general potatoes did not at first take a place in the rotational system, but were grown partly for reclamation purposes, partly as a means of providing relatively cheap food for farm workers – even in East Lothian by 1794 it constituted a third of the food of the 'common people'[106] – and partly for feeding horses, cows, poultry and pigs. Carrots were also tried as a field crop as early as the 1780s in Ross-shire, when they were 'rare in Scotland, and an

54. b. A tattie lifting squad.   C300

absolute novelty in the north'. Though Robert Hall of Fowlis fed horses on them instead of corn, this was a fairly isolated instance.[107]

In certain areas, such as Fife, but most of all in South-West Scotland, the potato became the basis for a great expansion in pig-rearing. Whereas Galloway had 150 pigs in 1780, by 1794 it had 10,000, and the bacon industry became well established there.[108] Later, other districts followed suit. Nigg in Ross-shire was growing potatoes to feed pigs for the market day by the 1840s, but pig prices got too low by 1845 and the potato acreage dropped.

In the Highland areas and in rough, boggy or moory ground in the Lowlands, potatoes were cultivated in lazy-beds. This technique, essentially, belongs to smaller-scale farming and to poorer folk who had no equipment beyond the basic hand tools. The potatoes were often dibbled in, sometimes as whole potatoes, sometimes as sections with good eyes, cut off with a knife, or scooped out with a spoon-shaped tool that was in use for a time around 1800. In the Lowlands and on the bigger Highland farms, however, they were planted in drills, as for turnips, the tubers having to be placed in position by hand. It was not until the 1930s that mechanical planters began to appear on the market, though even then their rate of adoption was slow.

The lifting of potatoes in October to November may be done with specialised hand tools like the Hebridean *croman* and *crocan*, even at the present day. The *croman*, at least, involves the same technique as the hand-hoes and muck-hacks that were commonly used for lifting in Caithness in the early 1800s.[109] The *cas-chrom* itself might be used to slacken plants, but much more common, already by 1800, was the three-pronged graip, with slightly flattened prongs.

Drilled potatoes were also taken up with graips in the Lowland parts, but it was more usual to open the drills for the 'tattie pickers' with the drill-plough. Special potato ploughs, with two sets of fingers that lifted and spread the roots, had been developed by the middle of the century, and the spinner type of lifter, still in use in many places (Fig. 54), was patented in 1855, and later improved by firms like Wallace & Sons, Glasgow. When the Highland and Agricultural Society of Scotland held a trial of potato diggers on a farm near Perth in 1896, six Scottish firms competed – J. Bissett and Sons of Blairgowrie; William Dewar of Killis, Dundee; Low, Duncan & Co.; James Mollison, Ruthven; James Robertson of Coupar-Angus; and R. Stewart, Buttergask, Coupar-Angus. All worked well, and all won a silver medal.[110] The elevator lifter appeared in the late 1920s, and more recent still is the potato harvester with a large, rotating gridded wheel that cleans as well as lifts. The difficulty of mechanically separating potatoes, stones, and hard lumps of earth, however, has made it impossible to avoid using the hands and eyes of men and women, and at the harvesting season large numbers of 'tattie pickers' are still required, though the war-time custom of giving school children a 'tattie holiday' to gather this valuable food crop has relatively recently been given up.

The storage of turnips, and even more of potatoes, brought new features to the farm. A section of the barn was often boxed off on the smaller farms as a store, or else barrels were used. Outside, potato pits were made, covered with straw and earth, in shape like the elongated roof of a house (Fig. 55a), and sometimes special 'tattie hooses' were built. In Papa Stour, Shetland, there are surviving examples of such houses about 12 feet (3·6 m.) long by 7 feet (2·2 m.) wide, built partly into a slope, with stone walls and a roof of wood and thatch like a normal house. Here, however, potato pits were more often circular, and dug into the ground. Potato houses in Fife, around 1800, were about 15 feet (4·5 m.) wide by 8 feet (2·4 m.) high. Stone-lined, completely

A

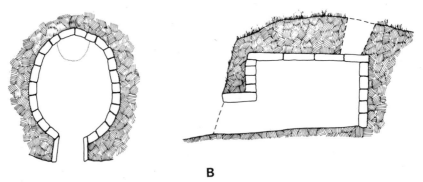

B

55. **a.** Sorting and weighing potatoes from the pit.   C1113
b. A stone-built underground potato pit at Blackhills, Glenesk, Angus.   C1193

underground pits were also made. They resemble small souterrains, and were known in Roxburgh and Fife about 1794–1800.[111] Examples survive in Glenesk, Angus. (Fig. 55b). A hay stack could be built on top for insulation.

One of the features of the potato is the great range of varieties that is still being added to. Whereas in 1697 only knotty red and oval white varieties had reached gentlemen's gardens, by the 1790s there were the round red, round white and broad white, the long kidney, the pale red and white streaked Tartar, the dark purple blacks or blackamores, the Lancashire Manby, and the Killimancas or Jeanies. By the 1850s the common Orkney red was one of the disease-free strains being developed in Orkney.[112] From there, potatoes were being exported to Shetland, Leith, London and the Isle of Man. The Angus area also produced some prominent potato men, like William Paterson of Dundee, who were importing potatoes from several countries and developing new disease-resistant varieties such as the Victoria, marketed in 1863, and the Champion, marketed in 1876. Another prominent name was Archibald Finlay of Markinch in Fife, who produced the Up-to-Date in 1891, the British Queen, the Majestic, and the Eldorado. Potatoes became and have remained a prominent part of the Scottish contribution to farming, and from about 1918 field inspection of crops was started under the Scottish Board of Agriculture, to help to stamp out disease and maintain the country's reputation as a source of healthy seed-potatoes that also gave high yields. However, in the remoter parts of the country, older breeds are still grown. The black potato can be found in Shetland, the Beauty o' Hebron in Caithness, Kerr's Pink in the Hebrides, and several more.

7

The Shieling

IN 1786, a traveller was approaching Loch Hourn by sea. 'About sun-set', he said, 'we cast anchor in an open road, at the mouth of the loch, and seeing a decent looking house, with sundry huts at some distance, Macdonald and myself bent our way thither, as if certain of a good reception, of comfortable lodging, and a whole budget of news. When we got to this place, a dead silence pervaded the whole village; the windows and doors of the principal houses were shut; we knocked in vain, nothing that had life was seen or heard from any quarter . . . we were informed by a transient traveller that the people of the village had just gone to the shielings.'[113]

Anyone familiar with the Highlands would have known that the village was empty because the people had gone to the hills with their animals for the summer grazing, as they did between June and August each year. The men came back later to do the work that was required about the village, leaving the women and old folk to look after the stock, and meantime, the crops in the unfenced fields were left to grow in peace from the depredations of animals.

This annual movement of people and stock to the summer grazings is very old, not only in Scotland, but in many parts of the world. It can be traced in this country back to and beyond the twelfth century through place names ending in, for example, -shiel, -ary (Gaelic airidh), and -setr. Shiel is a Norse word that entered Scotland from the Northumbrian dialect of English, -setr came directly as a result of the Scandinavian settlement of the Northern and North-Western parts of Scotland from the end of the ninth century AD, and -ary or airidh is Gaelic. The varied origins of these names suggest that the practice of transhumance may have reached this country from three directions, and indicate its widespread nature.

It is likely that the early expansion of the settlement pattern was aided by the shieling system. Following the establishment of fixed settlement sites in prehistoric times, the subsequent expansion may have taken place first through the use of sites occupied only in summer, and then by their permanent settlement. This expansion process went on in some places, such as the Highland villages of Aberdeenshire and Banffshire, until the end of the eighteenth century.

From some unknown period until the 1700s, and in Lewis until the 1900s (Fig. 56a), the annual movement to the shieling grounds was an

56. a. Milking at a Lewis shieling, ante 1928. The cow is eating a titbit, perhaps some seaweed or weeds gathered from the grain. The stone walls are surrounded by turf. C1228
b. A shieling on a mounded site at Uishal, near Shawbost. XVIII. 32.18.

integral part of the life-cycle of every farming community, a means by which the cultivation of crops was brought into balance with animal husbandry. It was this balance that helped greatly to determine the earlier pattern of settlement, not only in Scotland, but also in Scandinavia, in the Carpathians, around the Mediterranean, and wherever transhumance involving a seasonal alternation between a farming village at lower levels and the summer grazing huts in the hills was carried on.

In looking at the history of the Scottish countryside, it is necessary to keep in mind a sliding chronological scale. Up to the period of the Clearances, change in the Highland zone was relatively slow as compared with the

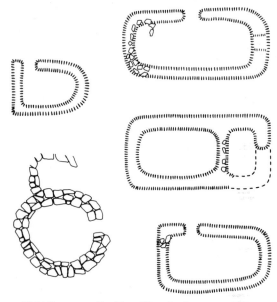

56. c. Diagrams of shielings near Lochlee, Glenesk, Angus.   C3740

Lowlands. As a result settlements of the farm-village type, parallel to those that still exist widely in other parts of Europe, have remained till the present day – even though they have been subjected to considerable modification – but in the Lowlands such settlements, which had once been numerous, had effectively vanished by about 1800, in the course of the agricultural improvements. Some form of shieling system once formed part of many such Lowland villages, for example in the Borders and in Angus, but here it disappeared relatively early. In the Highlands on the other hand, the system survived much longer, especially in Lewis where many folk of middle age have direct personal knowledge of it, as the last bastion in Britain of an age-old tradition.

Whether or not the shieling system was common in early times, it is likely that it would have been re-organised after the arrival from England in the twelfth century of Benedictine and Cistercian monks, of whom the latter in particular introduced an organised system of agriculture, with extensive arable and sheep farms, and villages of workmen and bondmen to carry on the work of the granges or home farms. Possibly place-names like Nether Shiels and Over Shiels (north-west of Stow) point to the earlier existence of the shieling system, but it is equally if not more likely that they relate to the huts of shepherds looking after flocks for monasteries and later for secular farmers, as paid employees. The custom of going to the hills in summer as a family unit disappeared early in the Borders. To some extent, existing shieling grounds were taken over for arable purposes in monastic times, but they were chiefly used for sheep. This was due to the extensive development of wool-production and the wool-trade from the twelfth century, when great quantities of wool began to be shipped to Flanders by the Border monasteries, through the ports of Berwick and Musselburgh. If the shieling or hill grazing system of the Borders is associated chiefly with sheep, this is largely due to economic demands.

In Highland Scotland, on the other hand, the emphasis was not on sheep, but on cattle. This was also due to economic factors that came into play in the course of the seventeenth century, when there was a substantial increase in the export of black cattle to England. This became one of the country's main staples, satisfying the demands for food of the rapidly growing city of London, and of the army and navy.[114] Between the Union of the Crowns of Scotland and England in 1603, and the Union of the Kingdoms in 1707, it was said that the country 'was little else than a mere grasing field to England'.[115] Just as the monasteries, in organising the grazings on the Border hills, brought about what might be called the Border clearances, transforming a shieling system into hill grazings, so also did the later secular land-owners start to bring about the same effect in the Highlands, though they usually allowed the mixed stock – sheep, goats, and cattle – of their tenants to go to the hills alongside their black cattle, so that for a time hill grazing and the shieling system were able to co-exist.

In this way the wider world of economics came to impinge on the domestic shieling system, whose character changed in two ways, due to the encouragement of cattle-raising for trade, and later, the disappearance of goats and of the small flocks of little native sheep, which were actively discouraged when the lairds started to bring in improved sheep types, Blackface and Cheviot, from southern Scotland, for their own purposes. These two factors brought about the characteristic emphasis on cattle as the shieling animals, but it is the family or rather groups of families with a mixed stock of sheep, cattle and goats that best reflect the old, indigenous form of transhumance.

Information is available for several regions. In seventeenth-century Angus, small heritors from Glenisla, holding of the Abbey of Coupar went to the distant glens bordering on Braemar with their cattle. Here they built small huts for themselves, and threw them down when they left. They lived on milk and whey, a little meal, and what venison or wild fowl they could catch.[116] A century later, shieling huts had become more sophisticated, and some were fairly substantial. Alexander Ross, the Lochlee schoolmaster who wrote the poem *Helenore*, has described an interior:

> On skelfs a' round the wa's the cogs were set,
> Ready to ream, an' for the cheese be het;
> A hake was frae the rigging hinging fu'
> Of quarter kebbocks, tightly made an' new.
> Behind the door, a calour heather bed,
> Flat o' the floor, of stanes an' fail was made.[117]

In the glens, the sites of shieling huts can still be seen, for example between Wolf Craig and Hunt Hill in Glenesk on the road to Lochlee (Fig. 56c). Here, at the foot of a steep slope, by a stream, is a group of foundations. The older ones, some of which have mounded up to a considerable height during the centuries of their use, are oval in shape, often with a smaller oval storage hut or chamber attached. The later ones are rectangular, about 29 feet (8·8 m.) long by 12 feet (3·6 m.) wide, with rounded corners, some-times with two compartments, and with a smaller hut measuring about 18 by 12 feet (5·4 × 3·6 m.) standing near by, but not attached. These date from the second half of the eighteenth century and are of the kind described in *Helenore*.

In the high-lying parts of North-East Scotland, especially Banffshire, a system prevailed that was closely controlled by the estate. In the seventeenth and eighteenth centuries sheep as well as cattle went to the grazing because the system was in part domestic, and each farmer on the estate had the right to graze a certain number of animals. The farmers themselves were glad to concentrate on cattle, since at these levels the arable land rarely produced enough grain for a year's meal, and sales of cattle were necessary before any extra meal could be purchased, and before the rent could be paid.

An important part of the system here was the herding, which overlapped the domestic shieling system. It was customary for landowners to send up their herds a week or two in advance of the stock, to prevent the encroach-ment of cattle from other people's shieling grounds, and to keep off the numerous horses that roamed around at that period. There were similar herding arrangements in Sutherland and Inverness. These herds were paid employees, for it was to the advantage of the lairds to ensure some control of the shieling grounds, but the basis of production remained the family or farm unit.

As long as rents were forthcoming, there was no great reason for change.

But a factor that began to break down the system, as it also did in parts of Sutherland in the eighteenth century, was the further spread of the area of permanent settlement. Either former grazing areas in the valleys, well manured by the droppings of farm stock, became the sites of individual farms, or else farm leases began to specify that parts of the shieling areas linked with individual farms should be cultivated. Such linked shieling areas were being excluded from farm leases in the 1780s, to be continued as separate units. By the third quarter of the eighteenth century, the spread of cultivation and of the permanent settlement pattern through the conversion of shieling areas into farm units, was leading to the dissolution or at least limitation of the system in a reasonably natural evolutionary way. In the North and West, however, the breakdown or eradication of the system was due to other factors, and was often more revolutionary in character, as a result of the development by estates of sheep-farms and later of deer-forests, but either way, the influence of the lairds was the main factor in bringing to an end a type of economy which, though domestic in character, nevertheless provided an essential basis for a subsistence balance in pre-industrial forms of agriculture.

Perthshire also had its own characteristics, some of them conditioned by the distances between the parent farmstead or village, and the shielings, which could be up to 20 miles away. This sometimes led to the existence of two sets of shielings, one being immediately above the head-dykes. In spring, when the first grass appeared, the nearer shielings were made use of first. This also happened in Lewis, where the first move was to the near-by spring-shieling hut, the *tigh earraich*, which was big enough to contain not only the herds, but also a number of animals.[118] The existence of shielings close at hand as well as further off led to better utilisation of the grazing resources, and had advantages in spring, when the animals were running very short of fodder and a bite of early grass was becoming a necessity.

In this way, there was a kind of double movement, but even where there was only one shieling area, there could still be a double movement. The first involved the sending of young horses, dry mares, and animals not needed for farmwork, a week or two in advance, along with boys to herd them. It was probably this factor that led to the employment of herds in Strathavon just before the season started properly. At the first or 'small flitting', the men also went to the grounds to repair and thatch the huts, and see to a stock of fuel. It was one of the boys' jobs to pull heather which, 'when packed close, standing right and uppermost, within board frames, or borders of stone on the beaten clay floors, was so good to lie on as a spring mattress, and far more fragrant'. The milk cows and women came up later at the second or 'big flitting', when all had been prepared for them.[119]

Sometimes the huts were used in winter as well as in late spring and in summer, by herds who remained to look after yeld or young cattle or horses which were allowed the full freedom of the shieling area after the milk cows had gone. This practice was known in Glenlyon in 1727, and also in Caithness.[120] In this way, the shieling system could be combined with a system of hill grazing with herds, maximising the use of the available fodder in the hills, and easing the strain on the fields around the parent settlement.

In Perthshire, the very remoteness of some of the shieling grounds was one factor in the breakdown of the system, for already by the end of the eighteenth century the custom had begun of joining two or three such remote areas together and letting them 'as grazing to a shepherd, who attends his flock, by residing all the year round on the spot, in a substantial house of good masonwork, which in many instances is covered in blue slate'.[121] Such areas became disjoined from the farms and were let as separate sheep-farms, to which the place name Newton was sometimes given.

In the north of Scotland, one of the more striking differences, as seen on the ground, is that some of the shieling areas, for example in Assynt, were enclosed by a dyke. In Perthshire, the individual grounds were grazed in common, but in Assynt the 246 shielings recorded in the 1760s were divided between 42 joint-farms, and 'every one has his particular Space of Pasture, for which, if it be not a Part of his Farm, he pays'.[122] Several of these shieling grounds eventually became croft land, in extension of the permanent settlement pattern, in a manner that emphasises their individual use.

However, individual allocation lasted only as long as the cattle were there, and as long as patches of corn were being grown. Outside this period, the grounds became common grazings. But since the corn growing period was longer than the family's normal period of stay, men called *poindlers* were hired in April to deal with straying animals, and to move from shieling to shieling taking care of the corn. In Inverness-shire, the Badenoch people had *poindlers* in 1767 to look after the grass.[123] Whenever one shieling was taken over by the transhumant families, he moved on to look after the next. The *poindlers* corresponded in part to the Banffshire herds, and a similar purpose was served by the little flitting of Perthshire.

Assynt shielings were also marked by the more or less regular cropping that went on around them, especially but not exclusively on those that lay nearest the farms. When John Home surveyed them in the 1760s, he said of the Inver shielings that they were better adapted for tillage than the village's infields, giving better yields. The impression is given of a well controlled system, calculated to get the most out of the shieling grounds as an essential complement to the infield. The need for this is underlined by the cold statistics – a population of 1,718 existing on 2,202 acres of infield required all the extra grain they could grow on their 1,506 shieling acres, if they were to keep themselves in meal. In other areas, such as Argyll, Ross, and Inverness, as in Perthshire, shielings tended to be higher lying – in Morvern they averaged 720 feet above sea-level[124] – and there was little or no question of cropping that would initiate individual allocation and use.

THE SHIELING ORGANISATION

The movement of people and stock to the shielings is spoken of as an occasion of delight, the highlight of the year. People in Lewis who have experienced shieling life always speak of it with nostalgia. The day for the journey was a day of high excitement and community effort that made hard work a pleasure. In the Western Islands, the stock are said to have travelled in sequence, first the sheep, then the younger cattle, then the older cattle, followed by the goats, if any, and the horses, on whose wooden pack-saddles all kinds of equipment was carried. The men carried spades, timber, heather-ropes that had been previously twisted by hand, and other things required to repair the huts. In some places, such as mainland Argyll, the roofing-timbers were brought home and taken back again each year. It was the work of the men to repair the huts in which their women folk lived, either in advance, or on the day of the flitting. The women carried bedding, dairy utensils, and oatmeal. Their long skirts were drawn up under a belt to let them walk more freely, and they knitted stockings as they walked along. They also took with them spindles and distaffs for spinning wool, for this work also went on at the shielings, and this was where young girls could learn the art of spinning with such equipment. In Perthshire where there was a possibility of taking light peat carts, spinning wheels were carried, and the bleaching of previously woven cloth was also a shieling occupation. The women and sometimes the herds also collected roots, herbs and lichens for making dye. The shieling period, therefore, was not wasted in terms of the domestic textile industry, for much of the preparation of yarn for winter weaving could be done then. There was no real break in the normal series of household activities – only the milieu was changed.

Once the huts had been prepared for occupation, and the *souming* or allocation of stock per family had been checked by the village officer or constable, as happened in the Hebrides, fires were lit again, and after a meal, often with cheese, and perhaps with a prayer and a hymn, the men returned to the village or *wintertown*. There, they had various jobs to do, depending on the area. In the Highlands and Islands, many went off to the herring fishing in the nineteenth century, but if they stayed, there was plenty of work to be done. Since the stock was away, no time was lost in herding the beasts away from the crops growing in the mainly unfenced fields and beds. The hay crop could be seen to, houses repaired and re-thatched, and leather tanned for making shoes and harness. An aspect of the close interplay between wintertown and shieling was that 'sanitation for man and beasts was one of the results of the yearly removal of most of the population and of the stock to the summer grazings'[125] and indeed there was a good opportunity to clean out the byres when the animals were away. In some places, for example Lewis, one of the men's jobs was to remove soot-impregnated bere-straw thatch from the roofs of the dwelling houses, in order to spread it as top-dressing on the potato shoots that were beginning to appear in the small fields. The more soot there was in the thatch, the better it was for manure, and for this reason no turf was laid on the roofing timbers below the thatch, nor were there any chimneys to carry out the smoke from the hearth in the centre of the floor. All the smoke could then accumulate as soot on the straw of the roof. Fresh straw was put on when the new crop was harvested, and the women would come back from the hills to well-aired houses, cleanly thatched with yellow straw. The stock, sleek from the hills, could forage over the harvested fields, and pick up anything that had been left behind.

The custom of using thatch as manure annually was once widespread in the Highlands and Islands, but had died out in most parts by about 1800. It survived nearly a hundred years longer in Lewis in spite of various attempts by landowners to eradicate the custom. It was precisely in this area, where house and byre, thatch, crops, and hill grazing were so closely and so functionally integrated that the shieling system itself survived longest.

The Decline of the Shieling System

The shieling system declined as a result of several factors. In the valleys of mainland Scotland, the spread of cultivation played a part, but this was a contributory and not a primary reason. Much more fundamental was the ending of the old run-rig form of cultivation – when several tenants occupied a piece of land with its arable and its grazing in common – and its replacement by today's pattern of individual farming units. Where each farmhouse and its outbuildings stood in the midst of its own fields, the shieling system became superfluous, for improved cropping techniques, the use of sown grasses, the better processing of hay, and so on, made these units reasonably self-sufficient within their own enclosures. Nevertheless the value of hill grazing is still recognised and many Lowland farmers run hill farms, with a close working link in terms of stock between the two. This, however, is on an individual and not on a community basis, and the people who look after the stock are paid employees. This kind of change, the conversion of shieling areas into hill grazing farms, has characterised the edge of the eastern Highlands of Scotland since the late eighteenth century.

It also happened, especially in the central and eastern Highlands, that there was an intermediate stage, when the hills were used for domestic transhumance and for hill grazing together, either contemporaneously, or one following the other, the herds remaining with non-milking stock after the cows and the women had gone home. This kind of duality of use goes back at least to the early eighteenth century and may be older. It can, for example, be observed in Skye in the seventeenth century. Here, because of the demand for cattle by dealers from the Lowlands, the traditional date of return from the shielings at the beginning of harvest was brought forward to mid-August. A cattle fair was established at Portree in 1580, and the dealers came here to buy cattle, which they then swam across to the mainland and drove on foot to the fairs at Falkirk and Stenhousemuir in mid-September. To support this trade, the grazing of herds of black cattle on the moors and hills of Skye was perhaps going on alongside the summer grazing of the stocks of individual families even by the early sixteenth century, when *marts* for winter slaughter were already being exported to the Lowlands. The value of cattle went on being appreciated in Skye, for Lord Macdonald was complaining in 1798–1800 about the number of squatters and others who grazed cattle in summer on his Skye estates without paying for the grass, and John Blackadder, who surveyed the estates at that date, summed up the local idea of economics thus: that each farm should grow enough to support the possessors without their having to go to the market for grain, and that the grazing or yearly cost of cattle should pay the rent. The important part played by cattle was recognised by both crofter and laird, and the Skye pattern was parallel to that in Strathavon in Banffshire – that is, it was a mixture of domestic and commercial.

The emphasis on cattle, therefore, gradually brought about change in the domestic shieling system. This emphasis does not appear to have existed prior to the sixteenth century. John of Fordun spoke of the upland districts along the Highlands in 1380 as full of pasturage grass for cattle, and abounding in wool-bearing sheep and in horses. Hector Boece described Buchan as a profitable land for sheep in 1527.[126] In Angus, the other half of what later became the Aberdeen Angus cattle area, the manuscript Kinnaird Farm Stock Book shows that there were considerable flocks of sheep in the second half of the sixteenth century, though it was mainly cattle that were being sent to the hills in summer. In East Lothian, it was chiefly the good store of sheep that impressed Camden in 1695,[127] but by this time the cattle trade was already beginning to bring about changes in the Highlands. It does not follow that the cattle trade actually led to an expansion of the shieling areas, for cattle grazing could go on alongside the family based transhumance system. It is more likely that the eighteenth-century increase in the use of shielings was due to population expansion, but this came at a time when both the shieling, and the kind of socio-agrarian system it supported, were nearing the end of their days.

Only in one area, the island of Lewis, did the shieling system survive into the twentieth century. There is probably no single explanation for this, but rather a mixture of circumstances. There were few evictions in favour of sheep farmers in Lewis, partly because the lairds, the Seaforths, had been disinclined to turn the people off in the early days of the sheep farming boom, and because Sir James Matheson had a paternal approach to his tenants in the second half of the nineteenth century.

In Lewis, the population increased by 139% in the period 1755–1801, as against an average increase of 48% in the Highlands as a whole. At the present day the island contains 2,299 farming units of under 5 acres each and 1,022 of under 10 acres.[128] There is, therefore, a higher percentage of small units here than in any of the other Highland counties. In practical terms, this has meant that self-sufficiency was and to a great extent still is impossible for the individual units. Though at present a livelihood can be got from ancillary activities (weaving, fishing, work as roadmen, postmen, etc.), and from Government subsidisation of certain kinds of stock and crops, this was impossible before the 1880s. Then, a subsistence livelihood could only be assured if the individual units worked closely together as community groups. It is likely that the strength of this tradition of community activity, and the real need for it in view of the smallness of the farming units, helped to keep the shieling system going. Even this, however, would have been impossible but for another factor, the rough, boggy terrain that made Lewis difficult to exploit for sheep farms.

THE SHIELING HUTS

There are various Gaelic names for shieling huts – *bothan, builteach, màr(r)ag, sgitheil*. Two other names, *àiridh* and *ruigh*, have the same kind of dual sense as the word shieling – that is, they may apply to the grazing area, or to the seasonal dwelling house on it.

Shieling huts generally occur in groups, reflecting the original joint-farming nature of the parent villages. Occasionally single ones may be found, taking advantage of some small, inaccessible spot of grazing, but the majority are grouped beside streams or lochs, convenient for water and trout, and the high mounding (Fig. 56b) of the foundations of huts in good situations is clear evidence of long continuity of use. What this amounts to in time is hard to assess. A shieling mound excavated in Skye showed a sequence of three huts, that is, there were three phases of more or less complete re-building, between each of which there must have been several seasons of annual repair. Such a sequence of occupation might well take place within a hundred year period, which would take the Skye huts back to about 1750, since transhumance had more or less died out there by 1850. In terms of relative chronology, mounded huts are obviously older than those that are not mounded.

Broadly speaking, shieling huts can be divided into two groups. The earlier group has a round or oval form, the later group is four-sided, and roomier. The building materials are turf and stone, with the necessary roofing timbers. An eighteenth-century illustration of shieling huts in Jura shows a construction in the shape of a wigwam, made of branches or wattle covered with sods.[129]

Many good examples of the older 'beehive' huts survive in Lewis, some of them almost complete. At the base they were built with double walls, up to 6 feet (1·8 m.) thick and standing 3 feet (0·9 m.) high. Above this level the walls were built single, in courses each of which was laid to oversail the one below so that the walls gradually drew in to form a cyclopean arch in the shape of a beehive or egg. At a height of about 8 or 9 feet (2·4–2·7 m.) the stones were so close that they could have been locked by a single stone on top, but an opening was left here to let out smoke and to admit light. The internal diameter was 7 to 8 feet (2·1–2·4 m.), and the height about 6 to 7 feet (1·8–2·1 m.). An example recorded in Harris in 1856 had one door measuring 3 feet high (0·9 m.) by about 2 feet (0·6 m.) wide, with four recesses in the walls to hold milking utensils. Quite often, even in the smallest examples, there were two doors, between which the fire was lit. The wind direction determined which door was to be used. Much of the floor area was bed-space, with a front of stone topped by turf that served as a seat before the fire.

As a rule, there was a smaller hut associated with the main one, and sometimes entered from it. It served as a store for milking equipment, milk, cheese and the like. Where the shieling was not too far from the sea, it was a common practice to carry up a few creelfuls of seaweed that was given to the cows during milking to encourage them to stand still. In Lewis the seaweed was kept in such a little hut, which was then called *tigh-an-fhaomainn*, the seaweed house. Otherwise a titbit of grass or weeds pulled from amongst the growing corn or potatoes, or a backbone or two of fish that had been dried for salting, were given to the cows. The same hut could also give shelter to new-born calves.

Such beehive huts were fairly widespread in Scotland. Surveys made in Perthshire and Sutherland have shown that in many cases the old beehive huts went out of use as dwellings when bigger four-sided huts were erected, but remained as store-houses. Another point of chronology is that it is sometimes the shieling huts nearer the village or farm that are four-sided, while those further off, on shieling grounds that had been turned into sheep-farms, were never altered from their older round or oval forms. The nearer shielings either remained longer in use than the remoter ones, or were built only after the remoter ones could no longer be used.

In Lewis, four-sided huts were still being built in the twentieth century. They are distinguishable from older four-sided huts by the fact that they are built like small houses complete with gable chimneys, a feature almost unknown in earlier times. The arrangement of two doors near the gable containing the hearth, however, was carried on, along with the wall-recesses for utensils, and the allocation of nearly two-thirds of the floor as bed-space. According to a description from Argyll, 'one end of every hut was banked up some eighteen inches from the rest of the floor, and part of it covered with heather-tops for a bed. The heather made a fragrant springy couch, and, as it was to be used in June weather, a thin blanket to cover it, and another to cover the sleeper, were all that were needed for comfort. The remainder of the banked up space served as a seat'.[130]

The shieling huts, therefore, have changed in the course of time, but nevertheless preserve in their structural forms features that may help to provide some understanding of earlier dwelling house types. The beehive huts in particular can be paralleled by structures in several countries that go back to the prehistoric period. With this ancient building tradition goes the shieling tradition itself, and the study of both brings history and archaeology together. It is, in fact, one of the basic keys to an understanding of the history of the more pastoral areas of Scotland.[131]

GRASS AND HAY

Though the shieling system was geared to making the best possible use of the grazings, the strange thing is that so little attention was paid to laying in a stock of winter fodder. Lowland farmers showed little skill in hay-making till the mid-nineteenth century, but in the Highlands hay was hardly being made at all, except for bog- and meadow-hay cut in patches from which the stock had been excluded from May till July. In the 1770s John Home wrote that thousands of cattle had perished in Sutherland for lack of winter hay, and though hay was cut 'by the most industrious people . . . when the Seasons are favourable for winning it',[132] this was far from being sufficient. The fact was that the hay was harvested only after the grain had been reaped. It coincided with the potato work, and with the seasonal rain. It was treated almost as an afterthought.

It was cut, in the Hebrides, with sickles, some of which were left-handed.[133] In the Northern Isles scythes with long, straight handles and short broad blades were used, and in the Lowlands hay was also mown with scythes (Fig. 57a), though as it was intended for seed, the sickle replaced the scythe because it was thought to shake the seed less. Mechanical horse-drawn mowers came into use after the 1850s.

In several parts of Scotland, it was once the custom to form small haycocks as soon as the hay was cut, or to toss it up loosely, though in the Lowlands it had begun to be left for a day or two in swathes already by the 1790s. But on the small crofts, the old method of tossing and shaking the hay and making small cocks entirely by hand may still be seen. Bigger scale farmers had forks and rakes with which they turned the swathes and combined a number of them into *windrows* (Fig. 57a) containing, according to Henry Stephens, the grass of five ridges. The first small hay-cocks were set up on the centre ridge, about 2 feet (0·6 m.) high, and were in a day or two amalgamated into bigger ones, about 6 feet (1·8 m.) high. These could be tied with a *thumb-rope*, twisted out of the side, to keep the top from being

A

B

57. a. The hay, which has been scythed across the rigs, is being made into windrows. From Stephens, 1855, II, 236. C276

b. The hay is being threshed with flails for seed before being stacked. A horse drags the haycocks to the stackyard with a single chain. From Stephens, 1855, II, 242. C278

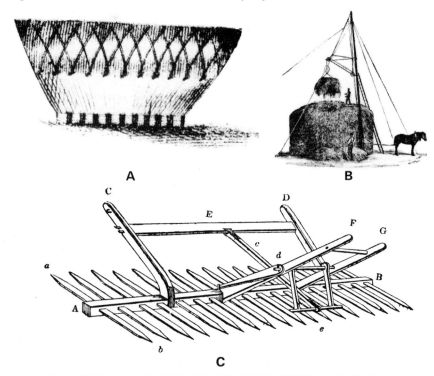

58. a. A rectangular hay-sow in Midlothian. From G. Robertson, *Agriculture of Midlothian*, 1795. C3921

b. A patent rick lifter by John Wallace & Sons, of Glasgow. C872

c. An American hay-rake or *tummlin' tam* introduced in 1828. From *Prize Essays of the Highland and Agricultural Society*, 1832, IX. C3032

d. Using a *tummlin' tam* in the Peterhead area of Aberdeenshire. Per Mrs. Simpson, Peterhead. C4026 blown off. The size of the hay-cocks varied according to the district and the season. There was often a third stage of building in the field, when *tramp-coles* or *tramp-ricks* were made, before the final transfer to the stackyard.

Here, hay was built on foundations as for stacks of grain, and was thatched and roped in the same manner. In parts of Central Scotland and the Borders large rectangular sows were common (Fig. 58a), and in the North and West very much smaller versions can still be seen – for example, the Shetland *diss* and the Caithness *gilt*. Elsewhere round stacks were usual, but where hay-knives were used to slice the hay for feeding the animals, the rectangular shape lent itself better to the cutting process.

In the course of its various turnings, cockings, and re-cockings, hay was handled by hand or with forks, and straight poles could be used, as in Skye in 1845, for moving hay-cocks entire. With horse-power, a hay-cock could be moved by a single chain taken round it (Fig. 57b), and linked to each end of a swingletree so that it could be dragged along the ground. The double-toothed American hay-rake (Fig. 58c–d) was first introduced by Archibald Ronaldson of Saughland in 1828,[134] and later *tummlin' tams* with single teeth became more common. These gathered hay across the swathes. At first this and the horse drawn stubble rake were much used in South-East Scotland. They seem to have reached Scotland before other parts of Britain. In the later nineteenth century various haymaking machines came on to the market for swathe-turning and tedding, but most of these were made outside Scotland.

Other advances were made in the quicker transport of hay by using bogeys on to which large hay-cocks could be pulled intact (Fig. 59a), replacing the horse and cart and the skilful building of loads of hay (Fig. 59b). Systems of ropes and pulleys and tripods also helped to hoist the hay (Fig. 58b) on to the stacks on the bigger farms of South Scotland.

The cultivation of sown grasses for hay goes back to the early eighteenth century, when Thomas, 6th Earl of Haddington, brought a Dorset family to East Lothian to teach enclosing and the management of grass seeds – an effort that was resented at first by the people. It did not spread very quickly, though it reached Islay in 1761, and Sutherland in the 1770s.[135] It was adopted on improved farms in the Highlands since it was seen as a means of rearing increased numbers of black cattle, but the lack of enclosures was a great hindrance. People like Mr. Grant of Corremonie were obliged to arrange for constant herding to keep his neighbour's cattle off his improved grass.[136]

Whereas meadow hay was mown in September to October, cultivated hay was cut in early July and generally treated with more respect. However, it was not until well through the nineteenth century that the regular sowing of grass-seeds and the regular making of hay for winter fodder became a part of the annual activity of most small farms.

A

B

59. a. A hay rick lifter. The rick is pulled on to the bogy by a horse dragging on the rope that passes round the front pulley. By J. Wallace & Sons of Glasgow.   C873

b. Four skilfully built cart-loads of hay at Harwood Farm, West Calder, Midlothian. Per A. Hamilton, from Jean Walker.   C2092

FODDER

In pre-enclosure days, it was practical to have the animals on the hills till the crops were grown and harvested. Some of them, for example horses needed for draught, were kept at home, and in that case they were suppered in the stable, often on thistles pulled from amongst the growing corn, by hand or by wooden thistle-tongs. When the crop had been gathered in and the corn-yard secured, both horses and cattle were allowed to wander freely around the buildings, picking up what they could. In the Lothians this was *lang-halter-time*.[137] In effect, the whole territory of the community then became common grazing.

Where the cows did not go to the shieling in the summer, they grazed on

the tether, as they still do in islands like North Ronaldsay in Orkney. A
tether peg of wood or iron was used, called a *baikie* in North-East Scotland
and *backie* in Caithness, from Gaelic *bacan*, a tethering stake.[138] Sheep were
also tethered, sometimes three at a time on an iron ring. The tether ropes
had swivels in them to prevent entanglement. Besides protecting crops in
unfenced fields, this also allowed controlled grazing in later days.

In the hardest periods of winter, animals nearest the coast were probably
best off, for they could be given seaweed, raw or parboiled, and kale- or
cabbage-stalks. In the Hebrides, dried fish-bones were fed to the cows in
the byre – 'when a cow comes in wet, cold and shivering, a fish-bone is given
her to chew. This chewing tries her to the utmost, and soon upon the point
of every hair of her body stands a bead of perspiration, while from her rises
a cloud of steam'.[139] If a cow was to calve before Whitsun, by which time
the year's supply of fodder would have fairly well given out, a few sheaves
of barley would be held in reserve for her. But the ordinary run of cattle
did not get as good treatment as the cows, and the supply of winter fodder
was critical in deciding the number of stock that could be maintained.

Improvements in agriculture brought a range of new possibilities into
play – turnips and potatoes, hay, straw in greater quantities than before –
and better food and better overwintering possibilities not only allowed
greater numbers of stock to be kept, but also gave an opportunity for the
breeds to be improved. In areas of small to medium-sized farms, however,
the desire to keep more beasts for sale meant that the fodder supplies were
stretched to the utmost, and had to be supplemented. One of the crops much
used for this was whins, a colourful, if somewhat prickly, crop.

Bailie Young of Perth erected a mill for crushing the shoots of whins in
1778.[140] Many of these were set up later, as far north as Inverness-shire, and
as far south as the Borders, but with a concentration in the North-East,
where they remained in use till the late nineteenth century. Some were on
the cider-mill principle, with an upright stone, about 4 feet (1·2 m.) in
diameter by 1 foot (0·3 m.) thick, revolving in a shallow circular trench
about 16 feet (4·8 m.) in diameter. A wooden pole, swivelling in the middle
of the circle, passed through a hole in the centre of the stone, and was pulled
by a horse or ox harnessed to the end of it (Fig. 60a). Other whin-mill stones
were about 4 feet (1·2 m.) wide, conically shaped to turn in a circle. Year-old
shoots of whins – and sometimes shoots of Scots fir – were cut and laid in the
path of the stone, being turned and watered occasionally. An acre of whins
could keep six horses for four months, on twenty minutes bruising daily,
according to the practice at Hillhouse, Kirknewton, Midlothian in 1795.[141]

Where farmers had no whin-mills, the shoots were crushed with a flail
whose beater was strengthened with strips of iron, or by a wooden mallet
on a block, the mallet having a face shod with edge-wise strips of hoop iron.
In Perthshire, they were crushed in a large trough of wood, with 'cross

hatchets'. A furze-machine with rollers and a drum with cutting blades was made by Dr. Mackenzie of Kinellan, Ross-shire, in 1840 (Fig. 60b). A Ross-shire farmer, Gordon of Udale in the Black Isle, sowed whin seed on his poorest land in the 1870s, cut the crop with a mower, and crushed it with a machine called Mackenzie's Gorse Masticator, made in Cork.

Whins were and are a natural crop in much of Scotland, but French furze

60. a. A whin mill with its driving beam at Whitelums, Gartlie, Aberdeenshire.   C4053

seed was brought from France for sowing in Ireland, and in eighteenth-century Galloway the grandfather of McDowal of Logan brought the first seeds in. The crop was fed to either horses or cattle. Though considered by some to be as good as turnips, and though it went with the days of improved agriculture, it remained in most places a supplement when fodder was scarce.[142]

DROVING

In the days before a road-network had developed, on which wheeled vehicles could travel, cattle were particularly valuable because they supplied their own means of locomotion. They could walk to the markets, even if the markets were far away. The cattle trade with England, and the needs of the

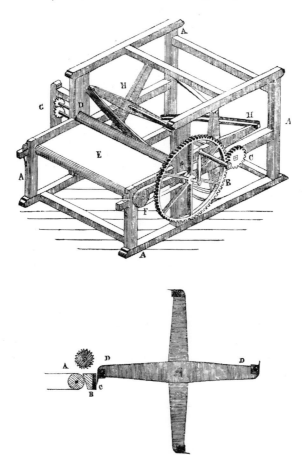

60. b. A furze-machine, with feeding rollers and a drum with cutt'ng blades, made by Dr. Mackenzie of Kinellan, Ross-shire, in 1840. From *Quartlerly Journal of Agriculture*, 1840, XLVIII, 226.

larger Scottish towns for meat, led to a fairly intricate system of cattle dealing, droving and markets, especially in the second half of the seventeenth century. In 1663, Skene of Hallyards in Midlothian recommended the Dunblane market on Whit Monday for buying oxen cheaply for fattening by grazing, so that twice the price could be got for them by Martinmas.

61. Ferrying cattle at Kyleakin, Skye. C1882

Edinburgh was good for milk cows on Trinity Monday, and Linlithgow on Magdalene Day for oxen, cows, young cattle and other stock.

The long roads travelled meant that the cattle arrived lean and hungry at their destinations – 'Highland bones to be covered with Scottish and English beef'.[143] Whether the itinerant drover bought them on the spot directly from the tenants, or through the tacksman or proprietor, the journey still had to be undertaken. In some cases the Highland cattle, *kyloes* from the West or *norlands* from the North, had to take to the water. Drovers swam cattle from Skye across Kyle Rhea. The old method was to get them to the shore at low water and tie them in groups of five to eight in line ahead, the lower jaw of one being fixed by a twisted withy to the tail of the one in front. The withy of the foremost beast was held by a man at the rear of a four-oared boat. From more distant islands, such as Islay, they were transported in open ferry-boats (Fig. 61). A visitor to Port Askaig in 1824 found 'the shore was covered with cattle; and while some were collected in groups under the trees and rocks, crowding to avoid the hot rays of a July evening, others were wading in the sea to shun the flies, some embarking, and another set swimming on shore from the ferry-boats; while the noise of the drovers and the boatmen, and all the bustle and vociferation which whisky did not tend to diminish, were re-echoed from hill to hill, contrasting strangely with the silence and solitude of the surrounding mountains'.[144]

Droving was only finally ended by the steamer services, in relatively recent times. The last herd out of Knapdale was driven to Stirling one autumn in the 1920s, on a Glasgow holiday when the cars drove the animals off the road.[145]

In 1794, it was estimated that there were 30,000 small black cattle in the Hebrides, of which a fourth was exported annually and brought in money to pay the rents. They were left outside all the time to fend for themselves except for the provision of straw or coarse hay, only the milk-cows and calves being housed. By 1811, the estimate had risen to 110,000, of which a fifth was exported annually, at a price of abou t£5 each. The cattle fairs and markets held in May were for bullocks and heifers, and dry cattle, those in October for brood-cows.[146]

About a quarter to a fifth of the cattle on the farms consisted of calves. According to the old reckoning two cows could bring up one calf between them. If a calf died, it was the custom to skin it and put the skin over another calf, otherwise the cow would refuse to suckle the stranger. At Dunrobin, Sutherland, in 1781, calves not needed for veal were allowed to suck the cow, and there were four women to milk, feed calves, clean the milk-vessels, and make cheese and butter. In Glenmorison, Inverness, calves were kept separate from the cows, contrary to the normal practice, but were allowed to suckle after milking time. At Balnagowan, Ross-shire, calves were raised one to a cow and then kept in herds of 80 to 100 in a grass enclosure, getting turnips in winter, and hay and straw in frost. In early summer they were sent 40 miles off to the hills bordering Assynt, to return in October. They were sold at 4 years old here, whereas in the improved islands in the Hebrides, bullocks were sold to itinerant drovers, or at the Dumbarton or Falkirk markets, at the age of three, and heifers and cows at all ages, from two up to ten. From the 1780s, therefore, much attention was being paid to calf rearing in improved areas. This accompanied the attention being paid to cultivated hay, for adequate winter fodder meant better milk supplies for feeding calves, and for butter and cheese.[147]

8

Milk, Butter and Cheese

IN 1605, Sir Thomas Craig wrote that the Highlanders could supply cheese to the Lowlands when cereals were short after a bad harvest, and that they lived solely on cheese, flesh and milk.[148] Sixty years later, Skene of Hallyards pinpointed a further regional emphasis when he said that 'kys milk is best for butter, and yows milk best for cheiss, for kys milk will give both mor butter and better butter than yows milk, and yowis milk will give both mor cheiss and better cheis than kys milk. They use in Cunninghame to make cheiss of kys milk, but it is not good.'[149]

Three points appear from this: that there were regional variations in the production of butter and cheese, that both ewes and cows (Fig. 62a) were milked, and that cheese, like butter, was an important food. Both butter and cheese commonly appear in early charters and rentals, and in grants and regulations in the Acts of the Parliament of Scotland from the time of David I in 1147 onwards. The export of cheese was forbidden by James VI in 1573; in 1661 Charles II required 2 oz. of bullion to be brought to the mint for each 5 cwt. of cheese exported, and under William in 1701 and Anne in 1705, the import or use of Irish, English or foreign butter was forbidden. Both cheese and butter also formed a regular part of the *teinds* or tithes that had to be paid to the Church. The quantity of cheese paid as part of secular rents was such a regular feature, that the word *kain*, a payment in kind for rent, came to mean a certain quantity of cheese, about 60 cwt., in Argyll, Ayrshire, Dunbartonshire, and Galloway, and the dairyman who paid his rent in cheese was a *kainer*.[150] The development in sense underlines the dairying emphasis of South-West Scotland. Milk was also a normal part of the rent in areas like Shetland, where only a little cheese was made before the eighteenth century, and almost none after.

Since butter, and especially cheese, are easily portable, they were particularly useful for trade. The twelfth-century Assisa de Tolloneis laid down tolls of a halfpenny for a load of butter or cheese on horseback,[151] and a farthing for a load on a man's back. From Caithness, quantities of butter made up in the shape of globes were carried in open boats to Moray, up to about 1800, and 'the pastry of the baker's shops of Elgin and Forres, were then enriched with their importation'. At the same period Moray was also buying butter and cheese from Banffshire, and cheese was being imported by grocers from Cheshire and Gloucestershire.[152] Already by the 1730s large

A

B

62. a. Milking a cow in Uist. Cathcart collection.   C1737
b. Carrying milk with a shoulder-yoke, at Gormyre Farm, Torphichen. Per A. R. Jones.
     C1125

quantities of Cheshire cheese and butter were being bought from two Aberdeen merchants, Farquharson and Leslie, for the Grant of Monymusk estate. Supplies, therefore, were carried over very long distances to areas where dairy farming was not developed, and possibly places like the cheese warehouse adjacent to Gray's Close in Edinburgh, marked on a plan dated 1790,[153] were staging posts in this trade between England and the north of Scotland. The scale of the demand at Monymusk was such that cheese was consumed at a rate of 3 lbs. a day, and butter at an even higher rate in the summer months on the estate. In Berwickshire in the 1790s there was a trade in firkins of salted butter, made by both farmers and hinds and sold in small quantities in Edinburgh, Berwick, and Dunbar.[154] Ayrshire butter and cheese were sold in the markets at Ayr and Paisley. Quantities of butter salted in kits, and cheese, were going along the three miles of turnpike road leading from Renfrewshire into Glasgow by 1794, and in Caithness in 1812 Mr. Traill of Hobbister was making Dunlop cheeses for sale in Edinburgh, using Ayrshire cows and employing Ayrshire dairywomen.[155] Till after 1850, Scottish sheep farmers were making use of 'Orkney grease butter' mixed with tar as a salve for smearing sheep, the butter having been paid as part of the rent in kind, and of poor quality as a result. Much later there was another kind of movement – that of buttermilk, carried in *soor-dook* carts from the country to the towns. The last of these carts were seen in the Lothians about 1948, though butts of *soor-dook* were also carried by rail. Town dairies have often continued to deliver milk by horse-power to the present day, and local transport on the farms, using shoulder-yokes, has only recently been given up (Fig. 62b).

THE MILKING OF EWES AND GOATS

Skene of Hallyard's Manuscript of Husbandrie shows that cheese was commonly made of ewes' milk in his time, and seems to have been preferred to cows' milk cheese, though plenty of that was also made, especially in Cunningham. The difference in quality is reflected by a difference in price. When cows' milk cheese cost 4/- a stone in Tweeddale in 1794, ewes' milk cheese cost 7/-.[156] With butter, the positions were reversed, and ewes' milk butter was generally used with tar for smearing sheep, like the second-rate cows' milk butter that was paid for rent.

By the end of the eighteenth century, the milking of ewes had virtually come to an end, surviving longest in eastern Scotland in areas like the Lammermuirs where farmers still milked ewes in 1794 to get butter for sheep-salve, and cheese for retail to the shops. In the Highlands, Samuel Johnson saw both goats and sheep being milked in Skye in 1775. A *meal* or single milking of goats' milk amounted to a quart, and was thinner than cows' milk; that of a ewe amounted to a pint, was thicker, and was not consumed unless boiled.

All the goats' milk, if not used in liquid form, was made into cheese, either by itself, or mixed with ewes' milk and sometimes warm cows' milk. A nineteenth-century description of the Glenlyon shielings in Perthshire speaks of four kinds of cheese – of cow, sheep or goat milk alone, or of all three combined.[157]

In the Lowland areas the folding and milking of ewes for cheese-making came to an end by about 1800, the custom surviving longest in higher parts like the Lammermuirs and the head of Annandale. In the Highlands there was a fifty year time lag, and though the introduction of the Border sheep breeds effectively ended the old custom, nevertheless in Rannoch and the Braes of Lochaber goats continued to be kept for milk and cheese. Even with the Blackface, the old tradition died hard, for it was common to gather the ewes into fanks once or twice after weaning to milk them, to keep the household supplied with cheese.

BUTTER AND CHEESE

Though the salted butter supplied by Renfrewshire farmers to Glasgow was said to keep fresh for a year, butter is nevertheless a perishable commodity, easily affected by heat. Women taking fresh butter to market would wrap it in a rhubarb leaf to keep it cool, or immerse it in a well, perhaps leaving the name 'Butter Wallie' behind as a souvenir. The same need for coolness and for longer-term preservation must explain the numerous finds of 'bog-butter' that have turned up in various parts of Scotland, often wrapped in a cloth and put in a wooden container. A sample from Poolewe was wrapped in the outer bark of a tree.[158] Bog-butter appears to have been unsalted, hence the need to immerse it in a boggy pool, where the owner lost it and where peat solidified over it in the course of time. Some of it contains many cow hairs, like butter seen on a croft in a northern island in the 1950s, when a knife blade had to be taken through it several times to clear it. This process had a name – to *hair* the butter – which goes back at least to 1700 and was known from Peebles to the Northern Isles.

The old way of churning butter in the shielings and in the houses of the wintertowns was to put the milk in a small wooden tub or earlier an earthenware *craggan* covered with a tightly tied sheep- or goat's skin. Then, according to a manuscript account of 1768 relating to Skye, two women seated opposite each other tipped it alternately half up and then dashed it back down, till the milk broke into butter against the sides. It could take nine or ten hours.[159] Straw was used to cushion the shock or, in the shielings, the work was done on the bed. According to a report from Loch Ailort, butter was sometimes made by shaking in a leather bag.[160] A Moray method, said to have lasted till about 1770, was simply to whisk the milk with the bare arm in an iron pot.[161] Such methods remained long where much of the community work

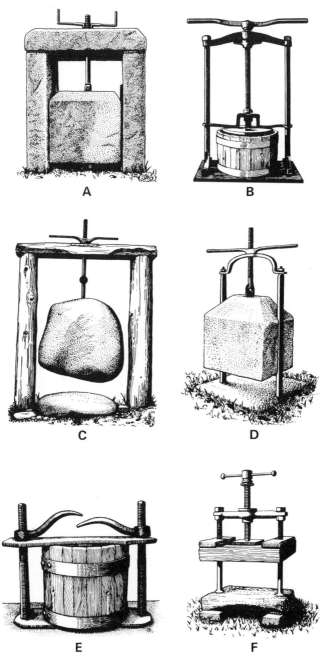

63. Cheese-presses in Angus: a. Mill of Aucheen, Glenesk; b. and e. Braeminzion, Glen Clova; c. Crossbog, Glen Clova; d. Delnamer, Glenisla; f. Gella, Glen Clova. From *Scottish Studies* 1963, Vol. 7/1, 47–56.

depended on women, and upright wooden plunge-churns were still innovations in the islands quite late in the nineteenth century.

The feature of a plunge-churn is that it is worked by a plunger, the head of
which is round or cross-shaped, with holes to let the liquid pass through, and
often shaped with some art (Fig. 64a). Churn-staffs and by implication
plunge-churns are referred to in England from about 1475, and in Scotland
a list of goods in an Edinburgh Testament of 1636 includes 'ane kirne staff'.
Milk churns are recorded from 1478, though there is no way of knowing
the type if the staff is not mentioned.[162] Churns in the Northern Isles (Fig.
64c) and Hebrides are wider at the top than at the bottom, and have no lid.
Elsewhere they are more nearly straight up and down, and are fitted with
lids. In the last days of their existence square plunge-churns were made, as
local joiners lost the skill of working with staves, but they were more difficult
to keep clean.

By the 1790s, patent barrel churns and box churns were already in use in
most Lowland counties, and began to replace plunge-churns, though some
of these still remain in use in the islands of the North and West. On big dairy
farms churning was even adapted to water-power and horse-power, and
circular horse-walks and gearing were used to rotate the dashers in big
wooden or earthenware churns, made by firms like J. Kirk, Bannockburn by
1835, and Peter Robert Drummond in Perth by 1851.[163] Cheese was made
with milk of various kinds, using a variety of materials as rennet. Probably
the stomach of a calf was most common, but that of a lamb, hare, deer or sow
would also do, or even the gizzard of a fowl. Plants like autumn crowfoot
could also be used. The curd was broken and usually salted, but there was
evidently a scarcity of salt sometimes. The little ewes' milk cheeses of St.
Kilda were, like the goats' milk cheeses of Jura, cured with the ashes of
seaweed in the eighteenth century, and before that the people of Heiskir were
salting their cheese with barley-straw ashes. In the Highlands it seems to have
been normal to make the cheeses without salt, and to salt them afterwards
for a few days in a wooden keg.[164] Other additives at the curd-breaking stage,
to give flavour or produce a mould, were a bowlful of mashed potatoes or of
oatmeal, or a handful of caraway seeds or mustard.

Soft cheeses and crowdie were eaten soon after making and did not have
to be pressed much. It was enough to hang them in a cloth to drip and dry
in the air. If cheese was to be kept for some time, however, all the whey had
to be squeezed out, and pressing was a necessity. To do this, the curds were
put in a wooden cheese-vat, with a cheese-cloth round them. The vat had a
wooden lid, a little narrower than the vat, so that pressure could be applied,
by laying on stones at intervals of increasing weight (Fig. 64d) – a method
observed in Orkney in 1961, and used by Sir Alexander Gordon of Lesmoir's
dairy maids in 1759.[165] More advanced was a method of pressing ewes' milk
cheeses in Roxburgh in the 1790s. It involved putting the curds into a

stout canvas bag which was placed under a long plank on the end of which the dairywoman sat or stood, seesawing up and down till the whey had been extruded. The curds were then broken, salted, and placed in a vat for pressing. Most of the presses were of long planks, fixed at one end, and weights were placed on top of the other end as for a steelyard. A 99-stone cheese press that could be moved up and down with a screw had been set up

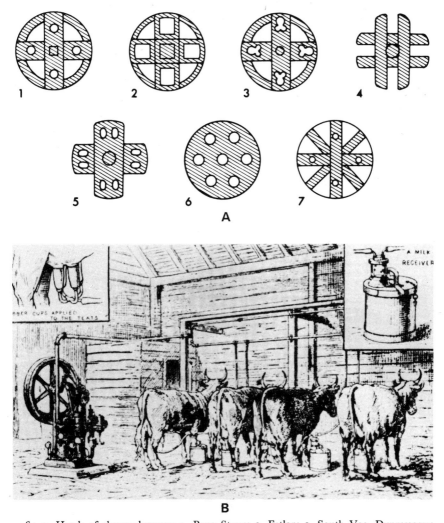

64. a. Heads of churn-plungers: 1. Papa Stour; 2. Fetlar; 3. South Voe, Dunrossness; 4. Burwick (1–4 all from Shetland); 5. Locheport, North Uist; 6. Auchterless, Aberdeenshire; 7. from D. Ure, *Agriculture of Dunbarton*, 1794.   C4150
b. The Thistle Mechanical Milking Machine in Renfrewshire. From the *Journal of the Royal Agricultural Society of England*, 1895.   C1130

C

D

64. c. Mrs. Helen Stout using a plunge-churn at Busta, Fair Isle, 1962.

d. Pressing a cheese with stones as weights at Appiehouse, Stenness, Orkney, in 1961.

at Faldon-side, on the analogy of similar presses in Renfrew, Ayr and Lanark, but otherwise this type was rare in Roxburgh. Ewes' milk cheeses could be up to 3 stones each in weight, and some of the store-farmers made up to 200–300 stones annually.[166]

Heavy stone cheese-presses, screw-operated, first appeared in the dairying South-West and spread from there to other parts of the country, becoming very general after 1800 and remaining in common use in the North-East (Fig. 63) till the 1930s. Cast iron presses, on the screw or steelyard principle, were also common over East-Central and South-West Scotland. One dated 1814 was used at Cortachy Home Farm Dairy in Angus, and a cast-iron one, with a pinion and rack, was on view in Drummond's Agricultural Museum in Stirling in 1835.[167]

It is no surprise that the only Scottish dairy breed of cow, the Ayrshire (Fig. 65), evolved in the later eighteenth century on the small dairy farms of the South-West. Their ability to produce milk from moderately good fodder made them ideal for answering the demand for milk and milk products from the rapidly growing industrial towns, and in turn there was a demand for Ayrshires by farmers around such urban centres. At the same time, Ayrshire or Dunlop cheese became the country's national cheese. It was a mild, sweet-milk cheese, not superseded until the introduction of the Cheddar system from Somerset in the 1850s. The by-product of cheese-making, whey, was used to feed horses, cows, and above all pigs, the Ayrshire bacon industry going hand in hand with dairying.

Another part of the South-West underwent a different kind of influence. Though a native of Ayrshire set up a dairy producing good Ayrshire cheese in the parish of Johnstone in Dumfriesshire, nevertheless Cheshire cheese was the important type there in the 1790s, because of an Annandale laird who encouraged Cheshire people to settle on his estate at Middlebie, Hoddam and Dornock, for this purpose.[168]

The importance of milk to the South-West was further emphasised by the establishment of a dairying school near Kilmarnock in 1889, which later became the Dairy School for Scotland.

The stone or iron cheese-presses went with the days when the bulk of the milk was still processed on the farms. Their decline came about the time of

65. Ayrshire cows at Colm's day fair, Largs, 17 June 1913. Per Mrs. S. D. Mensing.
C2890

the First World War, when large creameries working on pooled milk supplies were established, when foreign cheese had begun to be imported, and when grocers' vans, selling the commercial product, were reaching every part of the country. However, home cheese-making continued in many country districts between the Wars, and actually increased for a time after 1939 when cheese was rationed and the movement of vans was restricted. It was about this time that the spring-loaded metal Don cheese-press became fashionable, though other types of hand press, especially one with two planks and two screws, remained in common use. Home cheese-making on any scale is now virtually dead, though grocers' shops in country towns still sell a few local farm cheeses.

The Milking Machine

It has been claimed that the milking machine is a Scottish invention, though an American one was exhibited in 1862. This was in the form of a metal bucket with four teat-cups, and two handles by which a vacuum could be created. Experiments had in fact been going on since about 1840 in Germany, Denmark and Sweden.[169] But Scotland did play a considerable part later on. In 1891, Stewart Nicholson of Bombie in Kirkcudbright, who died in 1961 at the age of 96, showed his invention at the Show at Doncaster, and won a silver medal. The teat-cups he used were of cows' horns, with india-rubber cushions. These were connected by flexible pipes to an airtight milking pail from which air could be extracted by a hand or power operated pump. Suction was continuous, however, and the difficulty was that too much pressure could congest the teat with blood.

Nicholson's idea had been in his mind since 1888, but the first milking machine patented in Scotland was one made by a sanitary engineer or plumber, William Murchland of Kilmarnock, in 1889. This also involved continuous suction. One was set up on the farm of Haining Mains and another at Newton Farm, near Glasgow. They worked adequately, though there was some opposition from female milkers, of whom there was a scarcity in the district.

The milking machine became a practical proposition when the pulsator principle was evolved by Dr. Alexander Shields of Glasgow in about 1895, reproducing the sucking action of a calf. In 1900 an improved type based on this first Thistle Mechanical Milking Machine (Fig. 64b) was tried out, and this, the Kennedy and Lawrence Universal Cow Milker, proved to be the world's first really practical milking machine. In 1905, J. & R. Wallace of Castle Douglas won a prize for their machine, and continued to adapt and improve it afterwards.

It was, therefore, the South-West of Scotland that helped to make the running in this field, and in spite of early opposition by the workers, it led to a considerable lessening in the amount of hand-work that had to be done in byres – the kind of work, indeed, that made the migration of Ayrshire farmers to the Lothians and to the South of England, away from the intensity of dairying, a matter of note in the later nineteenth century.[170]

Milk Dishes and Derivatives

Though butter and cheese were at the same time major foods and articles of commerce, milk as such was far more perishable, and much less easy to transport, without special equipment and organisation. It therefore played a considerable part in the everyday diet of the locality. Indeed, since the right to keep or graze a cow applied to almost every class in the pre-enclosure farming communities, the milk products, fresh or preserved in some way, were the main defence against hunger. The cow was the form of social security of the period, as long at it was in milk, and later on, milk supplied by the farm was part of the wages or one of the perquisites of bothy men and married servants.

Milk was used directly as a drink or as an element with other dishes like porridge and brose, and barley broth. Milk puddings of the 'semolina' type appeared only in the later nineteenth century, when commercially processed materials became available in the shops.

In times of adversity, when the absolute maximum had to be squeezed out of available resources, milk was processed as a hunger food to give it bulk, by frothing it up. Either milk or whey was boiled in a pot over the fire, and was then wrought with a stick about 12 to 18 inches (30–45 cm.) long with a cross-head round which a horse-hair band was fixed. The stick, which was twirled rapidly between the palms of the hands, was a *fro' stick*, in Gaelic *loinid* or *ròn*. The froth, in Gaelic *omhan*, scotticised into *oon*, was worked up, according to Martin Martin in 1695, five or six times, the froth being apparently supped off the top with spoons each time.[171] Sometimes there was nothing else to eat at a meal. *Oon* was also made of goats' milk, sometimes with a lump of butter added.

It was not always a food of necessity, however. When Captain Thomas was surveying archaeological remains in the 1860s, he was given a drink of frothed milk at a Loch Roag shieling. The sour, thick milk under cream kept for butter was also frothed into a cooling drink called *sgathach*. On the east coast from Moray down to Angus the *fro' stick* was used to whisk a mixture of cream and whey which was then sprinkled with oatmeal and eaten. The Gaelic equivalent was *fuarag*. Such 'froh milk' or 'vrocht milk' was being made within living memory, and still in 1951 a *People's Journal* correspondent could recite the rhyme that gave the knack of working the *fro' stick*: 'Not too high, not too low, not too fast and not too slow'. At the present-day, such sticks may be bought in the open market in Sofia, Bulgaria.

When a cow had newly calved, the first milking was sometimes put into a dish, flavoured with salt or sugar, sprinkled with cinnamon on top, left to set to a custard-like consistency, and eaten for supper. This was *beesnin-* or *beestin-cheese*, or *calfie's cheese*.

In the Northern Isles, when the butter had been taken out of the churn, hot water was added to the buttermilk, producing a white, cheese-like substance called *hard milk* in Fair Isle. This was hung in a cloth, and the liquid left was drunk as *bland*. This must be a very old custom. *Bland* had the great virtue of being able to be kept for a long time, and it fermented to a sparkling stage, when it was used as a refreshing drink and was recommended as a cure for consumptives. A barrel of bland was referred to in the Shetland Sheriff Court records for 1604. It was the drink the Shetland fishermen took to sea with them when they were at the line fishing in their open *sixareens*, six-oared boats.

Various preparations of coagulated or soured milk were also drunk or eaten. Sweet-milk curdled deliberately by adding sour-milk or butter-milk was called *ost-milk* or *eusteen* in Shetland. Another Shetland dish was *clocks*, a preparation of new milk boiled for hours until it became thick, brown and clotted. Gallons of milk produced only a moderately-sized dish of *clocks*, which 'not even its exceeding goodness can justify for being a most absurd waste of good milk'.[172]

9

Everyday Food

As long as wages were wholly or partly in kind, there was an intimate relationship between food and wages, and this relationship in turn reflected the resources and farming organisation of the area. The earliest clear statement of farm-servant wages dates back to 1656, when the Justices of the Peace for Midlothian drew up an Assessment of Wages, which also showed the hierarchy of workers at the period, The pay scales were:

1. A *whole hind*, maintaining an able fellow servant so that between them they could see to the work of the plough, got a house with a kail-yard, 15 bolls of oats, 6 firlots of pease, enough ground to sow 6 firlots of oats and 1 firlot of bere, and grazing for two or three cows.

2. A *half-hind*, who got half of these wages, plus 2 firlots of oats.

3. A *shepherd*, who got a house and kail-yard, 8 bolls of oats, a boll of pease, an acre of land for sowing grain, and grazing rights as for the hinds. He also had to maintain a servant.

4. A *tasker*, who threshed the grain with the flail. He could be employed for a few weeks only, in which case he got as wages a twenty-fifth part of the grain he threshed. If employed full time on a large farm, threshing in winter and doing other farm-work, especially harvesting, at other times, then he got, in addition to his portion of the grain, a house and kail-yard, a boll of pease, grazing for one animal, and food for himself and his wife during harvest.

These grades, especially the first three, were those with the highest skills and responsibilities. It was incumbent on two of them to maintain a fellow-servant. Perhaps the term *whole-hind* reflects the arrangement whereby the old Scotch plough was worked by a minimum of two – that is to say, the job implied the ability to see to the work of the plough. All had wives, who were expected to work as well, and it was their work that paid for the rent for the cot-house. They worked hard for their home, for according to the document, they 'are to Shear dayly in Harvest, while (until) their Masters Corn be cut down. They are also to be assisting with their Husbands in winning their Masters Hay and Peats, setting of his Lime-kills, Gathering, Filling, Carting and Spreading their Masters Muck, and all other sort of Fuilzie (manure), fit for Gooding and Improving the Land. They are in like manner to work all manner of Work, at Barnes and Byres, to bear and carry the stacks from the Barnyards to the Barnes for Threshing, carry meat to the Goods (stock) from the Barnes to the Byres, Muck, Cleange and Dight the Byres and Stables, and to help to winnow and dight the Cornes.' They scarcely had much time left to prepare food for themselves and their families. They worked, therefore, as close family units, and were closely tied to their farms and conditioned in their way of life and dietary habits by the nature of their wages, in which oats played a prominent part, as well as the produce of their cows.

The remaining farm-servants in the Midlothian list were unmarried, and lived in or received their food in the house. They included plough-men, farm lads, female servants, and maids. Unlike the married workers, they were paid partly in money, but also got food and board. They therefore shared the food the family ate, though in 1656 this did not differ very much from the food eaten by married servants, which was based on the produce of the soil (oats, bere, pease, beans), and of the cows (milk, butter, cheese), with meat and fish occasionally.[173]

Some idea of the etiquette in farm-kitchens of the period may be got from a later account of a Selkirkshire farm. When the farmer died in 1745, the goods listed in his testamentary inventory included four beds, two fitgangs (long foot stools before the beds), three big and four small chests, one aumrie (small cupboard), two cupboards, a wool wheel, a lint wheel, a clack reel, a big table, an oval table, a long settle, six chairs, four stools, two meal arks, three tubs, a flesh boat, four butter kits, three cogs, six milk bowies, two stoups, two kail pots and a kettle, a brass pan, a salt fatt (vat), a brander, a girdle, a ladle, a sowens sieve, a babrick (probably the same as *baw breid*, baking board), a meal skep (straw container), two basins, a pewter stoup and jug, six pewter plates, three trenchers and a dish of earthenware, eleven wooden trenchers, six plates, six wooden caups (bowls), twelve horn spoons, eight pewter spoons, six dozen bottles, a crook and clips for hanging pots above the fire, a pair of tongs, and a flesh hook. At this date, the farmer had three ploughs and employed three male and three female servants.

This range covers sleeping, sitting, and the storage, preparation and eating of food. These were the important things. In a later description of the same farm-kitchen, it was said that the *goodman*, the head of the household, sat at the head of a long, stout table that was placed near the window. Possibly this is the one referred to in the inventory. Next to him were his wife and family, with the servants at the lower end. At dinner, two or three large wooden bowls of broth were served, and supped with short horn spoons or *cutties*. Next some wooden trenchers were put on the table and a piece of boiled meat put before the goodman, who carved it with a clasped knife and fork that he always carried. Knives and forks were at this time still exceptions rather than rules, and the meat that was distributed was eaten with the fingers. This lack of cutlery is a point to be considered in looking at the range of everyday food made in earlier days. After the meat had been eaten, the broth was replaced on the table and supped along with barley bannocks. On other days, cheese, butter, milk, salt herrings, or oatmeal dumplings might replace the meat. As yet, potatoes were no more than a garden dainty, and played no part in the daily diet.[174]

On this Selkirk farm, the farmer's family and the unmarried servants had their meals together, though they kept their separate places at the table. Even in the 1840s in Berwickshire, several remembered how the master shared out butcher meat for the rest to eat with their fingers.[175] But agricultural improvements gradually led to increased segregation of masters and men, and the economy of the farm-house began to be organised, as in Fife about 1800, to 'put an end to that indiscriminate intercourse in respect of sitting and eating, which was common in former times'.[176] Some of the parish ministers regretted the move away from the family board with the goodman presiding, for 'his presence and conversation produced the most beneficial effects on the manners and morals of the domestics'.[177] In Peeblesshire, old habits died hard, for though in general farmers and men ceased to eat together after about 1750, one small laird who died about 1830 always dined with his servants until after his second marriage. His new wife was more fashion-conscious, and he had to compromise by taking tea for breakfast with his wife in the parlour, and eating his porridge afterwards with the servants in the kitchen.[178]

The increase in social differentiation was also accompanied by differentiation in eating when the men who had formerly been in the house were moved into *bothies*, where they slept and ate by themselves. For this reason, in lieu of the food and board they would formerly have got in the house, they now had to have a proportion of their wages in kind, usually in the form of oatmeal and milk, with an allowance of fuel for the fire, though it was still not uncommon on farms in the 1790s that the farmers' wives prepared the servants' food with their own. Increasingly, however, they came to have an allowance of victuals instead. The situation in the Carse of Gowrie, the heart of the bothy area, in 1794, was characteristic: that the men got an English pint of sweet milk daily, or two pints of buttermilk, for breakfast, dinner and supper, with an allowance of thirty-six ounces of oatmeal per man, along with salt or 1/– in lieu.[179] The result of this was that the unmarried ploughmen and farm lads came to eat oatmeal in one form or another three times a day. *Brose* was a preferred dish because it was easily prepared by pouring boiling water on to oatmeal, with a little salt, in a wooden bowl, to be eaten with milk over it (Fig. 66). Though oatmeal had always been a prominent part of the Scottish diet, it had never been used as exclusively as in the special kind of situation that the bothy system created. So much emphasis came to be laid on oatmeal that in 1869 a Report on the Dietaries of Scottish Agricultural Labourers reckoned that it formed the main article of daily subsistence among 90% of the families of the working classes in Scotland. In the better bothies a little variety was possible – for example, in one Angus

A

B

66. a. The morning brose at Gormyre Farm, Torphichen, West Lothian. Per A. R. Jones.
C1123
b. A *caup* with newly made brose for breakfast on an Aberdeenshire farm in the 1960s.

bothy in 1813, the ploughmen had porridge or brose for breakfast, oatcake with butter or skimmed milk, cheese, and milk, for dinner, and sowens or potatoes for supper, but even so, oatmeal was the major element. The eating of too much oatmeal was alleged to produce a skin eruption popularly known as the 'Scotch fiddle', but this prevalent skin disease, scabies or the itch, was really due to a tiny burrowing mite.[180] The diet was not, in fact, an unhealthy one, and there is little doubt that country workers were better off than their counterparts in the towns.

Single farm-workers, therefore, were considerably influenced in their diet by agricultural improvements and new social standards. They were at first, because of their way of life, less affected than married servants and farm folk generally by the very fundamental and widespread change brought about by the introduction of the potato, which became a general element in the wages and food of married men.

BREAD

Some of the arable districts of Scotland have been outstanding for their fertility from early times, and it is little wonder that these areas quickly attracted monastic farmers. South-East Scotland, the Carse of Gowrie which has been called the granary of Scotland, the Laigh of Moray, as well as parts of Fife and Easter Ross, are amongst such districts, all of them characterised by the fact that they grew wheat. Elsewhere oats and bere were the standard crops. It was in these wheat-growing areas that the bigger farms were established in the days of agricultural improvement.

It might be expected that bread made of flour would have been eaten here, but wheat was more of a cash crop, for sale rather than for home consumption. Nevertheless white or wheaten bread was eaten by the higher classes, who had baking ovens in their houses, or who could afford to buy bread from the bake-houses in the towns and cities. It was rare for others in the country districts to taste white bread, though the manuscript Old Cambus Accounts (Berwickshire) for 1596 note that white bread was baked with eggs for the supper and dinner of servants who had travelled some distance, perhaps as seasonal labour.

One of the points of interest in this context is that the food provided by farmers for shearers in harvest was better than the everyday fare. Wheat bread with ale was specified in 1794 for the supper and dinner of shearers in Berwickshire (Fig. 25b, Ch. 3), and for the breakfast and dinner of those in Angus. Twelve loaves, made in the bake-house from 8 lbs. of flour, provided breakfast for twelve reapers there. These loaves were 10⅔ oz. each. In Roxburgh, in 1798, shearers got a 20 oz. loaf of coarse wheat with a bottle of small beer for dinner. In sixteenth-century Moray, a wheat loaf weighed 22 oz. Social improvement in Angus by 1813 is indicated by the fact that wheat bread was becoming more common, and the farmers were keeping a proportion of the second quality wheat (having sold the best) to be ground into wheat for the baking of scones.[181]

However, the further from the wheat growing areas, and the further from the towns, the more dependent all classes were on the local produce, so that in Caithness it could be said in 1812 that the upper classes ate as in South Scotland, except that oatmeal or barley-meal cakes were used in place of wheaten bread. Change was imminent, though, for there were two bakers, one in Thurso and one in Wick, who had started to import flour.[182]

Wheat bread was a prestige food, eaten at first by the higher classes, that sank in the social scale in the course of the nineteenth century, though eaten by the lower classes before that on special occasions, including harvest shearing (Fig. 25, Ch. 3). At first its social descent took place in the towns and cities – where already by 1805 in East Lothian mostly only wheat bread was eaten. Even in small towns, its rate of adoption was rapid, and was accompanied by a spread in the number of baker's shops. In Wigtown, for example, there was only one baker about 1755, but four or five forty years later.[183] It later spread in the country districts as well, reaching the houses of farm servants last of all, in the course of the later nineteenth and into the twentieth centuries. Even in Fife, where there were fourteen mills in 1800 producing 40,000 bolls of wheat flour a year, it was long before the lower classes could turn regularly to wheat bread, except on festival occasions like baptism and marriage.[184]

The eating of wheat bread can be used to pinpoint social gradations at different periods of time, and also, if sufficient comparative data can be got, differential rates of diffusion through the social strata and through the different regions of the country. However, it is never enough to look only at such prestige foods, but also at the kind of food these replaced on a permanent or occasional basis, since these are fundamental to any assessment of local conditions, especially when wages were paid partly or wholly in kind.

Apart from wheat with its relatively limited distribution, the main crops in Scotland were bere, oats, and to a lesser extent rye. Pease and beans have also to be reckoned as bread crops, but more in the Lowlands than in the Highlands and Islands. Both pease-meal and bean-meal bread were made. It was common to mix bere-meal with about a third to a quarter of pease- or bean-meal, and to bake it with salt and water, but no yeast, into round cakes about an inch (2·54 cm.) thick, on an iron girdle, which, according to John Major in 1521, was a thin, round iron plate, about an ell in diameter (45 inches, 1·1 m.), supported by three feet, each of which was bifurcated.[185] It was also possible to bake such bread in front of the fire by leaning it against a toasting stone (Fig. 67c), of which some nicely carved examples have survived. In Fife, about 1785, bread made of bean- and pease-flour mixed

B

A

C

67. a. Baking round oatcake *bannocks* at Turnabrane, Glenesk, Angus, 1967.

b. Oatcakes being baked over a peat fire at Gorthfield, New Pitsligo, Aberdeenshire. The rounds are cut into quarters on the girdle, and hardened off on an iron toaster. 1960.

c. A carved stone *bannock* toaster from Angus, dated 1791. National Museum, ME237.

with bere-meal was eaten partly by the higher and entirely by the lower classes. In Moray in 1811, bere-meal was mixed with bean-, pease-, rye- or wheat-flour on the coastal stretches, but inland such mixing did not take place and the normal bread was oatcakes, said to be of two thicknesses. This no doubt implies two baking methods, one on the girdle (Fig. 67a-b) and the other in front of the fire.[186]

The different kinds of flour were mixed by hand, or else cereal grains and legumes could be deliberately grown and ground together. This kind of mixture was called *mashlum*, and is known from the fifteenth century. Its distribution was mainly eastern and southern Scotland. The *mashlum* areas, therefore, are the main farming areas, from Cromarty to Galloway, but even within the limits of its context some social variation can be observed. Already by the seventeenth century the use of pease-bread or bean-bread alone was confined to the poorer people and similarly about 1800 in Angus, Fife and Moray, at Dingwall, and in parts of Perthshire, where, however, the thin flaccid bannocks of pease- or bean-meal were eaten by all classes, though becoming rarer.[187] The subtle pressure of prestige led to its earlier disuse in the fertile south-east than further north. In general, however, the evidence suggests that *mashlum* was deliberately sown by farmers, in relatively small quantities, as a crop from which bread could be made for the servants. Its occurrence, therefore, indicates a kind of farming organisation that involved hired labour, and it is not in any way a sign of a retarded area.

Oats, Bere, and Drink

For most of Scotland, bere and oats were the main crops. Bere or barley was the drink crop. When John Major described the British skill in brewing ale in 1521, he elaborated on the Scottish technique that produced ale of greater strength. Orkney had an especially high reputation, for according to Hector Boece in 1527, her malt made the best ale in Albion. A visitor to Orkney between 1614–18 said the ale was strong, whitish in colour, and tempered with herbs.[188] It was in part due to this skill of the Orcadians that bere went on being grown as a crop there into the twentieth century, and it was a main reason for retaining the little corn drying kilns long after they had vanished in most other places.

Shetland, in contrast to Orkney, was doubly unfortunate, for drink as well as bread was scarce. Such spare barley as there was went to make bread, and it was said in 1701 that many never tasted ale or beer, but only *bland*. Some Hamburg beer could be got from traders, however.[189]

In most of Scotland, in the days before tea and coffee, ale was the standard drink, along with milk, and if milk was scarce it was used to wash down porridge or sowens. In the Highlands, much of the barley went into whisky making, though in Cromarty, George Ross erected special buildings about

1780 for the brewing of ale and porter, much of which was exported to Inverness by sea. At Ferintosh, belonging to Forbes of Culloden, great quantities of aquavitae were made under the exemption from duty granted before the Union. When Andrew Wight was carrying out his surveys in 1781, he estimated that about a thousand small distilleries were in operation, leading to neglect of the farmers' land. In true business fashion, not only was much bere imported and malted as Ferintosh bere, but also quantities of whisky made elsewhere were carried to the market as Ferintosh.[190] In Hebridean islands like Coll, Tiree, Islay and Gigha in the 1790s, much of the barley went into distilling whisky for export, so that grain had to be imported for meal and seed in the spring.[191] Much of this distillation was illicit, but even when legal it was a profitable and a useful means of paying the rent, though duties applied in the course of the nineteenth century made small-scale legal distillation uneconomic, and many of the major distilleries came into being at this time.

Tales of illicit stills and smuggling are legion, and may be exemplified by the activities of the people of Abriachan on the north side of Loch Ness. They were said to be the best at making whisky in the North Highlands, with the possible exception of the people of Strathglass, though they were without exception the most cunning smugglers to escape the Inland Revenue Officers. In this steep land, they were adept at building bothies for making the malt underground, or in the face of steep rocks accessible only to themselves and to agile goats. A drying kiln was set up in the woods or on the moor, and a portable hand-mill let them grind their malt on a hill-top or in the heart of the wood. They had learned the art of distilling their whisky in broad daylight, using old stumps of burnt heather and juniper bushes to make a fire without smoke. It was a fine way of leading an open-air life.[192]

But in spite of all this, a survey of the earlier printed sources for the Highlands and Islands gives a strong impression that bere, though the main crop until the sixteenth century, was used not primarily for ale or whisky, but for food. Where the extent of arable was limited, bere was a preferred crop, for it gave a better yield in meal than oats did, and the seed-yield ratio was better. The standards usually quoted for Scotland are 1:3 for oats and 1:4 for bere, though the intensive lazy-bed form of cultivation undoubtedly gave higher yields than the average for Lowland Scotland.

The sources suggest that by the end of the seventeenth century, the oat crop was spreading and had caught up on bere, though the situation may simply reflect a more intensive use of bere for distilling. In this spread, the Highlands were coming more into line with the Lowlands, where bread and bannocks and bere-meal dishes had already fallen out of favour, apart from the widespread use of bere as the major constituent of barley broth, and in brewing ale. In the Highlands, as amongst the poorer classes in the Lowlands, bannocks of bere-meal and bere-meal porridge tended to be eaten more than oatcakes and oatmeal porridge, till well into the nineteenth century. Bere-meal scones and bannocks can still be got on the farms and crofts of Caithness and Orkney, but the old custom of making two qualities, noted in 1812, as a mark of social distinction, has died out – that is, for the family, fine bere-scones made at sixteen to the pound of meal, and for the servants, thicker scones of more coarsely ground meal.[193]

As often happens with food that falls through the social scale, there comes a point where it may come back as a prestige element in the diet, or as a health food. In 1799 in Perthshire, when bere-bannocks were the common bread of the Highlander, and oatcakes were eaten by those of middle rank, at the same time twice-shelled and refined barley cakes were to be seen on the tables of the affluent.[194] At an even earlier period, in the early seventeenth century, bere-meal porridge was considered good for the health of Border ladies, and for school children.[195] It appears not to have been commonly eaten by the end of the eighteenth century, going gradually out of use as living standards started to improve.

Freshly made bere-bannocks have a slightly astringent taste and are very palatable, though they harden quickly. When the Orkney branches of the Scottish Women's Rural Institutes took part in an exhibition at the Royal Highland Show near Edinburgh in June 1973, the baking of bere-bannocks, brown in colour and 10 inches (25 cm.) round by about half an inch (1·3 cm.) thick, was demonstrated. However, they differed from those of earlier days, which 'bore little resemblance to those of the present, well raised with butter-milk and bicarbonate of soda, and having mixed with the meal a proportion of flour. The old-time housekeeper knew not of baking powders, etc., so she was content to make the dough with cold water from the spring. These water-bannocks, as they were called in later days, were indeed sweet to the palate, but tested one's ivory to a considerable extent.'[196]

That bere-meal has laxative properties is still known and recognised, as by an old Caithness lady who said she took a bit of bere-bannock every morning, and it kept her right all day.

Though the use of oatmeal has been seen for the last two or three centuries as a mark of Scottish nationality, there is no doubt that it came much more into fashion from the eighteenth century, partly because bere lost face as a food, and partly due to an increase in the absolute acreage of oats, as improvements led to more land reclamation. It formed a major element in the everyday meals of nearly all classes. According to a description of a typical Aberdeenshire farmer's daily fare in 1782, meat was never seen except at baptisms and weddings, at Christmas and on Shrove Tuesday. The usual diet was oatmeal, milk and red-cabbage in winter, and kail in summer and spring. The daily routine was:

'*Breakfast*. Pottage made of boiling water, thickened with oatmeal, and eat with milk or ale. Or brose, made of shorn cabbage, or cole-worts, left over night. After either of which dishes they eat oat-cakes and milk; and where they have not milk, ale, or small beer.'

'*Dinner*. Sowens, eat with milk. Second course, oatcakes, eat with milk, or kale. Sowens are prepared in this manner. The meally sid, or hull of the ground oat, is steeped in blood-warm water, for about two days, when it is wrung out, and the liquor put through a search (sieve); if it is too thick, they add a little fresh cold water to it, and then put it on the fire to boil, constantly stirring it, till it thickens, and continuing the boiling till it becomes tough like a paste. In the stirring they mix a little salt, and dish it up for the table.'

'*Supper*. First course, during winter season, kale-brose, eat about seven at night, while, at the fire-side, the tale goes round, among the men and maid servants. Second course, kale, eat with oat-cakes, about nine. During the summer season, there is generally but one course, pottage, and milk, or oat-cakes, and kale, or milk. Kale is thus prepared, red-cabbage, or cole-worts, are cut down, and shorn small, then boiled with salt and water, thickened with a little oatmeal, and so served up to table. Brose, is oatmeal put into a bowl, or wooden dish, where the boiling liquor of the cabbage or coleworts are stirred with it, till the meal is all wet. This is the principal dish upon the festival of Fasten-even, which is emphatically called Beef-brose-day.

'In harvest they sometimes have a thick broth of barley and turnip, in place of sowens, and if near a sea-port, frequently some kind of fish, which they eat with butter and mustard. . . . The Clyak-feast, or, as it is called in the south and west, the Kirn . . . is celebrated a few days after the last of their corns are cut down, when it is an established rule that there must be meat, both roasted and boiled.'[197]

There was, therefore, a strong emphasis on oatmeal in many shapes and forms, and the meals described here were common to both the farmer's family and his staff. Conditions differed, however, in different parts of Scotland. Workers in contemporary Ross-shire, maintained in the family, were being given two meals a day, and if a third was allowed it was of thin *brochan*, a gruel of oatmeal, with bere-meal bread marking a regional survival. Sowens were eaten for dinner. Work began at 4 or 5 a.m., breakfast was at 11 a.m., dinner at about 3 p.m., and work stopped at 7 or 8 o'clock in the evening.[198]

In Orkney, the feeding was less spartan, but the work equally long. The morning piece when work began about 3 o'clock was a bite of bere-meal bread and a drink of butter-milk. Breakfast at 8 a.m. was of boiled sowens or porridge, with a bowl of milk. Dinner, at 3 or 4 p.m., was of fish and potatoes boiled in one pot, or pork and kale, or potatoes and herring after potatoes came into use. Work came to an end at 7 or 8 p.m. and supper then was mashed potatoes and milk, or kale and potatoes, or kale and 'knocked' corn.[199]

In Roxburgh about 1798, the diet of married servants, cottagers and shepherds, consisted of bread, oatmeal, potatoes, milk, cheese, eggs, herring,

salted meat. The bread was of barley- and pease-meal, kneaded into bannocks and toasted over a fire. Oatcakes were similarly made, but thinner.
Wheaten bread, ale and whisky were taken only at baptisms and weddings.
House-servants had breakfast of oatmeal porridge or sowens with milk;
dinner of broth and boiled meat warm twice a week, or of re-heated broth,
or milk, with cold meat, or of eggs, cheese, butter, and bread of mixed barley
and pease-meal; supper was as for breakfast, or in winter there might be
boiled potatoes mashed with a little butter and milk. [200] This range highlights
clearly the superior productivity of the south-eastern parts of Scotland. At
the same time, the diets of the four areas noted here, all recorded in the days
before or just at the beginning of the introduction of the potato, show considerable regional variety, rather different from the impression of uniformity
in the rural diet, whether inland or on the coast, whether highland or lowland, reported by R. Hutchison in his 1869 Report on the Dietaries of Scotch
Agricultural Labourers. It seems fairly certain that this move to greater
uniformity, based on oatmeal and milk, and potatoes, is a direct result of
increasing social differentiation between the farmer and his servants.

MEAT

The available sources all suggest that the eating of fresh meat, except on
festival occasions, was rare amongst the rural population in the 1790s.
Though it had become more widespread by the 1840s, it was still far from
being an everyday item in the diet, least of all amongst the poorer classes.
As always, however, there were distinct regional variations. In 1633 it was
said of the Shetlanders that 'in the Winter time they feed strongly upon
Fleshes, for the Country affords many Cows, Sheep, and Swine, and plenty
of Fowles'. [201] If this is so, then there was a deterioration in the standard of
the diet there during the next two centuries.

  In general, meat was rarely eaten fresh, but salted. The Shetlanders dried
theirs fresh or salted in little stone houses, *skeos*, built very open to let the
wind blow through. Elsewhere it was more often pickled in brine. In Lingay
in the Hebrides beef was salted in cows' hides, transported to Glasgow, and
there barrelled for export to the Indies. [202] This was a form of trade that
complemented the marketing of cattle on the hoof along the drove roads. As
a rule, however, animals were slaughtered about Martinmas and salted for
family use. Sometimes, as in Orkney, crofters in a township clubbed together
to buy a cow or ox at the Hallowmas market, which was pickled and shared
out for winter use. [203] In such cases, the amount of beef per head was strictly
limited, and used chiefly on special occasions. *Marts* were usually oxen or
cows fattened up for slaughter, often when they had come to the end of
their days as drawers of ploughs and carts and producers of milk and calves.
In the sheep-rearing districts, sheep served as marts, especially for the people

of poorer and middle class, who bought them, for example, at Hawick market about 1820. In the Highlands a goat used for this purpose was contemptuously called the 'poor man's mart'. In Ayrshire, sea-fowls from Ailsa Craig were salted as a mart for winter, like the gannets of Sula Sgeir.[204] Salt meat, therefore, of any kind, is to be reckoned amongst the contents of the barrels or tubs in almost every household in the days before new root and fodder crops enabled farmers to overwinter more animals, and to provide fresh meat at reasonably regular intervals, winter and summer.

One of the consequences of the spread of potatoes as a field crop was an increase in the number of pigs (Fig. 68), especially in the Northern Isles and Caithness, eastern Scotland, the Borders, and the South-West; and even in the Hebrides the prevalence of potatoes had encouraged the breeding of small swine by the 1790s,[205] in spite of the fact that the Highlanders were said to have detested the pig and its flesh. Though this antipathy remained in places, it did not prevent them from raising swine and driving them to the towns of the Lowlands to be sold and eaten. The people of Atholl, Strathardle, Glenisla and Glenshee sold them in thousands at the Kinrossie and Cupar markets to farmers, millers, and distillers, who had draff to feed them. Yet it was not only for their commercial value that they were appreciated. A writer of 1802 noted that Highlanders who formerly had a strong aversion to pork now relished it highly, and in Easter Ross – which is, however, more akin to the Lowlands – the people were very fond of swine. There were 'one or two at every cottage, and they are also very kind to them; they were generally tethered at the house door'.[206]

Most of the time, these small animals were half starved and left to fend for themselves, so that they were regarded as little more than game by agricultural writers. The Chinese and short-legged English breeds introduced by improvers got better treatment, being fed for the market on bran, potatoes, milk and meal to a weight of 8 to 15 stones, but the old native breed were fattened with corn about March to a weight of 80 lbs., before being slaughtered. The coastal districts of Sutherland had a bigger breed of light-coloured, long-eared hogs that fed in the pasture ground in summer and were fattened on corn, potatoes and pease in harvest and winter, for sale at 112 to 180 lbs. the carcass. Both kinds, one for home use, one for sale, were often kept in the house for their last week of life and fed solely on pease, which were thought to harden the flesh and fat.[207] This custom was also known in Denmark.

The pigs of the Northern Isles were small, arch-backed, brown-coloured, hairy creatures, tethered by one front leg or kept in styes built on the common grazings. Their numbers were sometimes restricted because they spoiled the grazing, but unlike in the Highlands, pork was a favourite dish, fresh or salted, and even the long bristles were used, for making ropes with which to collect birds' eggs on the cliffs, or to serve as tethers for horses and cattle, or for mooring boats. As elsewhere, mealy puddings were made out of the entrails.

A

B

68. a. Pigs on their way to the Thursday mart in Turriff.   C3677
    b. The pig has been killed and bled, scalded and scraped. At Greenlaw, Berwickshire.
Per J. Cowe.   C2055

In the Lowlands, most families came to keep one or two pigs in the course of the first half of the nineteenth century, or even earlier, though there were districts like Aberdeenshire where the country people retained a dislike of pork. Of particular interest was the way in which the married farm-servants came to keep pigs, often as part of their wages, and if this was not given, they might get two stones of pork in lieu, as in Gladsmuir, East Lothian, in 1845. To some extent the improvement in the living standards of farm-servants brought about by this increase of meat in their diet was a direct result of the introduction of the potato. It brought them, in terms of meat consumed, more into line with the farmers themselves, who had always been used to slaughtering an animal for winter use. But for long pork remained to the poorer classes what beef was to the better off in the country districts; and on a regional scale, it became to the Lowlands what mutton was to the Highlands.

Like the old breed of pigs, sheep were little attended to outside the South of Scotland, though they were universally kept for mutton and wool for the family. Enclosing in the Lowlands, and the spread of commercial sheep farming in the Highlands from the 1770s, brought the keeping of domestic flocks to an end. It is likely that before the agricultural improvements, the eating of mutton, even if only occasionally, was rather more common than was the case later, for numerous references in the First Statistical Account indicate that as enclosures spread, the keeping of sheep declined in the late eighteenth century. In most of the Lowland counties, at least in the arable areas, only small flocks were retained, either for the butcher if in the neighbourhood of a town, or for domestic use, but mainly by the gentlemen and bigger farmers. Mutton, therefore, kept on being a fairly regular element in the diet of the upper classes of Lowland Scotland, as it had been in the early seventeenth century when three Englishmen dined with Sir James Pringle in the Borders on 'big (bere) pottage, long kale, bowe or white kail, which is cabbage, . . . powdered (salt) beef, roast and boiled mutton, a venison pie in the form of an egg, goose, then cheese, a great company of little bits laid on a pewter platter, and cheese also uncut, then apples'. After the table cloth had been removed, beer was served.[208] There is not much to complain of here, even though nearly all the items were local produce. Only the scale and range offered at one time differed greatly from that of the normal meals of the farming population. Mutton played its part here in two forms, both apparently fresh, unlike the beef which was salted. It is amusing to think that one of the results of the enclosures was that the general use of mutton became more confined to the higher classes in the Lowlands whilst it remained a food of the common man in the Highlands and Islands.

FISH

Though fish was eaten around the coasts and in the islands, the difficulty of transport meant that for most of the farming population, salt-herring was the fish usually eaten, apart from any fresh-water fish they could catch, legally or otherwise. The comment made of the parish of Knockando in Moray in 1845, that fish was becoming more common among the country folk than formerly, seems to have been generally true, and may be partly due to the potato, which makes a good accompaniment to herring, whether salt or fresh; on the other hand, fluctuations in the movement of herring shoals meant that places like Kingarth in Bute, where herring had been the mainstay of the people for three-quarters of the year, had to do without them.[209] In 1869, dried or salt herring was still an element in the diet of farm workers in most counties, usually for dinner or supper, but in Midlothian and Lanarkshire also for breakfast. In New Deer parish, Aberdeenshire, where farm workers were said to fare poorly, a barrel of the cheaper herrings would be got, to be eaten with potatoes for dinner by the head of the household. Presumably the others had the well-known dish, 'tatties an' pint', that is, they ate their potatoes alone and pointed at the fish or at the hens outside.

The herrings could be cooked by being boiled in a large pot over the potatoes, and were then dished up all together into an 18 inch (37 cm.) square container, called a *clàr* in Gaelic, from which the family helped themselves. The flavour of such a meal is mouth-watering.

In some districts, fish had overwhelming importance, for example in Shetland, as long as the economy remained at or near the bare subsistence level. Here, as on the north and west coasts, the fish eaten in the houses were not so much the types caught from boats at sea, which were for commercial sale, as those caught close inshore, or by fishing from the rocks. This was known as *craig-fishing*, and was done at established points amongst the rocks. Although there were places like a cove in Lewis, mentioned in 1549, where men and women caught haddock and whiting with hook and line,[211] the kind usually caught from the rocks was coalfish. A rod with a fixed line was used, or else a circular *poke-net* on the end of a wooden shaft was lowered into the water, and raised after a bait of chewed or mashed limpets, or of potato mash, had been thrown over it to attract the fish. Similar nets, round or sometimes oval like the *tabh* used at Borve in Lewis, were also employed along the north and west coast. It was said of Canna in 1824 that the quantity of coalfish taken, often in such nets, was nearly incredible.[212] Towards the end of the harvest season when the coalfish were sweet and fat, providing food as well as oil for lighting, the people of Broad Bay in Lewis went to the shore at night to sweep the river mouths with blankets sewn end to end. Around 1845, twenty-four barrels of *cuddies* were got from two hauls of six blankets.[213]

For the ordinary folk of the coastal regions, coalfish played a most important part in the diet, indeed the main part in terms of fish consumed. In Shetland it was the mainstay of the people, filling the hungry gap before harvest in the days before the potato, when dried fish beaten small had to be used instead of bread.[214] Fish and milk were the bases of the summer diet, and though the potato brought an improvement, the catching of coalfish from the rocks or also with rods from small boats (formerly also with the *poke-net*), has remained a regular activity.

The fish were cleaned, washed, steeped overnight in salt water, put on wooden spits, and then hung up to dry in the wind or in the smoke of the

69. A fishwife and her customer at Corstorphine. Per G. W. Dey. C1801

fire. When hard, they were stored in a basket or sack till needed. For use they were soaked in warm water to get the skin off, boiled, and eaten with potatoes. A late evening meal of dried *sillock* (year-old coalfish), boiled black potatoes, and milk, is one of the pleasant memories of a visit to Fetlar in 1963. Coalfish were also eaten fresh, often being dipped in oatmeal and fried, or they could be fried or baked on the coals of the fire without being opened or cleaned.

In towns like Edinburgh, fishwives with their creels may still occasionally be seen, selling fish to customers, but they are a disappearing race (Fig. 69).

BIRDS AND POULTRY

In Scotland generally domestic poultry, especially hens and geese, were for long regularly included in rents paid in kind, either directly, or in the form of eggs and feathers. In places like St. Kilda where bird fowling was a main basis of the economy, wild fowl and their produce were also used in paying the rent.

In areas like the Northern Isles, geese were probably the main source of poultry-meat. They were also valuable for their feathers, and in 1792 there were exported from Stromness, Orkney, 4,424 lbs. of feathers, along with 240 smoked geese and 10 barrels of salted geese, which must have been rental payments.[215] In pre-enclosure days, geese were very common generally, and were herded on the grazings. The keeping of large flocks of geese by crofters in the Northern Isles still lies within living memory. They lived in little huts of stone or turf on the common grazings, and sometimes had small clogs of wood tied to their feet to keep them from flying off. In Orkney the importance of geese was so considerable that in the older houses goose-nests in the form of a row of recesses were built into the inside of the kitchen walls. Here the brood geese sat in comfort, enjoying the domestic scene.

Hens were sometimes also summered in turf hen-houses, as in Great Bernera in Lewis, in recent times, and in North Uist,[216] but for the most part they stayed about the houses, roosting on spars in the byres until hen-houses began to appear generally after about 1900. Apart from their use as food, hens were usually regarded as nuisances by the farmers, so that farm-workers in arable areas were often specifically forbidden to keep them. Nevertheless, accommodation for hens began to be included amongst the stone buildings in the steadings of improved farm-houses in the Lothians and Fife in the late eighteenth century, and about the same period something of an organised marketing and collecting arrangement for eggs began to appear in the south, marked by the appearance of hawkers, called *egglers* in Berwickshire. They travelled on foot, collecting from farmers, hinds and shepherds surplus eggs which they carried in creels on their backs. Later, in the mid-nineteenth century, Glasgow's demands for food encouraged a similar trade in the Western Isles. In Skye, where there had been no buying or selling of eggs before about 1840, women started to go around for them, giving 3/- a dozen, usually paid for in groceries, or in tea and tobacco, on the barter system (just as groceries got from travelling vans until the period between the Wars were often paid for in eggs in North-East Scotland). The eggs were sent in boxes by steam boat from Skye to the Glasgow market.[217]

The eggs of wild fowl were also very much eaten, wherever they could be got. In Shetland, eggs were said to keep fresh without preservation for many months. A seventeenth-century account of Dunrossness noted that in St. Ninian's Isle, gulls' eggs were boiled hard and eaten with vinegar. They were still being gathered in Shetland in the twentieth century, between the first and thirteenth of May. Fulmar eggs were also kept, and when scoured with fine salt, their flavour was like that of a hen's egg. In Orkney, guillemots' eggs were being gathered in places like Copinsay until the end of the nineteenth century, with a short-term revival shortly before 1914. The eggs were sold for 1/- a dozen in Kirkwall, but now the motives for the sale vere commercial, since the taking of eggs as an essential part of a subsistence :conomy was at an end.[218] The flesh of the guillemot was also eaten, and iccording to an old man from Deerness, 'there's nothing as good as a pot of <ale (i.e. broth) with an auk (guillemot) in it'.[219]

In the Western Isles, the inhabitants of Ness in the north of Lewis have long been going to Sula Sgeir for gannet feathers and carcasses for salting, but the place of all others for wild birds was St. Kilda, where, according to a writer of 1824, 'the air is full of feathered animals, the sea is covered with them, the houses are ornamented by them, the ground is speckled with them like a flowery meadow in May!'[220] Here, the birds and their eggs were harvested in a regular yearly cycle:

April	Killing of gannets and to a small extent of shearwaters on Boreray
May	1. collecting puffins' eggs on the Dun
	2. catching fulmars on Soay
July	Snaring puffins on Soay
August	Catching fulmars and gannets on Boreray
September	Catching young gannets on Boreray, at night, by knocking them on the head with a stick.

The birds were caught in various ways. Sir George Mackenzie of Tarbert noted in 1675 that a man lying on his back, with a long pole in his hand, knocked down the fowls that flew over him. Twenty years later Martin Martin described horse-hair nooses. For making nooses, and the ropes with which the men descended the cliffs, horse-hair was a valuable commodity, and a pound of it was sufficient for a woman to bait a marriage with. There were eighteen horses in St. Kilda at this time. Later records suggest that women often did the work of puffin catching with horse-hair snares with up to forty nooses on a three-foot length of rope. Nooses on the ends of long poles were also used for catching puffins, as well as razorbills, and gannets and other birds that were sitting on eggs and therefore less likely to be frightened.[221]

These activities, however, are a response to an extreme environment, which laid down its own conditions for the survival of the inhabitants. Elsewhere, wild birds and their eggs have been, at least within the last two centuries, more in the nature of supplementary foods, additions to the everyday diet, rather than an indispensable element in it.

KAIL

Kail was being grown from at least the fifteenth century. The name indicates a plant of the Brassica variety, but earlier references do not make it clear whether borecole, colewort or cabbage is meant. By the sixteenth century several varieties were being grown, distinguished by various prefixes – *cabbage kail, bowcaill, white kail, red kail, green kail, lang kail, hard kail* – and eventually 'kail' became restricted in sense to borecole, especially the curly variety, *Brassica oleracea acephala*.[222] The dialectal usage in the Northern Isles and Caithness is still, following the old custom, to call cabbage by this name.

Kail was an important article of diet, rich in vitamin C, a valuable anti-scorbutic in the days before the potato. It was the kind of greens used in making barley-broth, or it could be boiled and mashed by itself with the addition of butter, milk, salt, and pepper if available, or as a kind of porridge with oatmeal, and sometimes a piece of salt meat on top. Throughout the country, houses had their dyke-enclosed kail-yards for growing this valuable food, and from the time of the first written references in the fifteenth century until the coming of the potato in the eighteenth, the records are full of cases of the theft of kail and the breaking of kail-yard dykes. The close relationship of kail with the everyday diet is made abundantly clear by the frequent references to it in proverbs and sayings, and by the fact that it came to be used not only of the plant, but also of broth of various kinds made from it, and even of the main meal itself.

Most people grew their own plants from their own seed, though near towns there was often a lively trade. The old palace-garden in Kirkwall, Orkney, was rented in the 1790s in patches of 15 by 18 feet (4·5 × 5·3 m.), known as *hundreds* because this was enough for a hundred plants in ten rows of twelve in each (that is, the 'long' hundred). Outside the town, kail-yards might contain anything from four hundred to two thousand plants, always in an enclosed yard and never in the fields,[223] for such greens were too liable to be eaten by animals, quite apart from the birds, especially pigeons, which could soon strip a plant whether it was in an enclosure or not.

Amongst the features of the Northern Isles, and parts of Caithness and Lewis, on the common land outside the head-dyke that delimits the arable, are the small round or four-sided enclosures of turf and stone, with no means of access except by climbing in. In islands like Papa Stour where kail is still grown on this system, seed was sown in these enclosures or *plantiecruies* in September or August, and the growing plants were transferred to the yards by the houses from mid-April to mid-May.

In Caithness, moorland nurseries called *plant tofts* or *plant cots* were made in June, consisting of an eighth to a tenth of an acre surrounded by a 6 foot (1·8 m.) high dyke of sods. The surface was cut in July by a *flauchter* spade and the turf burned as a fertiliser which was then dug in with the spade. The earth was broken with a rake or small harrow, dung and peat ashes spread, and the seed sown and raked in. New plant tofts were made each year, the dyke of one side of an old one serving as one side of a new one. The old toft was dug over and sown with oats, so that this activity had the long-term effect of reclaiming moorland, like the lazy-bed cropping of potatoes. The cottagers and small farmers who were working such tofts in the early 1800s sold the young plants to farmers at 3d to 8d per hundred.[224] It was still the custom in the twentieth century for the inhabitants of Stroma in the Pentland Firth to buy their plants in bundles of fifty from people who maintained plant tofts in the Skarfskerry district on the mainland of Caithness.

SOFT FRUITS AND GARDENS

The gardens of ordinary folk contained kail in quantity, and probably a few berry bushes. Gooseberries or *grosers* were being grown in the form of hedges around Dundee in the early sixteenth century, and red currants or *rizzars* were available, as well as black currants and wild berries such as brambles and blaeberries.

Sugar was being imported into Britain from Alexandria, Cyprus and Madeira from the fifteenth century, and people like Andrew Halyburton, the agent for the Scots merchants at Middelburg, were sending kists of sugar with almost every cargo dispatched from the Netherlands to Scotland in the 1490s. In January 1496, 192 lbs. of sugar cost him £3.4.4. Sugar, however, was confined to the houses of the wealthy, or to the shops of the apothecaries as an element in medicine. Following the establishment of the East India Company, it became cheaper and more plentiful in the seventeenth century, and in the next century, supplies of sugar processed from beet were added to that from cane.[225] The result was a revolution in the diet, leading on the one hand to the sweets and puddings that formed the final course of a meal, and on the other to the making of jams and jellies as part of the annual cycle of domestic work in town and country alike. This was accompanied by a spread of soft fruit into the gardens of ordinary folk from the late eighteenth century onwards. This included the raspberries and strawberries that had formerly been largely confined to the gardens of gentlemen. Sir John Foulis of Ravelston was already selling excess garden produce, including raspberries, strawberries and red currants, to the Edinburgh markets by 1703.[226] He and other estate owners were instrumental in establishing the market gardening tradition in the Edinburgh area and around the other cities. But cottage gardening only came to the countryside a century later, though even then the gardens were stocked with kail, potatoes, onions, carrots and leeks for the broth pot, a few berry-bushes for jam and jelly, and rhubarb, rather than anything more exotic such as lettuce and other materials for raw salads, in which country people have been little interested until recent times. It can scarcely be doubted that the spread of cottage gardens and the positive encouragement of better gardening by the Highland and Agricultural Society and The Caledonian Horticultural Society, established in 1809, had a good effect on the range of the everyday diet.

The commercial growing of strawberries had begun at Roslin by 1812, but the real expansion in their cropping came after the 1870s when the strawberry industry developed in Clydesdale. The raspberry industry was concentrated more on the Blairgowrie district of Perthshire, especially after the adoption of new, disease-free strains in the 1920s, and in parts of Angus and Fife, providing fruit for the jam-factories of Dundee.

The fruit farms provided a specialised crop which like the grain harvest in earlier times, and the potato harvest, required a concentration of labour for the five or six weeks when the berries were ripe. Seasonal labour was supplied from the small towns at first, and then increasingly by groups of tinkers. Therefore this crop too provided a work link between town and country, and, via the industrial process of jam-making, added another commercially produced element to the tea-table.

Farm and Steading

By the standards of southern England, the farm houses and steadings of Scotland are relatively young. The face-lift given to the country by the agricultural improvements was so all-embracing that it swept away most of the older habitations, some of which were in any case built of impermanent materials like turf, wood, clay and wattle, and replaced them by neat, stone farm-buildings on new sites central to the ground that went with them. Most farm-buildings in Scotland do not ante-date the third quarter of the eighteenth century. It is chiefly on big mains farms on estates where improvements started early, and in areas like Orkney, that farm-houses and steadings of early eighteenth or late seventeenth century date may be found. But the majority of the farm-buildings in the countryside were erected in the course of the nineteenth century, and even the black-houses of the Outer Hebrides, however primitive and archaic they appear, were in some cases still being built no more than a hundred years ago.

There is not a great deal of information available about pre-improvement farms. Whereas the later arrangement was geometrical, earlier on the buildings were built in a line, or lay with their various elements scattered higgledy-piggledy, perhaps mixed up with those of other tenants in a joint-farming community. Living conditions certainly varied according to status, and not every house was like the one near Langholm visited by the Englishmen Lowther, Fallow and Mauson in 1629, with a wall of alternating turf and stone, a door of plaited wicker rods, and a fire in the middle of the floor,[227] or the farm servants' houses seen by John Ray the naturalist in 1601, which were 'pitiful Cots, built of Stone, and covered with Turves, having in them but one Room, many of them no Chimneys, the Windows very small Holes, and not glazed'.[228] Such huts almost certainly formed part of the farming hamlets or cot-towns, so much a part of the pre-improvement landscape, which housed all sorts of people, day-labourers, carters, hedgers, ditchers and thatchers, tradesmen like weavers, shoemakers and tailors, who not only did their particular jobs, but also provided a labour reserve for peak periods, especially at harvest-time. It was this kind of continued need that must have led, as mentioned earlier, to the late survival of labour forces of 76 and 87 on the farms of Coates and Hairlaw in Gladsmuir parish, East Lothian. By this date, however, most of the cot-towns had disappeared without trace, apart from the place-name 'Cottown' that was often left behind, and the surplus population had moved into the new or expanding villages or into the towns and cities.

The higgledy-piggledy farm arrangement disappeared with these hamlets. The linear form survived, however, especially in the north and west, for though many of the existing buildings are not very old, they carry on the older tradition, even if it is modified in one way or another.

IMPROVED FARMS

The first writer to discuss the layout of farm-buildings in detail was Lord Belhaven in 1699, though in terms of proposals rather than as a reflection of an existing situation. He suggested that the 'sit-house' or dwelling-house should lie east and west, with the windows facing south for warmth. The barns should lie at the west end of the house, with a north-south orientation. This meant that the barn-doors would be east and west opposite each other, to get full advantage of the prevailing winds for the winnowing of corn. In terms of East Lothian farming, three barns were recommended, one for wheat and barley, one for oats, and one for pease. The barnyard should be conveniently placed west of the barn, for preference on a piece of rising ground to help the corn in the stacks to dry.

The stable and byres should be placed at the opposite side of the close from the house, with their doors on the north side, facing the house, for convenient access. The remaining east side should be partly filled by the chaff-house, with the entrance to the close lying between it and the house. This meant that since high winds from the east were rare, the dunghill in the middle of the close was less likely to be spoiled, and furthermore, the entrance to the house was at the cleanest available position.

In describing the house, Belhaven recommended that the walls should be of stone and lime, not of stone and clay which, by implication, must have been the common mortar of the period. In spite of his injunction, clay mortar was still being used well into the nineteenth century in many parts of the country, especially for smaller farms and cottages. In 1699, sods and plenty of straw thatch were still the recommended roofing materials. Slates and pantiles did not become common till nearly a century later.

An essential part of Belhaven's ideal lay-out were the yards or gardens, which should be planted around with ash and elm trees, the wood of which could later be used for the upkeep of the house. They should lie on the north side of the house, and should contain cabbage and kail, which was such a common element in barley-broth that the broth itself was known as 'kail', along with potatoes and turnips, neither of which became field crops till half a century later, and a few 'Turkie Beans' or ordinary beans and pease to go with pork. Then came Belhaven's aristocratic comment: 'Leeks, Sybous and other curious Herbs not being for your handling.' They were more at home in the gardens of gentlemen.

This early description of a farm built around the sides of a square, with the dunghill in the centre, foreshadowed the kind of layout that became common later. It is a forward-looking scheme, that must typify the thinking of the more progressive lairds of the period, though there was as yet no suggestion that the dwelling-house should be sited anywhere but at one side of the close, with the midden before its door. The separation of dwelling-house and steading, sometimes with a clump of trees forming a screen between, was a sophistication that had to wait a few generations before it was adopted by the big farms, and then spread down the social scale until by the late nineteenth century it had crept right down the farming ladder to units of under 100 acres.

The expression on the ground of Belhaven's ideal can be seen from a 1793 description of an old-style farmer's mains in Midlothian. This was a set of low buildings in the form of a square. On one side was the house, with two or three rooms floored with earth, low ceilings, and a few small windows. On another side was the barn, which was cruck-framed, that is, the roofing timbers did not rest on the wall-head, but were carried right down to floor-level. They supported the roof independently of the walls. The walls were only about 5 feet (1·5 m.) high. Opposite the barn were the byre and stables. The stables had no internal divisions and the horses were kept and fed loose inside. The cattle, however, were each confined to an upright stake, but had no other partitions between them.[229] Examples of such byre fittings, and the bindings or *awban's* of wood or iron that tied the cows by their necks to the stakes, have survived in West Lothian and Peeblesshire almost till the present day, though outside South-East Scotland, partitions of solid boards or in Orkney, Caithness and part of West Lothian of stone, have long been the norm. Stone flags between the animals go back at least to Viking times, and the Northern Isles arrangement of stone or wooden dooks in the walls, with no partition, is even older.

The Midlothian farm differed from Belhaven's in that it had on the fourth side, near the midden, the servants' cottages. They were often built in alternating courses of turf and stone, each turf course acting as a bed for the field gathered stones above. This technique was widespread from the Borders up to Sutherland. Such walls could only support the heavy roofs of timber, sods and thatch if they were kept low, and they often had to be buttressed on the outside with piles of stones. In addition, upright poles were set into them, three or four feet apart, to take the roofing couples. Chimneys were not always present in such cottages, but if they were, they took the form of a 'hangin' lum', a wide wooden funnel pinned against a gable wall. Such huts averaged 12 feet (3·6 m.) square and were lit by the chimney opening and one narrow window.

Building improvements started first in the main grain-growing areas, and in districts where stock-rearing was encouraged by the proximity of markets. Around Edinburgh, a number of farms date from the first half of the eighteenth century, like House o' Muir farm on the Biggar road, with the date 1741 above the door, and deep skews showing that the house was thatched originally. The steading appears to be younger, however. The Hopetoun estate was pressing on with improvements at this period, and the Duke of Buccleuch was erecting excellent farm-houses with commodious offices. Many of the tenants of large farms in the Lothians were able to build their own houses – people like William Hunter of Gilmerton, and Alexander Carfrae, a tenant on the Marquis of Lothian's estate who, though a bachelor, set up a large residence for himself.[230]

Accommodation for the farmer and his family tended to be improved first, then for the farm-stock, and last of all for the farm-workers (Fig. 70a). Even in this sector, however, some improvement had begun by the 1790s. In Midlothian, huts of the type described by George Robertson had been partly replaced by larger ones, 16 to 18 feet (4·8–5·4m.) square, built of good mason-work, with walls 7 to 8 feet (2·1–2·4 m.) high. They were neatly thatched with straw, and some were ceiled, and had timber floors. Instead of lying adjacent to the midden, they now began to be built a hundred yards or more away from the farm-house, often several together in a row. The present pattern of farm layout, therefore, in which the accommodation for workers is, like that for the farmer, at a little distance from the steading, originated in the late eighteenth century in the southern parts of Scotland, and demonstrates – like changes in diet – an increasing degree of social differentiation between the farmer and his servants.

As former commons were reclaimed and old outfield land broken in for 'centrical farms', and the run-rig farm-towns and cot-towns were phased out, building activity was intense, not only on farms, but also in the villages. Simprin in Berwickshire grew from a population of 100 in 1770 to 351 in 1793, and as an indication of improving social conditions, every house had a clock, many people had watches, and loaf-bread, as opposed to oat-bread, was being brought from Edinburgh, Berwick, Duns, Coldstream and Norham.[231] New villages like Castletown in Roxburgh appeared. Built by the Duke of Buccleuch on the farm of Park, it had two streets crossing at right angles, a central square, and two smaller squares. It was started in 1793 and by 1795 had 23 houses, each with 2 acres of ground.[232] All of this activity gave a boost to a variety of trades. In addition, the contemporary division of commonties meant that the ready cutting of turf and sods for walling and for roof covering was no longer easily possible, so that slates and pantiles rapidly replaced turf and divot and straw thatch as roofing materials in the third quarter of the eighteenth century. The old trade of thatcher faded slowly from the scene, quarries for building-stone and for dyking flourished, and the slater, stonemason and dyker came into their own as rural craftsmen. As always, a range of causes produced a range of effects, though even in the prosperous parts where these changes first occurred, there were districts like Heriot and Colinton in Midlothian, where building-improvements had not

A

B

70. a. An improved farm, with the house and garden a little aside from the steading. Dwelling house and outbuildings are slated, but the cottar house, for two families, is still thatched, and is built away from the farm. From G. Robertson, *Agriculture of Kincardine*, 1813, facing 184. C673

b. A Midlothian farm-servant's house (two family) in 1795. From G. Robertson, *Agriculture of Midlothian*, 1795, facing 166. C3924

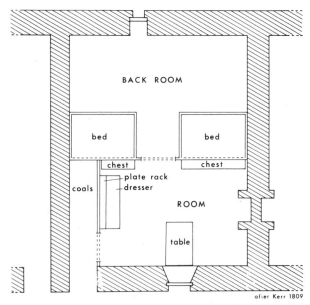

70. c. The interior of a Berwickshire farm-servant's house. The internal divisions are made the box beds. From R. Kerr, *Agriculture of Berwick*, 1809, 108.   C4074

advanced very far even by the 1840s. Nevertheless, by this date, farms had settled down into their present shape, with a good functional relationship between the hay-loft and stable, the turnip shed, the cow and feeders' byres, the barn with its threshing mill and grain loft, and the cart-shed.

FARM WORKER ACCOMMODATION

The improvements in the squarish farm-servants' houses in Midlothian in the 1790s matched similar changes in East Lothian (Fig. 70), where there were some two-roomed houses by 1752, though each room was occupied by a separate family, but in general the main period of betterment or rather renewal came in the 1840s or later. In Ratho, Midlothian, at that date, the farm houses and offices were good, but not the servants' houses, 'which generally, with a stinted economy, neither favourable to comfort nor delicate feeling, have only a single apartment for the accommodation of a family'. In nearby Currie, by contrast, the old 'wretched pig-sty like huts . . . are replaced by neat houses, with slated roofs, and divided into two apartments'. At Pencaitland in East Lothian, Lady Ruthven was erecting three-roomed houses, with a kitchen-cum-sleeping room, a bedroom, and a room for dairy produce and household necessities.[233]

Already by the 1830s, the Highland and Agricultural Society of Scotland

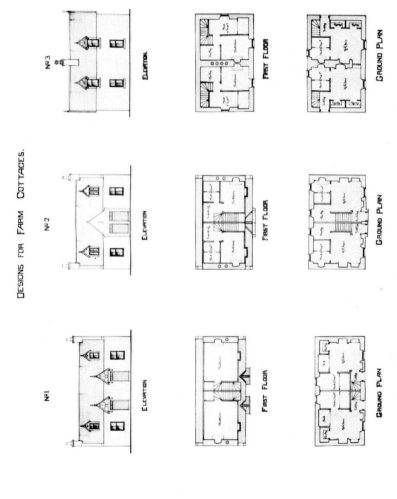

71. Designs for farm cottages on the Hatton Estate, Aberdeenshire, of late nineteenth-century date. The prices, marked in pencil, are £150–171.
C4101

was offering premiums for improved farm-servant houses, and the better keeping of their gardens. The Society had a strong influence on mid-nineteenth-century housing, like those erected at Yorkstone for Mr. Dundas of Arniston. These were for four families. They were arranged two by two in line with a space between for the coal houses, privies, and ashpit, accessible only by going outside. At Cauldcoats nearby, a double house was built, each unit with a rear annex containing a sink, a privy, and a space for coal, accessible from within.[234] With some modifications in sanitation, lighting, the provision of water, and more recently of television sets and aerials, such cottages are still to be found (Fig. 71). By 1861, George Hope of Fenton Barns, at a meeting on labourers' dwellings, 'spoke of the striking improvement which had taken place in labourers' cottages within his recollection. Instead of being four bare walls covered with thatch, having a small hole twelve or fifteen inches square, with a fixed piece of glass for a window, and a door covered with keyholes, made to suit the size of the lock of each successive occupant, on many estates they had been rebuilt in a commodious and comfortable manner'.[235]

For single men, things were not so good. As the high farming of the South-East developed and its characteristics spread into Fife and Angus from the end of the eighteenth century onwards, accommodation for single men and casual migrant labour was provided in *bothies*, which were rooms in the steading or sometimes in a separate building where the men both slept and ate, usually making their own food. Angus and the Mearns appear to have taken the lead in the development of the bothy system, which became common there and in parts of Fife, the Lothians, Berwickshire, the eastern parts of Ross and Cromarty, and in Caithness, where bothies for women outworkers were also to be found. The preference for married labour, allied to the ready availability of casual seasonal labour, restricted a development of the bothy system equivalent to that of Angus, in South-East Scotland, although married servants with large families lived there in single rooms in pantiled sheds that were the equivalent of bothies in their style and standard of comfort. William Cobbett noted a bothy for four single men near Edinburgh in 1832, and another near Dunfermline, with three wooden beds for six men in a space measuring 16 by 18 feet (4·8–5·4 m.). Coal for the fire lay loose in one corner, and there was a pile of potatoes beneath one of the beds. There was a large iron saucepan, and wooden bowls for the men's food.[236]

The bothy system survived in Angus until the tractor era, and many people still alive have practical experience of it.

Another kind of accommodation for single men, common on the small and medium-sized farms of North-East and West-Central Scotland, was known as the *kitchie* system. The men slept in a room in the steading close to their horses in the stable. The room was called the *chaumer* in the North-East, and in Morayshire a *berrick* (barrack). Chaumers were still being included in farms built in the early 1900s. The men had their food in the farm kitchen or 'kitchie', which gives the name to the system. In areas where the kitchie system prevailed, it was also common, or became common, for the single man to be complemented by married men living in cottar houses tied to the farm.

THE LONG-HOUSE

In the crofting counties, though there were many areas where the new norms in agricultural housing were adopted, especially on the eastern coastal strip, nevertheless there was a high survival rate for older building types. This was partly due to the fact that whereas in the Lowlands the farm buildings that went with improved farming and enclosures were designed and built as a rule through the estate, in the Highlands there was not this form of control. Tenants put up their own houses, even though lairds sometimes tried, not always with entire success, to lay down some basic rules. The Rules and Regulations of the Lewis Estate in 1879 required that:

> 'The dwelling-houses to be erected by the tenants . . . shall be of stone and lime, or of stone and clay pinned and harled with lime, or with stone on the outer face, and turf and sod on the inside, and roofed with slates, tiles, or straw, or heather with divots . . . each house to have at least two apartments, with a glazed window in the wall of each, and a closet or small room, with chimneys in the gables, or other opening for smoke in the roof; the thatch or covering not to be stripped off or removed for manure; the byre to be built at the end or the back of the dwelling-house, as the site may admit, and to have a separate entrance. In the byre a gutter to be formed for manure, which shall be regularly removed to a dung heap outside.'[237]

The provisions of the Crofters Holdings (Scotland) Act of 1886 did not improve the situation, for it meant that crofters, though renting their land from the laird, nevertheless could and did build their own houses, and were encouraged in this on the one hand by the right to compensation at waygo for improvements provided by the crofter, and on the other by the right to bequeath a tenancy, which meant that a home, once built, could remain in the family. The crofter was, in fact, statutorily required to provide a house, though he could not sell it since he did not own the solum. In this case, the law appears to have aided and abetted the strength of tradition in some areas, for in Lewis new black-houses were being built with house and byre under one roof and intercommunicating at least until 1898 (Fig. 73a), and as recently as 1947 about 40% of the Lewis homesteads maintained this arrangement; though change since then has been rapid.

The term 'long-house', applied to a building with house and byre under one roof, is convenient, though to some extent a misnomer, since such a

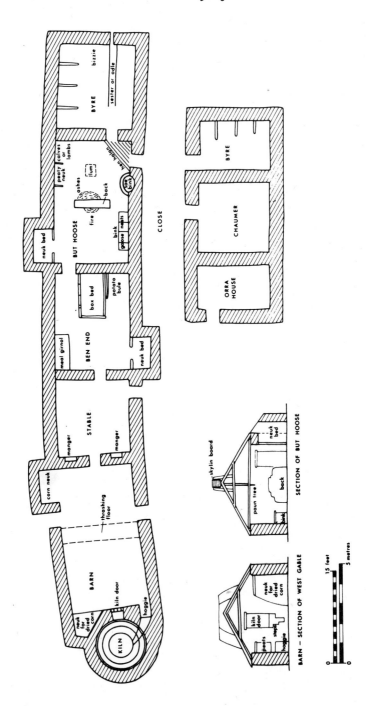

72. A long-house in Orkney, of early nineteenth-century date. All elements are intercommunicating. After J. Omond, *Orkney Eighty Years Ago*, 1911.

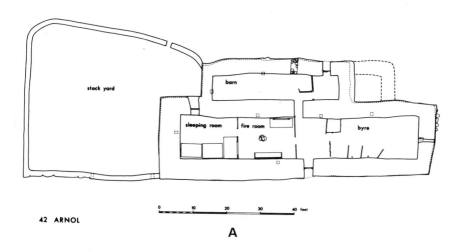

42 ARNOL

A

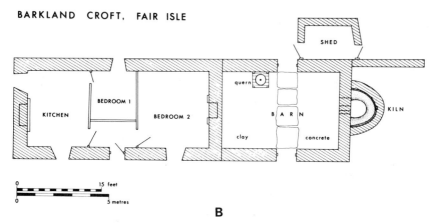

BARKLAND CROFT, FAIR ISLE

B

73. a. The black-house at 42 Arnol, Westside, Lewis. Adapted from a survey prepared by the Ancient Monuments Board of the Dept. of the Environment. C2304

b. Barkland Croft, Fair Isle, Shetland. Barn and house are in a straight line, with a corn kiln on one end. Surveyed by A. Fenton. C4076 house need not be long at all. The Hebridean black-house with its double walls and central fireplace is an example of the short type of long-house, rarely longer than required to hold house and byre end to end. Other buildings, often the barn, were added in parallel at the back. In Orkney and Caithness, on the other hand, the ultimate in linear development can be seen, with all the elements of the steading in one long intercommunicating row (Fig. 72). The sequence was byre, living room with fireplace, best-room-cum-bedroom, stable, barn with opposing doors for winnowing, and a circular corn-drying kiln at the very end. These should be regarded as evolved long-houses that go with conditions of improved farming, for they generally stand by themselves on their own land, and not as part of a township group. The 'normal' long-house, on the other hand, usually forms or formed part of a village cluster, as at Auchindrain in Argyll, or in early nineteenth century Angus. This was the joint-tenancy farming village, of the kind that agricultural improvement in Lowland Scotland swept away.

During the nineteenth century, partitions came to be set up between people and animals in the long-house, but the linear tradition remained so strong that it was carried over into modern types of croft buildings. These often have the dwelling house in the middle, with the barn and byre on either side, or barn and byre may be together at one side of the house, though no longer with direct communication from the house (Fig. 73b). At the same time, it cannot be assumed that existing buildings of a traditional long-house or long-house derived character in the crofting counties reflect the earlier appearance of farm buildings in pre-enclosure days in the Lowlands. The Orkney and Caithness forms are highly evolved. Black-houses like the one at 42 Arnol, Lewis, now preserved by the Department of the Environment (Fig. 73a), are just on a hundred years old and have been considerably modified – however archaic they may seem – in relation to older black-houses.[238] Any attempt to interpret back for other areas, on the basis of existing long-house evidence, can only be undertaken with great care.

Fuel for the Fire

AT the present day it is the price of fuel that comes under discussion, but in earlier times the question was rather one of availability. For much of Scotland there was no problem, for peat was plentiful in many areas, and is still in common use in many parts of the north and west. Something like 10% of the land surface remains covered with peat bog. But where the peat banks had been worked out, or where peat was not available, recourse had to be had to all sorts of alternatives.

FUELS OF NECESSITY

IN islands like North Ronaldsay and Sanday in Orkney, Heiskir, Muck, Tiree and Canna in the Hebrides, the people had to use dried horse and cow dung in their fires, supplemented by seaweed. Fires were lit, therefore, when required for cooking, for they could not have been kept alight all the time. Furthermore, the use of the dung in this way absorbed the manure that should have gone to fertilising the crops in the fields. In mainland Scotland the factor of poverty came more into play. The poor people in Galloway collected cakes of cow-dung, *bachruns*, from the autumn fields for winter use, and in Fife or Angus coal-dross or sawdust was mixed with cow-dung and dried in large cakes, called *dalls* or *daws*, in the sun.[239]

Equally if not more wasteful of resources was the custom of cutting turf with a *flauchter* spade (Fig. 8, Ch. 1) as a substitute for peat. The parish reports of the 1790s in the First Statistical Account make it clear that the peat supplies around innumerable farms and settlements were being rapidly used up or were already finished. Turf was cut for fuel from the shallow moors and even from the surfaces of the pasture and meadow grounds, though this had a disastrous effect on the grazing areas, especially since turf was cut not only for fuel, but also for building house walls, roofing buildings, setting up dykes, mixing with middens composted with byre-manure or seaweed, for bedding in the byres, and for burning (especially in North-East Scotland) as a means of fertilising the arable fields. Entries in Baron Court Books testify time and time again to the lairds' anxiety about the running down of resources in such a way. In 1604, the Earl of Erroll forbade tenants in Urie, Kincardineshire, to provide the inhabitants of Stonehaven with peat, turf or heather for fuel, the farmers being made answerable for their servants. This regulation was several times repeated during the following century and a half.[240] Possibly the outstanding example of the using up of the moorland and grazing resources – the importance of which for the old joint-farming communities can scarcely be overestimated – is the island of Papa Stour in Shetland, where in the course of centuries the land surface lying outside the township dyke, amounting to about two-thirds of the total area, has been cut and bodily carried on to the remaining third. The same process of peat and turf clearing went on over the centuries around every settlement, sometimes leading to the reclamation of land that could be used for arable purposes, and sometimes affecting the pattern of settlement itself, for fuel could not be done without. The using up of peat was time and again followed by the absorption of turf supplies at the expense of the grazing, so that the economy became wasteful almost to a point of no return. If this factor could be assessed, it would undoubtedly appear as one of the major incentives that led to the agricultural 'revolution'.

The cutting of turf, as of peat, involves equipment and organisation, neither of which was readily available to the poor. Their situation worsened, if anything, with agricultural improvement, which cut off from them their former resources of whin and broom, heather and scrub. Their distress, according to the minister of Eccles in Berwickshire in 1794, was 'unspeakably great'. In Tongland, Kirkcudbright, there was 'real distress for fuel, which many poor and shivering wretches suffer'.[241] In the towns, it must have been even worse.

PEAT

Where peat is easily accessible, and where there are manpower reserves to cut, dry and transport it, it is a cheap and obvious fuel. Without these two factors, it could be very expensive in time and labour, though as long as there was a tax on coal, until 1793,[242] its use continued. By 1792, coal was considered to be cheaper than peat in Stracathro, but away from the areas around the coal-seams that ran west in a belt from the Firth of Forth across the Clyde valley and into Ayrshire, and back from the points on the coast to which coal could be carried by sea from Scottish or English ports, peat remained the stand-by, even if its processing took up time required for agricultural operations. There were also jobs like the kiln-drying of corn for grinding, for which coal could not be used, though heath could serve if peat was scarce, as in Tullynessle, Aberdeenshire, in 1752. Till the 1760s in the same parish, and much later in the Northern Isles and in the Hebrides, smiths were also using peat to make charcoal for the forge.[242] This must have been the general practice where coal could not be got. For these reasons, besides the need for cooking and warmth, people were prepared to go long distances by land or sea for the necessary supplies of peat.

The techniques of cutting and drying peat varied from place to place, and different kinds of spades and knives were used, which can be related to particular areas. Peat banks were opened by clearing the heathery top layer to get at the soft peat below, using an ordinary spade by itself or along with a *flauchter* or turf spade. The cutting of the peat below could be done from the top of the bank or, if the bog was reasonably dry, from the front, by a horizontally operated breast spade. In Shetland the light peat-spade or *tusker* was worked by one man who not only cast the peats but also threw them into place to dry (Fig. 74a) from the blade of his spade. In all other

74. a. Cutting a peat-bank in Shetland. The man using the *tusker* also throws the peats out to dry.

parts of Scotland, the caster usually had a helper to take the peat off the blade and throw it up on to the bank, and often a third individual then laid it out to dry. An ideal team, described for the Western Hebrides in 1793, was of five people: one to cut, one to throw up the peat, one to spread it, one to pare and clean the bank, and one resting, ready to relieve the man on the peat-spade.[243]

Work in the mosses was and remains a community effort, with groups of neighbours and relations working together. In Lewis and elsewhere the one for whom the group is cutting peats on a particular day sees to the food, which is prepared on an open peat fire. Potatoes are roasted or boiled in

74. b. A central fire in Foula, Shetland. Photo: H. B. Curwen, 1902.

their skins, and water for tea boiled in a thick cast-iron kettle. Work is a pleasure in a moss, when the gentle wind wipes away sweat, or when in the shimmer of heat from the sun the hum of insects makes the human voice sound sacrilegious, and when in a moment of rest the eye glances over the glistening black lines of the opened banks, to the houses of the township far below, and the sea beyond.

Peats were spread out to dry individually, or were arranged in dykes at the top of the bank, with spaces in between. Single peats were set up in groups of three to five or more, with one on top, and later were built into small circular heaps, before the final move to the houses. The length of the drying stage, and its particular method, varied from place to place and according to whether the season was wet or dry. It has been estimated that fifty or sixty loads were required to maintain one fire throughout the year. In North Uist the cutting, drying and carting of this quantity was said to be equivalent to a full month of a man's time, though usually two neighbours cut together, each spending four or more days on drying and fourteen days on carting.[244]

The proper fire for peats is the fire in the middle of the floor. It may still be possible, but only just, to see such a fire outside a museum in places like the Long Island, and in places like Orkney and Shetland such fires were burning within the last two decades. In a room with a central hearth on which the peat is glowing, the heat holds the smoke just high enough for those who are not used to it to be comfortable, provided they sit down on a wooden chest or on the long wooden settle often found in such kitchens. The peats were laid on edge to last longer, and if there was a stone back to the fire, a turfy back-peat, full of sand and earth, was set against the stone to catch and throw out the heat. Above, fish could be hung all round to be smoked and dried at the same time (Fig. 74b).

In the course of the eighteenth and nineteenth centuries, the central fireplace came to be moved to the gable, or else the stone back was built up to form a gable. Built chimneys appeared, of wood or of wattle plastered with dung and clay, which were dooked into the gable wall like an inverted funnel (Fig. 75a), or else chimneys were built into the thickness of the gable. Black-houses were sometimes adapted by having stone chimney pieces thrust through their hip-ends, giving a curiously hybrid appearance, and new houses that were erected had built into them their own kind of dichotomy, for the kitchen fire on which the cooking was done was of the old, traditional type, burning peat, and often having a 'hangin' lum', whilst the best room, the scene of the personal occasions of baptism, marriage, death, and of visits from the minister, had a gable chimney and a coal burning fire. Where peat is plentiful, as in Kildrummy, Aberdeenshire, many houses still have their old peat-burning fireplaces at floor level,[245] and in Caithness peat-fires are still to be found with a deep 'lazy-hole' below for peat-ashes. It was, of

course, easier to use peat than coal when, as in summer, the fire was only lit
for cooking purposes. In Wigtown, in 1795, the 'better class' of inhabitants
used peat in their kitchens, and coal in their rooms. The carrying on of the
domestic industry of spinning in the parish of Dyke and Moy in Moray
encouraged the lower ranks to use coal early, since it provided enough light
for them to work.[246] In many places, where peat was getting scarce, only a
few loads were got to serve as kindling when lighting a coal fire. Wherever

75. a. A large *hangin' lum* with a grate at Tirlybirly, Glenesk, Angus. By courtesy of the
Glenesk Trust Museum.

75. b. A kitchen range, with swey and grate, at Stobo, Peeblesshire.   C222

coal' fires were in regular use, however, grates were made for them, as in Forglen, Banffshire, where it was said in 1795, that country folk had found the coal not to answer so well on the low hearth, though grates (Fig. 75b) were being installed in the chamber fires, and would probably be extended to the kitchens eventually.[247] But that change took a long time, for low peat or wood burning fires survived in the surrounding districts almost till the present day.

There was a close interrelationship between fireside equipment and the nature of the hearth. The built-in oven, common in most countries of Europe, and in Britain coming as far north as the North of England and the Isle of Man, never played a role in Scotland, except in the castles and big houses, where wheaten bread was regularly baked and eaten. Pot ovens could, however, be used with peat fires, set in peat embers with the lids covered with glowing peat, but mostly the flat iron girdle, round or square, with legs of its own or a handle for hanging it, was the main baking utensil for oatcakes and bere bannocks, which were to such an extent the everyday bread that oatcakes are still called 'breid' in North-East Scotland. *Branders* of open grid work were used like girdles for bere bannocks and for holding pots etc. above a fire at floor level. Alternatively, bannocks could be baked on toasting stones that sat on the floor before the fire, and when grates did eventually reach the kitchen fire, iron oatcake toasters were made to be hung on to them, for hardening off oatcakes baked on the girdle.

Transport

FARM transport, by its nature, bears a close relationship to local conditions and must be judged in relation to them. The kind of sledge known as the Jura car, for instance, with side struts fastened to the sides of a horse and their rear ends trailing on the ground, with a carrying platform linking the struts behind the horse, might well be considered a primitive survival, an example of the past in the present. And so it is in a way, for slipes or travois of this type go back to the Bronze Age and are known in many parts of the world, from Scotland to the plains of North America. They were illustrated by John Slezer in 1693 at Dunblane, Perthshire, and Arbroath, Angus, and appear to have been in widespread use in hilly areas. Yet the Jura car, though a link – perhaps the last one – in a long chain of succession, was nevertheless made, as it survives, by estate joiners, to carry the deer shot by sporting gentry off the trackless hills. No equipment or tool can really be described as primitive, where it is obviously serving a purpose that more up-to-date equipment cannot serve, or at least cannot serve better.

Transport methods are greatly affected by the presence or absence of roads. Where the ground was soft and peaty, or steep and rugged, transport had to be on the human back or on horseback (Fig. 76), the choice usually depending on the length of the journey. Creels of straw, rushes, docken stalks, heather, or willow were made for back-transport, generally by the people themselves as they sat around the fire in the evening. Such basket-making, and the allied craft of rope-twisting, were amongst the range of non-specialised craft skills required to keep a community functioning smoothly, using for the most part the raw materials that the neighbourhood could supply.

Similar creels, sometimes even a little smaller, were used in pairs on the backs of pack-ponies. A pad of sheepskin, of plaited grass, straw or rushes backed with cloth, or even a thin, grassy sod, was put on the pony's back, and over this was laid a wooden pack-saddle. There are two main varieties of saddle, the split-saddle in two interlocking halves, characteristic of the Northern Isles, and the crook-saddle of Western Scotland (Fig. 77a). The creels were hooked on to the crooks or horns of these saddles either directly, or by being placed in nets of hand-twisted bent-grass and straw. Besides creels, various types of panniers could be used, depending on the load to be carried. Creels were for peats, or for seaweed which could be mounded over the horse's back, or for dung, in which case they were often made with

A

B

76. a. A Ross-shire tenant with a creel-load of firewood talks to the factor. C812
b. A pack pony loaded with peat, in Fetlar, Shetland, 1904.

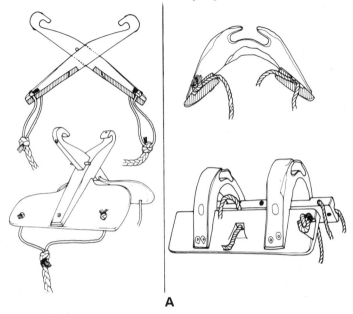

A

B

77. a. Wooden pack-saddles from *left*, Shetland; *right*, Islay.   C226
      b. A slipe at Loch-vana-choir, Perthshire. From A. Campbell, *Journey from Edinburgh*, 1802,
facing 106.   C3189

openable bottoms so that the load could be dropped straight down. In the Hebrides special deep baskets, of closely woven bent-grass, were used for carrying grain to be ground at the mill. Panniers were for loads like sheaves of corn, and must have been in very common use for this purpose in East and South Scotland until well through the eighteenth century. The equivalent in the islands, even in the 1900s, was a loop of rope and a load of sheaves on the human back (Fig. 34b, Ch. 3). Corn-sacks could simply be slung across the horse's back, and much of the grain taken to the Lowland ports for export was no doubt transported in this way, by tenants performing their long carriage duties.

For loads that had to be pulled rather than carried, there were a number of possibilities. On moderately level land, sledges were used for peat, dung, and corn – corn was sledged in Perthshire in 1778,[248] for example, before Lord Kames had improved the roads – with slipes (Fig. 77b) as the alternative on steeper land. These were much more restricted in their movements than a horse with a load on its back, and it also seems to have been the case that some kind of a road or track was preferred for the slipe. Both sledges and slipes were suitable only for short carriages.

If dung was to be carried, the sledge and slipe were adapted by adding a wickerwork creel as a container. It had a pointed base, which allowed it to be easily tipped over. A creel was also added for peats, but in this case it was square, more like a frame all round the body of the vehicle.

These vehicles, known as *kellach* sledges, have been used by various writers[249] to illustrate a stage in an evolutionary sequence that leads from the simple slipe with a roughly made platform, to the two-wheeled cart, since from at least the early eighteenth century, wheels of solid wood were being added to the ends of the rear runners of the slipe, to produce a simple two-wheeled cart with a wicker body. The wheels were not shod with iron and quickly wore along the grain to an uneven oval shape.

Besides *kellach* carts with basket bodies for dung, there were also *rung* carts, whose bodies were made of a framework of upright rungs (Fig. 78). They were more suitable for peat and corn, and were used in vast numbers. In the 1790s, there were 2,410 in Dingwall, 300 in Kiltearn, and 376 in Kiltarlity. In each case the wheels were attached right at the rear end, making these vehicles cart-like, but it is difficult to see them as part of the story of the evolution of the cart, since wheeled vehicles have been known since the fourth millennium BC in the Ancient Near East, and in Scotland at least from Roman times.[250] It is more likely that the addition of wheels to slipes is simply due to the influence of existing more conventional types of carts. The same kind of back-formation made its appearance much later in the small islands of Hoy, Graemsay and Flotta in Orkney, where, in the early 1800s, four wheels came to be added to sledges pulled by oxen, or more rarely horses. These were solid, not spoked, and were cut out of old ships' hatches

78. a, b, c. A slipe, *kellach cart*, and *rung cart*. From Captain Burt, *Letters from a Gentleman in the North of Scotland*, 1754.

(Fig. 79a). It is not impossible that the influence that led to the making of these four-wheeled wagons out of sledges came from the prairie-wagon of the United States, an area with which many Orcadians were perfectly familiar.

WAINS AND WAGONS

At the beginnings of the period of agricultural improvement in the seventeenth century or even earlier, at least two layers in the stratification of farm transport can be seen. The first is the kind involving carriage on the back, or in vehicles with runners or skids, the latter sometimes modified by the addition of wheels in areas of active marketing needs, for example in and around Inverness, and to such an extent in the fertile, corn-growing Laigh of Moray that rung carts were known in Banffshire as 'Morra' cairts' or 'Morra' coaches', and the first wheeled carts that reached Caithness in the eighteenth century came from Moray.[251]

The second layer is one to which little attention has been drawn, because the evidence is very scattered. It relates to estates and to the activities of landed proprietors, who required and were able to afford more substantial vehicles than their tenants, and who could supply the necessary draught animals. These were ox wains, with which heavier loads than normal could be carried over relatively long distances.

In Shetland, an area of back transport till the early 1800s, the lairds had a few ox wains. An early eighteenth-century inventory of the implements on the estate of the improving landlord, Sir James Stewart of Burray in Orkney, included one ox wagon and part of another, and a horse wain. In 1721, John Traill of Elsness in Sanday had six oxen for carts.[252] In Moray and Banffshire, oxen were being yoked abreast in wains with draught-poles about 1811–12, and in Aberdeenshire, Grant of Monymusk had wains pulled by four and six oxen in the early 1700s.[253] In Perthshire, in 1778, at Redstone farm, Stobhall and Lintibert farm, Muthill, there were wains pulled by two oxen and two horses, able to carry six bolls of marl for manuring land. Though wains were recommended by Andrew Wight for transporting lime and marl, he nevertheless acknowledged that the horses and cattle of the period were too small for draughts of any weight.[254] On some of the bigger East Lothian farms, wains were drawn by four oxen, with two trace horses in front, and a hind and goadman to control them. They could move 42 to 48 bushels of oats or barley when the roads were passable in summer.[255] In Berwickshire, ox wains were more common than carts up till about 1750, and small four-horse wagons had been introduced for long carriages, especially for transporting lime from the draw-kilns of Northumberland to improve the ground. These seem also to have been known in Midlothian, since it was said in 1793 that they were 'reprobated' there. In Oxnam parish, Roxburgh, wains drawn by two oxen and two horses, or four horses, were used for dung, corn,

A

B

79. a. An Orkney sled, with solid wheels cut from ship's hatches. Per Mrs. N. Macmillan.
b. Box carts with trace horses, for heavy loads of dung, at Strathmiglo, Fife. Per H. Cheape.

C537

hay, and wood. In Dumfries at the same period there were a few wagons with four or more horses.[256]

This evidence involves three main points. First, it applies to estate vehicles and must be related to the mains or home farms that served the estates directly. Second, the distribution of ox wains is in the south and east, and though Shetland and Orkney are included, the influence of mainland Scotland no doubt played its part there. Third, the difference between the terms 'wain' and 'wagon' in the southern counties is more than linguistic. It almost certainly indicates the presence of two types of vehicle, one of which, at least, can be linked with the development of farm transport south of the Border. The four-horse wagons appear to be examples of the four-wheeled wagons introduced to England from the Low Countries in the sixteenth century. They were at first intended for road transport rather than general agricultural work – for example, for the long distance transport of lime – and their presence indicates the existence of usable roads. In England, such wagons were adapted during the eighteenth century by local cartwrights for harvest work especially, and the splendid series of vehicles that is one of the high-water marks of English farming and the skill of English cartwrights came into being. For harvest purposes they replaced the smaller two-wheeled cart wherever the terrain was suitable, which meant that parts of Northern England, Ireland, and Scotland remained as two-wheeled cart rather than becoming four-wheeled wagon areas,[257] although there was a slight penetration of the wagon into South Scotland, for a short period only.

The word 'wain', on the other hand, is used in South-West England for a two-wheeled vehicle with a flat, platform-like body, equivalent in form to the *long cart* of other parts of Britain, including the southern half of Scotland, a type that can be traced back at least to the fourteenth century. It is reasonably certain that the word indicates a two-wheeled vehicle in Scotland as well, though few or no descriptions are available, apart from the fact that in Perthshire its wheels were 48 to 50 inches (1·4–1·5 m.) in diameter, and that it was drawn by a central pole, at the sides of which the oxen were yoked in pairs, and to the front of which one or two horses could be attached by traces.[258] It is likely that the needs of improving estates in transporting heavy loads of lime and marl extended the useful life of this vehicle well into the improvement period, as well as introducing the four-wheeled English wagon, however briefly, to Scotland.

THE TUMBLER

The wain was one of the main types of farm vehicle in medieval Scotland, where conditions, both social and geographical, were suitable for its use. Another was a form of box-cart known as a *tumbler* or *tumbril*, used over a wider area and at a lower social level than the wain. Eleanor, Countess of

Linlithgow, in writing to her daughter from Linlithgow Palace in 1612, said specifically: 'as for tumeler cairtis, thair is nan heir. As for my cairt it is broken bott I haif causit command thame to bring hochemes (collars) creills and tedderis with thame'.[259] In other words, she was being forced to use back transport. Tumblers could not be used on soft or hilly ground, which meant that their distribution was limited to the lower lands. By the 1790s, they had become little more than a memory except for the *kellach* carts of the north-easterly districts, which appear to be a kind of a cross between slipes and tumblers. The tumbler began to be generally replaced by better carts in South and East-Central Scotland in the first half of the eighteenth century, at the same time as the slipes of Moray, Nairn, Easter Ross and Inverness took a step towards improvement, following the fashion of the innovation centres in the South-East of Scotland, by being adapted for wheels, though these were often fixed individually, and not paired on the ends of axles.

The chief characteristic of the tumbler was that the wooden axle rotated with the wheels, which were not spoked, but were made up of three solid pieces of wood. If they were shod, it was not with complete rings, but with iron straiks nailed over the joints. The wheels were 2 or 3 feet (0·6–0·9 m.) in diameter, which meant that heavy loads, as of dung, did not need to be hoisted very high, though 'heavy' is a relative term since tumblers could scarcely draw 5 cwt. Tumblers also served an industrial purpose sometimes, as at Alloa in Clackmannan, where they were much used for transporting coal to the shore.[260] Instead of a central pole, tumblers had shafts, which were presumably extensions of the side timbers. They were drawn by horses.

Tumblers can be traced back to 1535 under that name, and even further under an older name, *coup*, from an Anglo-Saxon word with the sense of 'basket'. It has nothing to do with the later 'coup-carts' that could be 'couped' or tipped up. As small box-carts for carrying manure, *coups* are mentioned in 1494 in the Dunfermline Burgh Records.[261] The same vehicles and the same name are found in Northern England.

Tumblers or coups had small, solid wooden wheels. In their latter days in the eighteenth century they were confined to poorer areas and to poorer farms. There were, however, bigger and better quality carts with spoked wheels, like those illustrated by John Slezer in Angus in 1693. Spoked wheels revolved on the axle, not with it. They were expensive items, especi-ally since the wheel had to be shod with iron. In an Edinburgh Testament for 1622 reference was made to 'ane pair of quheillis with ane lang cairt, ane clois cairt, and ane stane cairt body'. That is to say, wheels were too expensive to be fitted to every cart, so they were made to be interchangeable according to the kind of load to be carried. This custom remained common, and still survives in areas of horse or ox transport in Central Europe to such an extent that a Polish writer has claimed that the otherwise useful distinction between two-wheeled carts and four-wheeled wagons has relatively little importance in his country.[262]

IMPROVED CARTS

Carts for relatively light loads and short distances usually had shafts for a horse (Fig. 79b), wains for heavy loads and longer distances had poles to which oxen were yoked by means of wooden yokes. The use of both poles and ox yokes died out about the same time, in the second half of the eighteenth century. Oxen did not then cease to be draught animals, however, but began to be yoked like horses between the shafts, by a special collar made to open at the bottom. For an ox with horns, it was impossible to put the collar on upside down and then twist it round, as for a horse. Collars and traces for oxen are first mentioned in the 1760s.[263] This adaptation is contemporary not only with new and improved cart-types, but also with improved ploughs. It took place first on the bigger farms, whilst the use of the yoke fell in the social scale till it was confined to the 'poorer sort' by the 1790s. Eventually even the 'poorer sort' adopted the ox-collar, which remained – along with the ox or some other bovid as a draught animal – on smaller farms in Fair Isle, parts of Orkney and parts of North-East Scotland until the 1940s. But in general, the horse was the main draught animal from the third quarter of the eighteenth century onwards.

During the 1700s, improvements in the construction of carts were rapid, as was the increase in their use, though not always without opposition. In Ayrshire about 1750, Lord Cathcart had carts made, but though he offered them to his tenants free, to improve his estates, few of them would accept the gift.[264] Inevitably, the improving estates, like Monymusk in Aberdeenshire, acted as innovation centres, but two other factors also played a part.

One was the effort made to improve roads in the second half of the eighteenth century, when the Commissioners of Supply were seeking to commute statute labour on roads, and Acts of Parliament were obtained authorising turnpike trusts. Before John Loudon McAdam came along in the early nineteenth century, road surfaces remained poor, and the value of roads lay more in helping agriculture than in helping communications. On a poor road a two-horse cart – that is, with one horse between the shafts and a trace-horse in front – would carry 18 to 20 cwt., and a one-horse cart 12 cwt. But given a good road, one horse could draw 24 to 30 cwt., according to a Midlothian writer of 1793, or 12 to 25 cwt., according to a 1796 report from Stirlingshire. The Falkirk carters, who before the days of the Forth-Clyde canal carried all the goods between Glasgow and the Firth of Forth, regularly moved 20 to 35 cwt. Their horses were fed high on beans, and lasted about two years.[265]

The second factor was the improvement in breeds of horses. The Lanarkshire breed of strong draught horse, the Clydesdale, had begun to spread in the late eighteenth century, and it was said that one of them could carry as much in a cart as two horses previously. As a result, by the 1790s, the old team of two horses had largely been replaced by one.

At the same time, the cart itself was becoming more sophisticated. There were two main types, the long cart for the hay and grain harvests, and the short cart, which could be either a close-cart or box-cart with a fixed body, or a coup-cart (Fig. 80), which could be tipped up to empty a load of dung, lime, or compost. To let the cart tip easily, it was desirable that the diameter of the wheels should be greater than in earlier times. Long-carts are relatively limited in their distribution. They centre on the areas of high-farming, mainly south of the Tay. To the north, and generally on farms of moderate to small

80. Harvest and box carts newly made by the firm of Allan of Murthlie, Perthshire. Per Miss J. Allan.

size, the box-cart was adapted for leading the harvest by the attachment of a movable frame of open spars that overhung on all sides.

Box-cart bodies also began to be made more roomy by local joiners, whose trade was greatly expanded by the demand for carts. Nevertheless, cart-wrights as such were rare in Scotland. In most cases, cart-building remained in the hands of general joiners. A good, joiner-made box-cart was expected to last about seven years.

Joiners, like smiths, worked either in their workshops, or on the farms (Fig. 81). Around 1812 there were travelling joiners in Caithness, who served the smaller tenants by making up carts for them. The tenants provided birch and fir, and got from the shops in the towns second-hand carriage-

A

B

81. a. Joiners assembling a cart-wheel at Currie, Midlothian. The last felloe is being knocked on to two spokes. Per J. Watt. C2595

b. Ringing a wheel at Brechin, Angus. Per Miss M. F. Michie.

wheels imported from Leith.[266] There was, therefore, a slight step forward in specialisation.

Some joiners gained wide reputations. The cart-bodies made by Alexander Manderson of Oldhamstocks were widely famed, and Samuelston cart wheels were considered to be everlasting.[267] A number of cart-making firms came into being, such as Jack of Maybole in Ayrshire, Kemp and Nicholson in Stirling, Allan of Murthly in Perthshire (Fig. 80), and so on, each producing vehicles to suit the needs of their regions, with recognisable differences between them. For example, a Peeblesshire cart was less deep than one from Ayrshire, with less slope in front, and the box was bolted to the shafts or *trams*.[268] This meant that if they got broken, as they easily could in the hillier ground of Peeblesshire, it was easier to replace them.

The joiner who made everything from carts to coffins became an essential part of every rural community. His workshop was never far from the smithy, and these two craftsmen combined to provide the full range of cartwrighting requirements. The joiner made up the body and shaped and assembled the nave, spokes and felloes of the wheel. The smith made the iron axle, which gradually replaced the wooden axle from the late 1700s, and ringed the wheel and the nave with iron hoops. There is no doubt that the demand for carts, as for ploughs, greatly helped to strengthen the position of these craftsmen in the community, and at the same time, Scottish craftsmen learned to produce carts that gained a reputation outside the borders of the country.

These were the 'Scotch carts' or 'Leith carts'. About 1800, they began to be exported to North-East Ulster, where the carriers of goods first took them on, and then the farmers. Though more expensive than the native 'Irish car', they carried twice the load. Their diffusion was also helped in Ulster by contemporary road improvements, as well as by the fact that the possession of a Scotch cart came to be a status symbol. This type of cart had fixed shafts that were extensions of the side-pieces, and spoked wheels about 4 feet (1·2 m.) in diameter that turned on iron axles. In effect, it was a smaller version of the long-cart.

More surprising, however, was the considerable export of two-wheeled carts by sea from Edinburgh to Essex in the late eighteenth century. In Eastern England, these Scotch carts replaced heavy carts that needed at least two horses to pull them. Two types were exported, the general purpose box- or coup-cart, and the long-bodied harvest-cart. They proved so popular that in the course of the nineteenth century at least two English firms, Crosskill of Beverley and Tasker of Andover, were producing Scotch carts in great quantities. Here, too, is a sphere of influence, along with Small's plough, Meikle's threshing mill, Bell's reaper (of which a version was also made by Crosskill of Beverley), and so on, in which Scottish farming had a considerable part to play outside the bounds of the country itself.

13

The Farming Community

SCOTLAND is a small country on the outer fringes of Europe, with a population that has increased from 1¼ million at the time of Webster's census in 1755 to over 5 million at present. In 1755, the pattern of settlement was rural, with 62% of the people living in the Highlands and Southern Uplands. Since then it has changed, so that now over 75% live in the industrial Central Belt. Not only was there a flow of people from the country into the towns and cities where employment in industry was available, but there was also much re-shuffling of those who remained.[269] In the eighteenth century, agricultural improvement was accompanied by the expansion or founding of villages in which domestic industries like weaving, lace making, and snuff-box making as well as fishing and water-powered industry, were carried on. Places like Simprin and Castleton in the south of Scotland, Cuminestown, New Byth and Huntly in Aberdeenshire – in all perhaps over 150 planned villages that appeared in the 1700s – added a totally new element to the landscape of Scotland, and allowed for the movement of people within their own area, as opposed to movement out of it.[270] The movement of people from the glens to the coasts as a result of the Sheep Clearances in the High-lands and Islands also kept at least a proportion within their original territorial area. A different kind of late eighteenth century movement was the settling of people displaced by the enclosing of farms on pieces of land at the edges of peat-bogs and moors, at low or no rents for the first few years, so that they could reclaim the land and bring it into a productive state. Many of the smallholdings, the 'crafties', of North-East Scotland, originated in this way.[271] The net result is that relatively few parts of Scotland have an indigenous population that can be traced back in its area of settlement for much more than a century to a century and a half.

These general movements were accompanied by changes at farm level, the one complementing the other. One effect of the blocking out and enclosing of farms was to cut off the land as a form of social security from unknown numbers, many of whom had to be re-absorbed elsewhere. Apart from the harvest period, when many extra hands were needed, technological improvements in the plough and the change from oxen to horses as draught animals alone made large numbers of farm workers redundant. The old Scotch plough with its team of up to twelve oxen needed two men to work it, but the new, lighter ploughs required only two horses, which now came to be controlled by reins. In part this was made possible by better and stronger breeds of horses, especially the Clydesdale (Fig. 82b) which was

82. Ploughing and harness medals: a. Highland and Agricultural Society, 1814, C1910;
b. Girvan District Agricultural Society, 1890, C1909; c. Insch, 1911, C1906.

widely bred in South-West Scotland, sold at the beginning of February each year at Lanark Fair and elsewhere, and spread through shows like the stallion show at Edinburgh in 1757, and another in the Grassmarket there in 1783,[272] from which period the systematic breeding of the Clydesdale is said to date. There was a contemporary spread of ploughs of James Small's type, and of improved one-horse carts. The result was that where a farm in the parish of Monikie in Angus, for example, was using five ten-ox ploughs in 1750, by the 1790s only three four-horse ploughs were required. For cultivation purposes, this was a reduction of fifty animals to twelve, and the manpower was probably reduced from ten to at least six at the same time. A farmer in the neighbouring parish of Muirhouse cut his staff from thirteen to five over the same period.[273] It was these displaced persons who went to swell the populations of the villages, towns and cities, or who in the more extreme situation in the Highlands and Islands migrated to the New World.[274]

Ploughmen (Fig. 83) remained in the hierarchy of farm workers, but some elements dropped out. One was the *tasker* who thrashed with the flail, made redundant on big farms by the advent of Andrew Meikle's threshing mill. By the 1790s, both the whole and half hind of the previous century had been widely replaced by married hinds, whose wages, however, were still largely in kind. In places a sum of money called sheep silver was given in lieu of an allowance of wool for domestic use, as well as a piece of ground for sowing lint-seed to be processed into linen at home, or in one of the lint-mills which proliferated in the second half of the eighteenth century. The wives still did outside work, but appear to have had more time for the distaff and spindle. Footwear was sometimes supplied by the farmer, like Mr. Begbie of Congalton Mains, East Lothian, in 1750–60, who seems to have retrieved and repaired shoes when a servant left.[275]

In the Borders the shepherd was an important figure, reckoned in 1797 to be £2 a year better off than the hind. That the yearly keep of a number of sheep as part of his wage was better than money is suggested by the fact that as recently as the 1960s there were shepherds who still kept a *pack* of 36 breeding ewes and 9 hogs as a major part of their wages.[276]

In the 1790s too, hedgers and ditchers appear, with wages equivalent to those of the shepherd. Some were regularly employed like hinds, others did customary work at customary prices, and broken work at stipulated daily wages. Their presence, and their financial rating, is clear testimony to the urgency with which the work of enclosing and subdividing was being carried on.

A class that came into its own first in South-East Scotland was the farm grieve, overseer, or steward. His wages varied from place to place according to its size and quality. Some were incomers from across the Border. Already by about 1754, three farms in the parish of Swinton and Simprin were

A

B

83. a. Five pair and an orra beast at Ingilston farm, Essie, Perthshire. Per M. F. Davidson.
C2388
 b. Alec Young with the first pair at the Moat, Auchterless, Aberdeenshire, 1917. Per R. Ewan.
C925

occupied by the Northumbrian stewards of three Northumbrian farmers. They maintained a certain state, keeping a social distance at a time when native farmers were barely distinguishable from their hinds in dress, attitudes and eating habits.[277] The advanced agriculture of Northumberland affected the Borders both through such direct infiltration, and through the movement of farm workers (Fig. 84a) back and fore, from the hiring markets at Duns and Berwick, so that some knowledge of Northumbrian farming practice could also have come in at this level.

Servants on the Scottish side benefited from the high wages on the English side, for farmers had to pay more to get them, and this in turn had an effect on their living standard. By 1797, farm servants had 'cast off their long clothing, tardy face, and lethargic look of their forefathers, for the short doublet, and linen trowsers, the quick step and life of persons labouring for their own behoof, and work up to the spirit of their own cattle, and the rapid evolutions of the threshing mill'.[278] But the ministers reacted petulantly. They deplored the tendency to expensive dress among young women, they suggested that 'a tax on silk, amounting to a prohibition of it among maid-servants, would be an advantage to them', they objected to the new pernicious habit of using tea, which even replaced porridge at breakfast time, and to the increase in dram-drinking, also amongst women of the lower class, due to its low price.[279] But these blessings or vices still had to spread from the South-East to other parts of Scotland in the course of the following century.

In the high farming areas of the South-East, it was particularly common to have female outworkers on the farms, equivalent to the tied dairywomen of the South-West. These outworkers, often called 'bondagers' (Fig. 84a), were the wives or female relatives of the hinds, or had at least to be supplied by the hind. Their work paid the rent for the house in which he lived. This custom was well on its way out by the 1860s. As early as 1845, a man called Thomson, from Tranent, led an attempt to organise the ploughmen of East Lothian to refuse to bind themselves to a farmer on feeing day unless they were relieved of the bondager system.[280] This formal attempt failed, but the farmers let the custom peter out gradually in any case. Nevertheless women outworkers went on being employed in these areas, with their characteristic dress: a wide-brimmed hat of black plaited straw with a rim of red rucheing, a neat blouse and drugget skirt, a striped apron, boots buttoned up the sides of the legs, and straw ropes twisted round the ankles in muddy conditions. They may still be seen occasionally in the fields, now wearing headgear with a hood at the front and a flap at the back, known in the Lothians as an *ugly* and in Lanarkshire as a *crazy*.

The consolidation of farms into units led to the creation of a fixed labour force with its own internal organisation and standards. The change from ox- to horse-draught, coinciding with this consolidation, brought into being the class known as horsemen. Under the stimulus of the Highland

and Agricultural Society, founded in 1784, and of the numerous local Agricultural Societies that sprang up around 1800, ploughing matches and harness competitions, pride in their horses and their turn-out, became part of the farm-servants' way of life (Figs. 21 and 82). As part of this movement a new trade appeared, that of saddler. The ministers of Fintry in Aberdeenshire, Edzell in Angus, and elsewhere, speak of proper harness coming into fashion in the 1790s, made by professional men. It is conceivable that the cost of decent harness was a factor in maintaining the ox longer as a draught animal, for it required only a wooden yoke. Earlier horse harness was home made, as noted by a Yorkshire visitor about 1679: 'their . . . harness is . . . all Wood from head to tail, Bridle, Saddle, Girths, Stirrups, and Crupper, all Wood; . . . their Bridles have not Bitts, but a kind of Musroll of two pieces of wood (that is, branks like those on a tethered cow); their Crupper is a stick of a yards length, put cross their docks, both ends thereof being tyed

84. a. Women outworkers near Cornhill-on-Tweed, Northumberland, about 1908–9. Per Mrs. Short.

with woven wood to the Saddle'.[281] Harness with ropes of twisted withies kept on being used with pack-saddles for long after in the Highlands.

As the agricultural improvements progressed, as the run-rig system with its reservoirs of on-the-spot manpower vanished, as enclosed individual farms with single tenants became the rule, as improved and new machinery – ploughs, mills, reapers, binders, etc. – came along, farm service ceased to be an integral part of a social system in which nearly every element had a stake in the land, and became instead a saleable and movable commodity. Socially, this was as much of a revolution as the change from run-rig to enclosed farms. Mobility developed to such an extent that unmarried men (Fig. 84b) changed their masters at the feeing-markets every six months, and married men (Fig. 85) moved every year. Movement was rarely outside

84. b. Bothy men in Angus. Per Bruce Walker.   C1467

a ten or twenty mile radius, so that the men gained a wealth of experience of the different farms and farmers in their districts, forming a kind of expanded community within their working context which meant that though farm service was of a very scattered nature in comparison with the close association of people in factories, nevertheless there was a real sense of brotherhood that expressed itself in different ways from time to time. The fact that they could sell their services, combined with their diminishing numbers, and under the stimulus of the activities of industrial workers and the propagation of extreme views through newspapers, books and journals, brought out some stirrings of self-assertion, sporadically in the eighteenth century, more consistently in the nineteenth, but effectively only in the twentieth.

SOCIETIES AND UNIONS

In 1807, a Ploughman's Society was established at Cluny Mains, Fife. It was essentially a Friendly Society, for the benefit of sick members, and was

85. a. An Angus farm-servant and his family. Before 1914. Per Bruce Walker.   C1460

strictly non-political, for 'any Member proving disobedient, or turbulent to the Laws, rousing or fomenting party spirit, in order to carry any particular point, contrary to the order and intention of these Laws, shall be fined Five shillings, sterling; and a repetition, double the sum, or expelled the Society, without the benefit of re-admission'.[282] The Bell's Wynd Society established in Glasgow in 1746 appears to be the earliest of such Societies. Like the Cow Clubs that existed in the Borders, they were forms of social insurance rather than means of exerting pressure on their employers.

About 1750, a certain 'Windy' Shaw was attempting to organise the discontented ploughmen in the Carse of Stirling. In 1834, 600 agricultural labourers and ploughmen in the Carse of Gowrie formed a union to secure a ten-hour day in summer and an eight-hour day in winter, with overtime to be paid at day-labourers' rates. The women of Sanquhar threatened in

85. b. An elderly farm couple in the Coupar Angus district.   C3430

1853 to stone any shearer who worked for less than 2/6 a day. In 1860, a short-lived Farm Servants' Union was formed at Dunbar, and in 1865, a Farm Servants' Protection Society in Midlothian. It asked for 15/– a week, paid fortnightly, with a free house, coals driven, and a month's food during harvest. This movement spread to the rest of the Lothians, Peebles, Berwickshire and Perth.[283] These sporadic efforts in South and Central Scotland are evidence of a strong feeling that better justice was needed for farmworkers, a feeling that was ultimately given unity through the Scottish Farm Servants' Union, founded by Joseph F. Duncan in 1912, and its monthly journal, *The Scottish Farm Servant*, which appeared in 1913. The revised Constitution, printed at Aberdeen in 1890, opens with the words:

> 'Brethren, – The time has now come for action. Too long have we stood idly by indifferent to our interests as a class', – and went on to state the Objects, which were:
>
> 'The establishment of Branches throughout Scotland. To consolidate and strengthen the influence and power of Farm Servants, Carters, and Labourers generally. To reform and improve our relations with our employers, and to obtain for Farm Servants Monthly Payments with Indefinite Engagements; Weekly Half-Holiday, except Six weeks in harvest. The Abolition of the Bothy System; the improvement of our Kitchen Dietary scale, and of our House and Sleeping accommodation. To protect the Interests of the Members of the Union by securing redress against oppression. To establish a Sick and Funeral Benefit Society, and Superannuation Fund for Trade Members.'[284]

These exhortations pin-point the worst features of contemporary farmservice, but it was not until far through the twentieth century that any degree of solidarity was achieved. In Dumfries, for example, the first Union lasted from 1913 to 1918, and was not re-started till 1935. In 1955 there were twenty-one branches in Dumfriesshire, a fact that itself points to the dispersed nature of farm service, which has become more and more accentuated as workers leave the land and farm-work is carried on more and more by machinery.

Apart from these official unions, there were also 'horsemen societies', which were strong in the North-East from the nineteenth century until the tractor replaced the horse from the First World War onwards. Horsemen societies were not the kind of unions that sought to gain their ends by threats of strikes or walk-outs, though sometimes the men might arrange for the 'supernatural' throwing of clods at dead of night, or the dancing of barrows across the close, in order to make an effect on a farmer's wife who fed them on too monotonous a diet or on 'steam-mill' oatcakes made thick and green with too much bakingsoda, or on a farmer who was making working conditions too hard.

To become a 'horseman', a form of initiation ceremony was necessary, after the young *halflin'* had served his apprenticeship. This took place in the barn in the middle of the night, and was usually conducted by four horsemen. The novice had to bring with him a loaf, a bottle of whisky, and a candle. He was blindfolded and led to the 'altar', which could be made by pressing a bushel measure on a sack of corn, and was then asked various questions to which correct answers had to be given, and an oath was taken, in the following terms:

'I of my own free will and accord solemnly vow and swear before God and all these witnesses that I will heal, conceal, and never reveal any part of the true horsemanship which I am about to receive at this time. Furthermore I solemnly vow and swear that I will neither write it nor indite, cut it nor carve it on wood or stone, nor yet on anything movable or immovable under the canopy of heaven, nor yet so much as wave a finger in the air to none but a horseman.

'Furthermore I vow and swear that I will never give it nor see it given to a tradesman of any kind except to a blacksmith or a veterinary surgeon or a horse-soldier. Furthermore I will never give it nor see it given to a farmer or a farmer's son unless he be working his own or his father's horses. Furthermore I will never give it nor see it given to a fool nor a madman nor to my father nor mother sister nor brother nor to any womankind. Furthermore I will never give it nor see it given to my wife nor daughter nor yet to the very dearest ever lay by my side. Furthermore I will never give it nor see it given to anyone after sunset on Saturday night nor before sunrise on Monday morning. Furthermore I will neither abuse nor bad use any man's horses with it and if I see a brother do so I will tell him of his fault. Furthermore I will never advise anyone to get it nor disadvise anyone from getting it but leave everyone to his own free will and accord. Furthermore I will never give it nor see it given to any under the age of sixteen nor above the age of forty-five. Furthermore I will never give it nor see it given unless there be three or more lawful sworn brethren present after finding them to be so by trying and examining them. Furthermore I will never give it nor see it given for less than the sum of £1 sterling or the value thereof. Furthermore I will never refuse to attend a meeting if warned within three days except in a case of riding fire or going for the doctor, and if I fail to keep these promises may my flesh be torn to pieces with a wild horse and my heart cut through with a horseman's knife and my bones buried on the sands of the seashore where the tide ebbs and flows every twenty-four hours so that there may be no remembrance of me amongst lawful brethren so help me God to keep these promises. Amen.'

In spite of the fact that the oath, which is related to the Masonic oath, should not be written, this version was written by an Aberdeenshire farm-servant who retired to London in 1908.

To conclude the ceremony, the novice got a shake of the Devil's hand, a stick covered with some sort of hairy skin, and was then given the Word, of which there were various versions, one of which was 'Both in one'.

CROFTERS

In 1878, R. S. Skirving included in his five classes of Scottish agricultural labourers those crofters and small farmers who personally cultivated the lands they occupied, helped mainly by members of their own family.[285] This group originated in various ways. In the early days of improvement there were small tenants who, it was considered, could not advance agriculture since they had other jobs such as that of hired carter, which often took them away from home at critical times for husbandry. A Berwickshire writer recommended in 1797 that such people should move to small possessions near towns and villages, or should become artisans, servants, or hinds to greater tenants.[286] This process of adaptation of the links with the land, involving a change to full-time employment rather than part-time employment combined with partial subsistence farming, was one of the continuing features of country life following the enclosure period. In East Central Scotland particularly, the *pendicle* became common, a small piece of ground held by a sub-tenant who was either a tradesman, or who paid the rent of his holding by working for the farm to which it was attached. The crofts of North-East Scotland were on a similar footing to the pendicles. They were, in their early stages of development in the late eighteenth and nineteenth centuries, occupied by people who combined work for a farm with the reclamation of their own spots of land from the moor or bog, and whose activities have helped to make the North-East the most continuously cultivated stretch of farm land in Scotland. The reclamation function eventually fell away, and multitudes of crofts have been absorbed by amalgamation into the farms, but till recent times, it was the personnel on these crofts – the smith, joiner, gravedigger, molecatcher, etc. – who provided the supporting services (as well as farm labour) without which a rural community could not easily function. Furthermore, such crofts or small-holdings gave a first foothold for those of ambition who wished to climb the farming ladder.

The main area for crofts, however, is the North and West. The seven counties of Shetland, Orkney, Caithness, Sutherland, Ross, Inverness, and Argyll have been collectively known as the Crofting Counties since the Crofters Holdings (Scotland) Act of 1886. A 'crofter' was defined then as a tenant of a holding from year to year, who resided on the holding, which should be situated in a crofting county, paying a rent not exceeding £30 a year, and whose successors should be his heirs or legatees. Subsequently there were various modifications, the upper limit of rent being raised, for instance, to £50 in 1911 under the Small Landholders (Scotland) Act.

Within the Crofting Counties, however, there is a great mixture of conditions. Orkney, Easter Ross, and the parishes of Cawdor and Croy in Inverness, for example, stand amongst the prominent farming districts of Scotland. The forms of occupation of the soil were various, and the occupiers ranged over *tacksmen* or tenants with leases, *bowers* who had grazing farms for milk cattle, *steel bowers* who according to the steelbow system of tenure received their stock and cattle along with their farm, the *pendiclers*, who in the north generally held their pieces of land from the chief tacksman, the *cottars*, with a house and portion of land but no cattle, who worked for a farmer and had their land tilled by him, the *crofters*, who controlled their own arable but had their cattle herded and tended along with those of the tacksman, and the *dryhouse cottars*, labourers who had no more than a house and kailyard.[287]

This range characterised the better farming districts of the Crofting Counties, as well as counties like Moray, but it was gradually simplified as agricultural improvement advanced, and was in any case simpler where the land was too poor to permit the mixture of bigger and smaller scale farming that the range indicates. In such areas, only townships of crofters have remained since the nineteenth century, the crofts totalling just over 19,000 at the present date. Their small size is emphasised by the fact that fewer than 5% of all crofts can provide full-time employment in agriculture, so that other forms of employment such as fishing, weaving, road-work, work as postman etc. are necessary, and a good deal of communal work is required in relation, for example, to sheep-shearing and dipping, and to peat-cutting, if these tasks are to be done expeditiously. The need for community effort varies regionally in relation to croft sizes. In Wester Ross, with 816 crofts below 5 acres and 287 between 5 and 10 acres, the need is greater than in Easter Ross where there are only 84 crofts below 5 acres and 85 between 5 and 10 acres, and where big farms are common, providing opportunities for employment and easy outlets for sales of stock by the crofters. The most intensively occupied crofting region of all is Lewis, with 2,299 crofts of under 5 acres, 1,022 between 5 and 10 acres, and only 19 of over 30 acres.[288] Conditions of life in the crofting districts, therefore, mean that the members of the farming community are much less specialised than their fellows in the Lowlands and in the farming areas of the Crofting Counties, though their ability to mix farming with fishing, shepherding, and to some extent gamekeeping, means that they have a wider range of skills. There is also in the crofting counties less of a farming class structure. The laird at one end and the crofter at the other have few or no gradations to separate or link them. They have no foreman or grieve to act as an intermediary between the farmer and the other men, and though the womenfolk did a lot of outside work, they had no specific name or status like the bondagers of the South-East. On the other hand the crofts did not have the 'landless' labourers of the Lowlands, though the crofter's stake in the land was often worth less than the wage earned by a Lowland labourer.

14

Conclusion

THIS book is concerned with the material culture of the countryside – the objects people made and used, the ways in which they used them, the houses in which they lived. Questions of functionalism, and of the fitness of the tools and equipment for the purposes they served, have been in the background throughout, and these, rather than value judgements in the light of later acquired knowledge, have dictated the approach. Pre-improvement implements were in general well enough suited to the kind of work they had to do. The old Scotch plough was not a crude tool of wood and iron knocked together without skill and knowledge, but a highly sophisticated piece of equipment adapted for the ridge and furrow type of cultivation. That it was capable of being modified in relation to terrain and availability of draught animals is shown by the evolution of the lighter version along the Highland line, and where it could not be used, there was a range of alternatives, all equally well adapted to their environments. The study of the functionalism of the material culture of the countryside in pre-industrial conditions is an exercise in the study of regional adaptation to the environment, whereas the power of the tractor means that it can operate standardised equipment made anywhere in the world, achieving its effect by force rather than by the acquired finesse of the older horse- or hand-operated tools.

The period covered is basically the seventeenth to the nineteenth centuries, when the rhythm of everyday existence was still controlled by the local environment. The integration of life with the habitat has subsequently become progressively less, but during the period reviewed, change was also very marked. It was, however, of an indigenous nature, arising out of local conditions. The adoption of the scythe as the grain cutting tool in the North-East was as much of an innovation in its way as the later adoption of the reaping-machine. Yet because this was an evolutionary rather than a revolutionary process, because it made use of an existing tool, it has been given little prominence in existing histories, even though it led to considerable change in the work-organisation. The importance of such indigenous processes of change can hardly be over-emphasised, for they provide an incisive view of local history at grass-root level, of a kind that can be less ambiguous than that gained from the study of documents alone, even though it is still necessary to learn how to interpret the material. And because of the grass-root level of approach, the patterns that emerge have positive value not only for comparisons between regions, but also for comparisons between different countries. There is no East and West when it comes to questions of man's response to his environment.

Some of the topics dealt with, such as the shieling, may conjure up romantic visions of mountain and glen. This is one of the many attitudes that have come to blur the true course of history, for those from outside the country as much as for the indwellers. If this book has an underlying purpose, it is to seek to look at the actualities of local and national history at particular moments in time, through the eyes and hands and skills of the people of the period.

References

Abbreviations:

Agriculture of . . .	= General View of the Agriculture of . . .
A.P.S.	= Acts of the Parliament of Scotland
D.O.S.T.	= Dictionary of the Older Scottish Tongue
Low	= D. Low *Elements of Practical Agriculture*
N.S.A.	= New (Second) Statistical Account
O.S.A.	= Old (First) Statistical Account
P.S.A.S.	= Proceedings of the Society of Antiquaries of Scotland
S.N.D.	= Scottish National Dictionary
Stephens	= H. Stephens *Book of the Farm*
T.H.A.S.S.	= Transactions of the Highland and Agricultural Society of Scotland

1   The Face of the Land

1. See M. L. Parry *Secular Climatic Change and Marginal Land* (typescript, Institute of British Geographers' Conference, Aberdeen 1972), and *Advance and Retreat of the Settlement Margin in Upland Scotland* (typescript, British Association for the Advancement of Science, Stirling 1974).
2. A. Symson *A Large Description of Galloway* (1692). 1823. 76.
3. A Fenton Seaweed Manure in Scotland, in *In Memoriam António Jorge Dias* 1974. III. 147–86.
4. *Selections from the Records of the Regality of Melrose* (Scottish History Society) 1914. II. 329.
5. J. Taylor *Journey into Edenborough* (1705). 1903. 99.
6. *A.P.S.* V. 420. X. 67b.
7. *O.S.A.* 1793. VI. 338–9.
8. F. F. Mackay *Macneill of Carskey Estate Journal* 1703–4. 1955. 61.
9. *N.S.A.* 1845. II. 335.
10. Cf. P. Gaskell *Morvern Transformed* 1968; A. Mackenzie *History of the Highland Clearances* 1883; J. Prebble *The Highland Clearances* 1963.
11. H. Fairhurst and G. Petrie Scottish Clachans II: Lix and Rosal, in *Scottish Geographical Magazine,* Dec. 1964; H. Fairhurst Rosal: a Deserted Township in Strath Naver, Sutherland, in *P.S.A.S.* 1967–8. Vol. 100. 157–9.

2   Tilling the Soil

12. K. Jessen and H. Helbæk Cereals in Great Britain and Ireland in Prehistoric and Early Historic Times, in *Kongelige Danske Videnskabernes Selskab* (Biologiske Skrifter III) 1949.

13. See G. Lerche The Ploughs of Medieval Denmark, and Pebbles from Wheel ploughs, in *Tools and Tillage* 1970. 1/3. 131–49.

14. S. R. Eyre The Curving Plough-strip and its Historical Implications, in *Agricultural History Review* 1955. III/1. 80–94.

15. H. Marwick Two Orkney 18th Century Inventories, in *Proc. of the Orkney Antiquarian Society* 1934. XII. 48.

16. N. A. Bringéus *Järnplogen som Innovation* 1962. 12 ff.

17. Dr. Singer *Agriculture of Dumfries* 1812. 646.

18. *D.O.S.T.* s.v. Harrow.

19. M. Martin *Description of the Western Islands of Scotland* (1695). 1884. 3.

20. A. T. Lucas Irish Ploughing Practices, in *Tools and Tillage* 1973. II/2, 72 ff.

21. J. Henderson *Agriculture of Caithness* 1812. 70; R. Heron *General View of the Hebrides* 1794, 51; J. Macdonald *Agriculture of the Hebrides* 1811. 181; G. S. Mackenzie *Agriculture of Ross and Cromarty* 1813. 250.

22. A Wight *Present State of Husbandry in Scotland* 1778. Survey I. I. 112.

23. W. Leslie *Agriculture of Nairn and Moray* 1811. 126–7.

24. J. Webster *Agriculture of Galloway* 1794. 15.

25. *T.H.A.S.S.* 1829. VII. 80.

3 *Harvesting the Grain*

26. *An Account of the Present State of Religion throughout the Highlands of Scotland* 1827. 36.

27. Sir J. McNeill *Report to the Board of Supervision on the Western Highlands and Islands* 1851. xii.

28. *A.P.S.* IX. 499. s. 94.

29. A. Murray in *Trans. of the Dumfries and Galloway Natural History and Antiquarian Society* 1965. XLII. 125–9.

30. J. E. Handley *The Irish in Scotland* 1943.

31. *Memoir of George Hope of Fenton Barns.* By his Daughter. 1881. 26–7.

32. *A.P.S.* VI. 25/1.

33. A. Lowe *Agriculture of Berwick* 1794. 45; Mr. Roger *Agriculture of Angus* 1794. 18–19.

34. J. A. S. Watson and M. E. Hobbs *Great Farmers* 1951. 47.

35. This combine harvester is preserved in the National Museum.

36. C. I. Maclean The Last Sheaf, in *Scottish Studies* 1964. Vol. 8/2. 193–207.

37. R. S. Barclay *The Court Book of Orkney and Shetland 1612–1613* 1962. 38.

38. M. A. Scott *Island Saga* 1968. 69.

39. F. Cruickshank *Navar and Lethnot* 1899. 13.

40. J. Slezer *Theatrum Scotiae* 1693.

41. G. Mackenzie *Agriculture of Ross and Cromarty* 1813. 162.

42. A. Fenton Ropes and Rope-making in Scotland, in *Gwerin* 1961. III/3–4. 1–15, 17–31.

4   Threshing the Grain

43. W. Alexander   *Notes and Sketches Illustrative of Northern Rural Life in the Eighteenth Century* 1877. 145.
44. W. Leslie   *Agriculture of Nairn and Moray* 1811. 180–1.
45. Stephens   1844. III. 989.
46. J. L. Buchanan   *Travels in the Western Hebrides* 1793. 155; *N.S.A.* 1845. XIV. 285.
47. J. MacTaggart   *Scottish Gallovidian Encyclopedia* 1824 s.v. Barnman's Jig.
48. See A. Bruce   *Agriculture of Berwick* 1794. 121; G. Buchan-Hepburn   *Agriculture of East Lothian* 1794. 147 ff; R. Kerr   *Agriculture of Berwickshire* 1809. 162; R. Somerville   *Agriculture of East Lothian* 1805. 75–7.
49. J. Bailey and G. Culley   *Agriculture of Northumberland* 1800. 51–61; P. Graham   *Agriculture of Kinross* 1814. 49.
50. N. Cartwright   The Meikle Threshing Mill at Beltondod, in *Trans. of the East Lothian Antiquarian and Natural History Society* 1968. XI. 1–10.
51. G. Robertson   *Agriculture of Kincardine* 1810. 238.
52. S. Smith   *Agriculture of Galloway* 1810. 370–80.
53. B. Quayle   *Agriculture of the Isle of Man* 1794. 22.
54. J. Bartyś   English and Scottish Farmers in Poland in the First Half of the Nineteenth Century, in *Agricultural History Review* 1967. XV/II. 98.
55. G. Berg   Tröskværk i Sverige före Andrew Meikle, in *Daedalus* 1970. 40–60.
56. Cf. E. J. T. Collins   *Sickle to Combine* (Museum of English Rural Life) 1969; The Diffusion of the Threshing Machine in Britain, 1790–1880, in *Tools and Tillage* 1972. II/1. 16–33.
57. D. Ure   *Agriculture of Roxburgh* 1794. 52.
58. Ross of Pitcalnie papers (Scottish Record Office).
59. G. Robertson   *Agriculture of Midlothian* 1793. 45–6.
60. J. Henderson   *Agriculture of Sutherland* 1812. 141, 156, and illustration facing 164.

5   Drying and Grinding the Grain

61. Bishop Leslie in P. H. Brown   *Scotland Before 1700* 1893. 165.
62. J. Robertson   *Tour through the Western Isles* (unpublished Communications to the Society of Antiquaries) 1768. II. folio 34.
63. A. McGregor   Notes on Some old Customs in the Island of Skye, in *P.S.A.S.* 1879–80. XIV. 143–4.
64. J. Boswell   *Journal of a Tour to the Hebrides* (1773). 1936. 138.
65. A. Carmichael   *Carmina Gadelica* 1928. I. 250–3; 1971. VI. 76; J. Landt   *A Description of the Feroe Islands* (c. 1798) 1810. 290; J. C. Svabo   *Indberetninger fra en Reise i Færø* (1781–2) 1959. Fig. X, Fig. XI facing p. 136.
66. For a diagram, see A. Fenton   Lexicography and Historical Interpretation, in G. W. S. Barrow, ed. *The Scottish Tradition* 1974. 248–50.
67. G. Gestsson   Gröf i Öræfum, in *Árbok hins Íslenska Fornleifafélags* 1959. 32–6, 86.
68. J. R. C. Hamilton   *Excavations at Jarlshof, Shetland* 1956.
69. Mr. Roger   *Agriculture of Angus* 1794. 20–21.

70. A. Wight *op. cit.* (1774) 1778. Survey II/I. 163–4.

71. *Session Papers, Petition J. Johnston* (19 Jan. 1781), Proof 15.

72. J. Headrick *Agriculture of Angus* 1813. 266.

73. S. Grieve *Book of Colonsay and Oronsay* 1923. II. 291–2.

74. C. Innes ed. *Black Book of Taymouth* (Bannatyne Club) 1855. 363.

75. G. Buchan-Hepburn *Agriculture of East Lothian* 1794. 145.

76. G. V. Irving and A. Murray *Upper Ward of Lanarkshire* 1864. I. 67.

77. E. C. Curwen Querns in *Antiquity* 1937. 133–51; J. R. C. Hamilton *Excavations at Jarlshof, Shetland* 1956. 71.

78. *O.S.A.* 1794. X. 356.

79. *Scottish Notes and Queries* Feb. 1903. IV. 126–7.

80. E. C. Curwen The Problem of Early Water-mills in *Antiquity* 1944. XVIII. 130–46; A. T. Lucas The Horizontal Mill in Ireland in *Journal of the Royal Society of Antiquaries of Ireland* 1958. LXXXIII. 1–36.

81. M. Martin *op. cit.* 1884. 204–5.

82. J. C. Svabo *op. cit.* 1959. 279.

83. W. Alexander *op. cit.* 220–1.

84. 39 George III, cap. 55.

85. W. Alexander *op. cit.* 147–8.

86. *D.O.S.T.* s.v. Miln.

87. *Accounts of the Lord High Treasurer of Scotland* (1947). I. 328.

88. A. Mitchell ed. *Geographical Collections* (Scottish History Society) 1907. II. 27; *O.S.A.* 1792. III. 127; *Scots Magazine*, May 1969. 88.

89. R. Belsches *Agriculture of Stirling* 1796. 12.

90. A. M. Maclean *Social and Economic Trends in Petty and Croy, from 1790 to 1850* (unpublished article); Sir J. Sinclair *Agriculture of the Northern Counties* 1795. 5.

91. *O.S.A.* 1791. I. 75–6; R. Kerr *Agriculture of Berwick* 1809. 43.

6 *Root Crops*

92. J. Wallace *An Account of the Islands of Orkney* (1693) 1700. 35.

93. *Scottish Notes and Queries* 1894. VII. 42–3.

94. J. Anderson *Agriculture of Aberdeenshire* 1794. 67.

95. D. Souter *Agriculture of Banffshire* 1812. 130–1.

96. J. Macdonald *Agriculture of the Hebrides* 1811. 217.

97. J. H. Smith The Cattle Trade of Aberdeenshire in the Nineteenth Century, in *Agricultural History Review* 1955. III/ii. 114–18; G. Channon The Aberdeenshire Beef Trade and London, 1850–1869, in *Transport History* 1969. Vol. 2. 1–23.

98. W. S. Hewison Holm Farm Diary, 1849–1868, in *Orkney Miscellany* 1954. II. 15–16.

99. J. Donaldson *Husbandry Anatomized* 1697. 117–18.

100. R. Belsches *Agriculture of Stirling* 1794. 31–2.

101. J. Macdonald *op. cit.* 234–5; J. Walker *Economical History of the Hebrides* 1808. I. 251.

102. R. N. Salaman *History and Social Influence of the Potato* 1963. 364; *O.S.A.* 1793. VIII. 4.

103. R. S. Adam *John Howe's Survey of Assynt* (Scottish History Society) 1960. 18.
104. P. Graham *Agriculture of Clackmannan* 1814. 286–7.
105. R. Belsches *op. cit.* 1796. 31–2.
106. G. Buchan-Hepburn *op. cit.* 1794. 79–80.
107. A. Wight *op. cit.* 1784. Survey IX. V/1. 242.
108. J. Thomson *Agriculture of Fife* 1800. 191; J. Webster *Agriculture of Galloway* 1794. 32.
109. J. Henderson *Agriculture of Caithness* 1812. 127.
110. G. E. Fussell *The Farmers Tools* 1952. 187.
111. J. Thomson *op. cit.* 1800. 188–9; D. Ure *Agriculture of Roxburgh* 1794. 32–3.
112. W. S. Hewison *op. cit.* 13–14.

7 The Shieling System

113. J. Knox *A Tour through the Highlands of Scotland* 1787. 93–4.
114. W. Ferguson *Scotland: 1689 to the Present* 1968. 168.
115. J. Walker *op. cit.* 1812. I. 307; W. Mackintosh *An Essay on Ways and Means of Inclosing, Fallowing, Planting, etc., in Scotland* 1729. X.
116. A. Mitchell ed. *Geographical Collections* (Scottish History Society) 1906–8. II. 36.
117. M. Wattie ed., *The Scottish Works of Alexander Ross* (Scottish Text Society) 1938. 82.
118. D. Macdonald *The Historical Geography of North Tolsta* (typescript) 1950. 91 ff.
119. D. Campbell Highland Shielings in the Olden Time, in *Trans. of the Inverness Scientific Society and Field Club* 1895–99. V. 68–70.
120. D. P. Menzies *The 'Red and White' Book of Menzies* 1894. 371; J. Henderson *Agriculture of Caithness* 1812. 146.
121. J. Robertson *Agriculture of Perth* 1799. 337, 340.
122. Captain Burt *Letters from a Gentleman in the North of Scotland* 1754 (1974 reprint) II. 132.
123. Gordon Castle MSS 1767, quoted in *Scottish National Dictionary* s.v. Poind.
124. P. Gaskell *Morvern Transformed* 1968. 14.
125. D. Campbell *op. cit.* V. 74.
126. John of Fordun in P. H. Brown *op. cit.* 1893. 11; Hector Boece in *Ib.* 76.
127. Gibson, E. ed., W. Camden, *Britannia*, 1695. 962.
128. A. Geddes *The Isle of Lewis and Harris* 1955. 239; A. Collier *The Crofting Problem* 1953. 48; *Land Use in the Highlands and Islands.* HMSO. 1964. 16.
129. T. Pennant *A Tour in Scotland* (1776) 1790. I. 216, 246.
130. K. W. Grant Peasant Life in Argyllshire, in *Scottish Historical Review* 1918–19. XVI. 150–1.
131. The substance of this section has been published as Wintertown és Shieling: Megjegyzések a Skóciai Transzhumanszról, in *Tanyák* (A Magyar Néprajzi Társaság 1974. Évi Vándorgyülése Szolnokon) 1974. 199–214.
132. R. J. Adam *op. cit.* 42.
133. R. Heron *General View of the Hebrides* 1794. 14.
134. *T.H.A.S.S.* 1832. 40–2.
135. J. Macdonald *Agriculture of the Hebrides* 1811. 261; R. J. Adam *op. cit.* 37.
136. A. Wight *op. cit.* Survey IX. V/1. 222–4.

137. A. Bruce *Agriculture of Berwick* 1794. 103; G. Buchan-Hepburn *op. cit.* 56.
138. A. Fenton in *Scottish Studies* 1959. Vol. 3/2. 226–8.
139. A. Carmichael *Carmina Gadelica* 1941. IV. 38–9.
140. A. Wight *op. cit.* (1774) 1778. Survey I. I. 169.
141. J. Anderson *Agriculture of Aberdeen* 1794. 116, 118; *Abridged Report of State of Agriculture in Midlothian* 1795. 14; J. Ritchie Whin Mills of Aberdeenshire, in *P.S.A.S.* 1924–5. LIX. 128–42.
142. M. Porteous History of Monivaird and Strowan, in *Archaeologia Scotica* 1882. II. 69; A. T. Lucas *Furze. A Survey and History of its Uses in Ireland* 1906; G. Buchan-Hepburn *op. cit* 1794. 53; *Prize Essays of the Highland Society* 1841. XIII. 226; J. Macdonald Agriculture of Ross-shire in *T.H.A.S.S.* 1877. IX. 110–17.
143. J. Macculloch *Highlands and Western Isles* 1824. III. 89.
144. *Ib.* IV. 420–1.
145. A. Fraser *Tayvallich and North Knapdale* 1962. 44–4.
146. R. Heron *op. cit.* 1794. 67–8; J. Macdonald *op. cit.* 1811.
147. A. Wight *op. cit.* 1784. Survey IX. V/1. 260–1, 301; Survey VIII. V/1. 136–7; J. Macdonald *op. cit.* 1811. 432.

8. *Milk, Butter and Cheese*

148. Sir T. Craig *De Unione Regnorum Britanniae Tractatus* (Scottish History Society) 1909.
149. *Agricultural History Review* 1963. XI/ii. 69.
150. *S.N.D.* s.v. Kane.
151. *A.P.S.* I. 668.
152. W. Leslie *Agriculture of Nairn and Moray* 1811. 309–10.
153. Scottish Record Office, R.H.P. 587/2, R.H.P. 587/1.
154. A. Lowe *op. cit.* 1794. 26.
155. *O.S.A.* 1794. X. 491; A. Martin *Agriculture of Renfrew* 1794. J. Henderson *op. cit.* 1812. 147.
156. T. Johnston *Agriculture of Tweeddale* 1794. 32.
157. *Trans. of the Gaelic Society of Inverness* 1887–8. XIV. 149.
158. *P.S.A.S.* 1881–2. XVII. 204–23; J. Williams Sample of Bog-Butter from Lochar Moss, in *Trans. Dumfries and Galloway Antiquarian Society* 1966. Vol. 43.
159. J. Robertson *MS Tour* 1768. II. Folio 40.
160. I. F. Grant *Highland Folk Ways* 1961. 215.
161. W. Leslie *op. cit.* 1811. 309.
162. *DOST* s.v. Kirn.
163. A. Martin *op. cit.* 1794. 14; *Catalogue of the Great Exhibition* 1851. I. 373.
164. *O.S.A.* 1792. III. 374; T. Pennant *op. cit* 1776. II. 246–7; M. Martin *op. cit* (1695) 1884. 10; M. Mackellar *op. cit.* 1887–8. 139.
165. J. H. Smith *Gordon's Mill Farming Club* 1758–64. 1962. 79–81.
166. D. Ure *Agriculture of Roxburgh* 1794. 65–8.
167. G. Michie and A. Fenton Cheese Presses in Angus, in *Scottish Studies* 1963. Vol. 7/1. 47–56.

168. J. McMaster   Scotch Cheese Making, in *T.H.A.S.S.* 1885. XVII. 214–8; W. Aiton   *Agriculture of Ayr* 1811. II. 457–8; B. Johnston   *Agriculture of Dumfries* 1794. Appx. xxxiii.

169. G. E. Fussell   *op. cit.* 1952. 195.

170. E. Lorrain-Smith   *Go East for a Farm* 1932.

171. M. Martin   *op. cit.* (1695) 1884. 202–3; J. Robertson   *MS Tour.* 1768. II. Folio 36.

172. B. Edmonston and J. M. E. Saxby   *Home of a Naturalist* 1888. 101.

9. Everyday Food

173. C. H. Firth ed.   *Scotland and the Protectorate* (Scottish History Society) 1899. 405–8.

174. *Scottish Journal of Topography* (1818) 1848. II. 28–30.

175. *N.S.A.* 1845. II. 77.

176. J. Thomson   *Agriculture of Fife* 1800. 92–3.

177. *N.S.A.* 1845. XI. 362.

178. *N.S.A.* 1845. III. 148.

179. J. Donaldson   *Agriculture of the Carse of Gowrie* 1794. 24–5.

180. W. N. Boog Watson   The Scotch Fiddle, in *Scottish Studies* 1971. Vol. 15. 141–5.

181. A. Lowe   *Agriculture of Berwick* 1794. 59; J. Donaldson   *Agriculture of the Carse of Gowrie* 1794. 24–5; R. Douglas   *Agriculture in Roxburgh* 1798. 88; J. Headrick   *Agriculture of Angus* 1813. 302.

182. J. Henderson   *Agriculture of Caithness* 1812. 259.

183. *O.S.A.* 1795. XIV. 482.

184. J. Thomson   *Agriculture of Fife* 1800. 177.

185. J. Major   *History of Greater Britain* (Scottish History Society) 1892. 11.

186. J. Thomson   *op. cit.* 177; W. Leslie   *Agriculture of Nairn and Moray* 1811. 172.

187. J. Robertson   *Agriculture of Perth* 1799. 162–3; J. Headrick   *Agriculture of Angus* 1813. 313; J. Thomson   *op. cit.* 1800. 180; W. Leslie   *op. cit.* 1811. 188.

188. J. Major   *op. cit.* 1892. 13–14; H. Boece in P. H. Brown   *op. cit.* 1893. 92; R. James   Description of Shetland, Orkney and the Highlands of Scotland, in *Orkney Miscellany* 1953. I. 49.

189. J. Brand   *Brief Description of Orkney, Zetland, Pightland Firth and Caithness* 1701. 76.

190. A. Wight   *op. cit* 1784. Survey IX. V/1. 238–9, 253.

191. R. Heron   *op. cit* 1794. 40, 42, 50, 53.

192. *Trans. of the Inverness Scientific Club* 1883. II. 312–13.

193. J. Henderson   *Agriculture of Caithness* 1812. 107.

194. J. Robertson   *Agriculture of Perth* 1799. 162–3.

195. R. James   *op. cit.* 1953. 54.

196. J. Firth   *Reminiscences of an Orkney Parish* 1920. 99.

197. F. Douglas   *General Description of the East Coast of Scotland* 1782. 168–70.

198. A. Wight   *op. cit.* 1784. Survey IX. V/1. 287.

199. J. Omond   *Orkney Eighty Years Ago. c.* 1912. 9–10.

200. R. Douglas   *Agriculture of Roxburgh* 1798. 191.

201. R. Monteith   *Description of the Islands of Orkney and Zetland* (1633). 1845. 18.

202. M. Martin *op. cit.* (1695) 1884. 69–70.
203. J. Omond *op. cit.* c. 1912. 10; J. M. E. Saxby *Shetland Traditional Lore.* 1932. 172.
204. *Scots Magazine* April 1820. 343; J. Ramsay *Scotland and Scotsman in the Eighteenth Century* 1888. II. 535; H. Ainslie *A Pilgrimage to the Land of Burns* 1822. 157.
205. R. Heron *op. cit.* 1794. 69.
206. T. Pennant *op. cit.* 1771. 10; J. Robertson *Agriculture of Perth* 1799. 325–6; W. Thom Journal of a Tour in the North of Scotland, in *The Agricultural and Commercial Magazine* April 1811. I. No. 4. 284.
207. J. Headrick *Agriculture of Arran* 1807. 325; J. Macdonald *op. cit.* 1811. 486; J. Henderson *Agriculture of Sutherland* 1812. 109.
208. C. Lowther *Our Journall into Scotland* (1629) 1894. 11.
209. *N.S.A.* 1845. V. 94.
210. R. Hutchison in *T.H.A.S.S.* 1869. II. 18.
211. R. W. Munro *Monro's Western Isles of Scotland* (1549) 1961. 87.
212. J. Macculloch *op. cit.* 1824. IV. 30–1.
213. *N.S.A.* 1845. XIV. 133.
214. J. Brand *op. cit.* 1701–3. 135.
215. J. Shirreff *Agriculture of Orkney* 1814. 148.
216. R. O'Malley *One Horse Farm* 1948. 94.
217. J. Hume *Agriculture of Berwick.* 1797. 124–6; *O.S.A.* 1795. XIV. 589; R. Gibson *An Old Berwickshire Town: History of the Town and Parish of Greenlaw* 1905. 221; *N.S.A.* 1845. XIV. 285, 313.
218. U. Venables *Life in Shetland* 1956. 16–17, 108, 110; H. Mooney Running the Lea, in *The Orcadian* 28. Sept. 1972. 4; J. R. Baldwin Sea Bird Fowling in Scotland and Faroe, in *Folk Life* 1974. Vol. II. 95.
219. H. Mooney *op. cit.* 1972. 4.
220. Macculloch *op. cit.* 1824. II. 195–6.
221. J. R. Baldwin *op. cit.* 60 ff.; the seasonal activities table is based on the diary of George Murray, Schoolmaster in St. Kilda, 11 June 1886–11 June 1887.
222. *D.O.S.T.* s.v. Kale.
223. *S.N.D.* s.v. *Hunder*; *O.S.A.* 1793. VII. 474.
224. J. Henderson *Agriculture of Caithness* 1812. 118–19
225. H. Hamilton *History of the Homeland* 1947. 67, 72, 82–3.
226. P. Minay Early Improvements in the Eighteenth-Century Lothians: the Efforts of the Inter-Related Foulis, Justice, Kinloch and Fletcher Families, in *Bulletin of the Scottish Georgian Society* 1973. Vol. 2. 3–46.

10. Farm and Steading

227. C. Lowther *op. cit.* (1629) 1894. 12.
228. Derham, W. ed. *Select Remains of the Learned John Ray* (1601) 1760. 187–8.
229. G. Robertson *Agriculture of Midlothian* 1783. 31.
230. A. Wight *op. cit.* 1783. Survey VI. III/II. 384, 430; for a study of the Hopetoun Estate, see I. Maxwell *Functional Architecture, Hopetoun Estate, West Lothian* (typescript) 1974. 2 Vols. (copy in Country Life Section of N.M.A.S.).

231. *O.S.A.* 1793. VI. 333.
232. *O.S.A.* 1795. XVI. 74–5.
233. *N.S.A.* 1845. I. 97; *Ib.* I. 551; *N.S.A.* 1845. II. 351–2.
234. Plans and Specifications of Cottages, in *T.H.A.S.S.* 1851. 245–80.
235. *Memoir of George Hope.* By his Daughter. 1881. 231.
236. A. Somerville *Autobiography of a Working Man* 1848; T. Johnston *The History of the Working Classes in Scotland* 1929.
237. Quoted in *Report to the Secretary for Scotland by The Crofters Commission on the Social Conditions of the People of Lewis in 1901, as compared with Twenty Years Ago.* HMSO. 1902. 38.
238. A. Fenton *42 Arnol. A Lewis Blackhouse.* HMSO (forthcoming).

11. Fuel for the Fire

239. A. Fenton A Fuel of Necessity: Animal Manure, in E. Ennen and G. Wiegelmann *Festschrift Matthias Zender* 1972. II. 722–34.
240. D. G. Barron ed., *The Court Book of the Barony of Urie* (Scottish History Society) 1892. 4, 27, 105, 130, 131–3.
241. *O.S.A.* 1793. IX. 332.
242. *O.S.A.* 1792. IV. 32; B. F. Duckham *History of the Scottish Coal Industry* 1970 I. 233.
243. Buchanan *op. cit.* 1793. 161.
244. W. Leslie *Agriculture of Nairn and Moray* 1813. 376–7; E. Beveridge *North Uist* 1911. 324–5.
245. *Third Statistical Account* 1960. 268 (Aberdeenshire).
246. J. Headrick *Agriculture of Angus* 1813. 505, 507; *O.S.A.* 1795. XIV. 485; *Ib.* 1798. XX. 223.
247. *O.S.A.* 1795. XIV. 545.

12. Transport

248. A. Wight. *op. cit.* (1773) 1778. I. 379.
249. Cf. A. C. Haddon *The Study of Man* 1898. 161 ff.
250. Cf. S. Piggott The Earliest Wheeled Vehicles and the Caucasian Evidence, in *Proc. of the Prehistoric Society* 1968. XXXIV.
251. J. Henderson *Agriculture of Caithness* 1812. 64–6; *Scottish Notes and Queries* 1900. II. 95.
252. H. Marwick *Merchant Lairds of Long Ago* 1939. 22.
253. H. Hamilton ed. *Life and Labour on an Aberdeenshire Estate 1735–50* (Third Spalding Club) 1546. 87, 108.
254. A. Wight *op. cit.* (1773) 1778. Survey I. I. 16, 107–8.
255. *N.S.A.* 1845. II. 375.
256. R. Kerr *Agriculture of Berwick* 1809. 172; G. Robertson *Agriculture of Midlothian* 1793. 45; *O.S.A.* 1794. XI. 328, footnote.
257. J. G. Jenkins *The English Farm Wagon* 1961.

258. A. Wight *op. cit.* (1773) 1778. Survey I, I. 57–8.

259. *D.O.S.T.* s.v. Cairt.

260. W. Fullarton *Agriculture of Ayr* 1793. 9; J. Ramsay *op. cit.* 1888. II. 199.

261. *D.O.S.T.* s.v. Coup.

262. B. Jewsiewicki Les types de chars utilisés en Pologne féodale du Xe au XVIIIe siècles, in A. Fenton, J. Podolák, H. Rasmussen *Land Transport in Europe* 1974. 304.

263. A. Dickson *A Treatise of Agriculture* 1770. I. 257.

264. W. Fullarton *Agriculture of Ayr* 1793. 40–1.

265. G. Robertson *Agriculture of Midlothian* 1793. 45; R. Belsches *Agriculture of Stirling* 1796. 40.

266. J. Henderson *Agriculture of Caithness* 1812. 64.

267. J. Martine *Reminiscences and Notices of ten Parishes of the County of Haddington* 1894. 93, 207.

268. Information from Mrs. I. M. Paterson, 1962.

13. The Farming Community

269. J. G. Kyd *Scottish Population Statistics* (Scottish History Society) 1952.

270. T. C. Smout The Landowner and the Planned Village in Scotland, 1730–1830, in N. T. Phillipson and R. Mitchison *Scotland in the Age of Improvement* 1970.

271. Cf. G. Kay The Landscape of Improvement . . . Agricultural Change in North-East Scotland, in *Scottish Geographical Magazine* 1962. Vol. 78. 105–7.

272. *Report on the Present State of the Agriculture of Scotland* (Highland and Agricultural Society) 1878. 160.

273. *O.S.A.* 1792. IV. 347–8; *O.S.A.* 1794. XIII. 163.

274. See G. Donaldson *The Scots Overseas* 1966; M. Gray Scottish Emigration: The Social Impact of Agrarian Change in the Rural Lowlands, 1775–1875, in *Perspectives in American History* 1973. VII. 95–174.

275. A. Fenton The Begbie Account Book 1729–70 in *Trans. of the East Lothian Antiquarian and Natural History Society* 1966. X. 26.

276. G. Littlejohn *Westrigg* 1963. 53.

277. *O.S.A.* 1793. VI. 333.

278. J. Hume *Agriculture of Berwick* 1797, 99–102.

279. *O.S.A.* 1792. IV. 387; *Ib.* 1795. XV. 641; *O.S.A.* 1791. I. 87; *Ib.* 1794. XII. 55.

280. A. Somerville *op. cit.* 1848.

281. T. Kirk *Modern Account of Scotland* 1679, pp. 5–6.

282. In Kirkcaldy Public Library.

283. A. Somerville 1848. *op. cit.*; T. Johnston *op. cit.* 1929. 355.

284. See G. Evans Farm Servants' Unions in Aberdeenshire from 1870–1900, in *Scottish Historical Review* 1952. Vol. 31. 29–40.

285. *Report on the Present State of the Agriculture of Scotland* (Highland and Agricultural Society) 1878. 134–8.

286. J. Hume *Agriculture of Berwick* 1797. 34–5.

287. R. W. Cochrane-Patrick *Mediaeval Scotland* 1892. 26.

288. *Land Use in the Highlands and Islands.* HMSO 1964.

General Bibliography

Note: This list is intended to fill out the background to the various chapters for those who wish to make a deeper study of some aspect of the subject. It also covers the sources on which this book is largely based.

Journals
  Scottish Geographical Magazine.
  Scottish Studies.
  Transactions and Prize Essays of the Highland and Agricultural Society of Scotland.

Standard Books
  County Agricultural Reports (two series for all counties, late eighteenth and early nineteenth century. For a list, see the bibliography in Symon, J. A., *Scottish Farming Past and Present*, 1959).
  First Statistical Account, 1790s.
  Second Statistical Account, 1845.
  Scottish History Society volumes.
  Sinclair, Sir J. *General Report of the Agricultural State . . . of Scotland.* 1814
  Sinclair, Sir J. *Analysis of the Statistical Account.* 1826.
  Stephens, H. *Book of the Farm.* 1844 and subsequent editions.

Bibliography
  Donaldson, G. Sources for Scottish Agrarian History before the Eighteenth Century. In *The Agricultural History Review.* 1960. VIII. 82–90.
  Hall, R. de Zouche, ed., *A Bibliography on Vernacular Architecture.* 1972.
  Hancock, P. *A Bibliography of Books on Scotland 1916–1950.* 1960.
  Mitchell, A. and Cash, C. O. *Scottish Topography* (Scottish History Society). 1917. 2 Vols.

Dictionaries
  Grant, W. and Murison, D. *Scottish National Dictionary.* 1931–   (post-1700 material).
  Craigie, W. and Aitken, J. *Dictionary of the Older Scottish Tongue.* 1937–   (pre-1700 material).

PEOPLE AND INSTITUTIONS
  Handley, J. E. *The Agricultural Revolution in Scotland*, Glasgow 1963. Chapter IV (Sir John Sinclair).
  Memoir of George Hope of Fenton Barns. By his Daughter. Edinburgh 1881.
  Ramsay, A. *History of the Highland and Agricultural Society of Scotland.* Edinburgh and London 1879.
  Watson, J. A. S. and Hobbs, M. E. *Great Farmers.* London 1951.

Cultivation and Land Use: General

Collier, A. *The Crofting Problem.* 1953.
Crofters' Commission Report. 1884.
Darling, F. Fraser. *Crofting Agriculture.* 1945.
Darling, F. Fraser. *West Highland Survey.* 1956.
Department of Agriculture. *Types of Farming in Scotland.* HMSO 1952.
Franklin, T. B. *A History of Scottish Farming.* 1952.
Fussell, G. E. *The Farmers' Tools 1500–1900.* 1952.
Gray, M. *The Highland Economy 1750–1850.* 1957.
Hamilton, H. *The Industrial Revolution in Scotland.* 1932. (especially Chapters I–III)
Hamilton, H. *An Economic History of Scotland in the Eighteenth Century.* 1963. (especially Chapters I–IV)
Handley, J. E. *Scottish Farming in the Eighteenth Century.* 1953.
Handley, J. E. *The Agricultural Revolution in Scotland.* 1963
O'Dell, A. C. and Walton, K. *The Highlands and Islands of Scotland.* 1962.
Salaman, R. N. *The History and Social Influence of the Potato.* Cambridge 1949, reprinted 1970. (especially Chapters XIX–XXI)
Smith, J. H. *The Gordon's Mill Farming Club 1758–1764*, Aberdeen University Studies 145. 1962.
Symon, J. A. *Scottish Farming.* 1959.

Plough and Spade

Fenton, A. Early and Traditional Cultivating Implements in Scotland. In *Proceedings of the Society of Antiquaries of Scotland.* 1962–3. XCVI. 264–317.
Fenton, A. The Chilcarroch Plough. In *Scottish Studies.* 1964. VIII. 80–84.
Fenton, A. Plough and Spade in Dumfries and Galloway. In *Transactions of the Dumfries and Galloway Antiquarian and Natural History Society.* 1969. XLV. 147–183.
Fenton, A. A Plough Type from the Outer Isles of Scotland. In *Tools and Tillage.* 1969. I/2. 117–128.
Fenton, A. Paring and Burning and the Cutting of Turf and Peat in Scotland. In A. Gailey and A. Fenton, ed. *The Spade in Northern and Atlantic Europe.* 1970.
Fenton, A. The Pleugh Sang: a Scottish Source for Medieval Plough History. In *Tools and Tillage.* 1970. I/3. 175–191.
Fenton, A. The Cas-Chrom. A Review of the Scottish Evidence. In *Tools and Tillage.* 1974. II/3. 131–149.
Jirlow, R. and Whitaker, J. The Plough in Scotland. In *Scottish Studies.* 1957. I. 71–94.
Marwick, G. *The old Roman Plough* (i.e. Orkney plough). 1936.
Megaw, B. R. S. Farming and Fishing Scenes on a Caithness Plan. 1772. In *Scottish Studies.* 1962. VI. 218–223.
Payne, F. G. The Plough in Ancient Britain. In *The Archaeological Journal.* 1949. CIV. 82–111.
Whitaker, I. The Harrow in Scotland. In *Scottish Studies.* 1958. II. 149–165.

Teams

Fenton, A. Draught Oxen in Britain. In Jacobeit, W. and Kramařik, J. *Rinderanschirrung* (Národopisný Věstník Československý). 1969. 17–53.

TECHNIQUES

Barrow, G. W. S. Rural Settlement in Central and Eastern Scotland: the Medieval Evidence. In *Scottish Studies*. 1962. Vol. 6/2. 123–144. (also in Barrow, G. W. S. *The Kingdom of the Scots*. 1973. Part III)

Caird, J. B. The Making of the Scottish Rural Landscape. In *Scottish Geographical Magazine*. 1964. Vol. 80. 72–80.

Dodgshon, R. A. The Removal of Runrig in Roxburghshire and Berwickshire 1680–1766. In *Scottish Studies*. 1972. Vol. 16. 121–137.

Dodgshon, R. A. The Nature and Development of Infield-Outfield in Scotland. In *Transactions of the Institute of British Geographers*. July 1973. No. 59. 1–23.

Eyre, S. E. The Curving Plough-strip and its Historical Implications. In *Agricultural History Review*. 1955. III/II. 80–94.

Gray, M. The Abolition of Runrig in the Highlands of Scotland. In *Economic History Review*. 1952. Vol. 5. 46–57.

McCourt, D. The Rundale System in Donegal. Its Distribution and Decline. In *Journal of the Co. Donegal Historical Society*. 1954. 47–60.

Thomson, W. P. L. Funzie, Fetlar: A Shetland Run-rig Township in the Nineteenth Century. In *Scottish Geographical Magazine*. December 1970. 170–185.

Storrie, M. C. Landholding and Settlement Evolution in West Highland Scotland. In *Geografiska Annaler*. 1965. Vol. 47. 138–161.

Uhlig, H. Old Hamlets with Infield and Outfield Systems in Western and Central Europe. In *Geografiska Annaler*. 1961. XLIII. 285–312.

BEGINNINGS OF IMPROVEMENT

Belhaven, Lord (ABC). *The Country Man's Rudiments:* or *An Advice to the Farmers in East Lothian*. 1699.

Cochran-Patrick, R. W. *Medieval Scotland*. 1899.

Donaldson, J. *Husbandry Anatomized*. 1697.

Fenton, A. Skene of Hallyard's Manuscript of Husbandrie. In *Agricultural History Review*. 1963. XI/11. 65–81.

Fenton, A. The Rural Economy of East Lothian in the 17th and 18th Century. In *Trans. East Lothian Antiquarian and Field Naturalists' Society*. 1963. IX. 1–23.

Fenton, A. Scottish Agriculture and the Union: an example of indigenous development. In Rae, T. I., ed. *The Union of 1707*. 1974.

Napier, A. The New Order of Gooding and Manuring of all Sorts of Field Land with Common Salt. In *Archaeologia Scotica*. 1822. II. 154–158.

Sanderson, M. H. B. The Feuars of Kirklands. In *Scottish Historical Review*. 1973. LII/2. No. 154. 117–136.

Smout, T. C. and Fenton, A. Scottish Agriculture before the Improvers – an Exploration. In *Agricultural History Review*. 1965. XIII/II. 73–93.

GRAIN CROPS AND PROCESSING
CUTTING

Bell, P. Some Account of 'Bell's Reaping-Machine'. In *The Journal of Agriculture*. 1855. 185–204.

Farquharson, J. On Cutting Grain Crops with the Common Scythe as practised in Aberdeenshire. In *Trans. of the Highland and Agricultural Society of Scotland.* 1835. X.

Fenton, A. Sickle Scythe and Reaping Machine. Innovation Patterns in Scotland. In *Ethnologia Europaea.* 1973/4. VII/I. 35–47.

Handley, J. E. *The Irish in Modern Scotland.* 1947. (Chapter VI. The Irish Harvesters)

Stephens, H. On the Flemish Scythe. In *Trans. of the Highland and Agricultural Society of Scotland.* 1829. VII. 244–249.

MILLS AND KILNS

Bennet, R. and Elton, J. *A History of Corn Milling.* 1898. (2 Vols.).

Clouston, J. S. The Old Orkney Mills. In *Proc. of the Orkney Antiquarian Society.* 1924–5. III. 49–54, 65–72.

Cruden, S. *Click Mill, Dounby.* HMSO 1949.

Curwen, E. C. The Problem of Early Water-mills. In *Antiquity.* 1944. XVIII. 130–146.

Donnachie, I. L. and Stewart, N. K. Scottish Windmills – An Outline and Inventory. In *Proc. Society of Antiquaries of Scotland.* 1967. XCVIII. 176–299.

Fairbairn, W. *Treatise on Mills and Millwork.* 1864. 2 Vols.

Fenton, A. Lexicography and Historical Interpretation (mainly on kilns). In Barrow, G. *The Scottish Tradition.* 1974.

Gailey, A. Irish Corn-Drying Kilns. In *Ulster Folklife.* 1970. 15/16.

Goudie, G. On the Horizontal Water-mills of Shetland. In *Proc. Society of Antiquaries of Scotland.* 1886. XX. 257–297.

Gray, A. *The Experienced Millwright.* 1806.

Gregor, W. Kilns Mills Millers Meal and Bread. In *Trans. of the Buchan Field Club.* 1892–5. III. 125–159.

Lucas, A. T. The Horizontal Mill in Ireland. In *Journal of the Royal Society of Antiquaries of Ireland.* 1953. LXXXIII. 1–36.

McCutcheon, W. A. The Corn Mill in Ulster. In *Ulster Folk Life.* 1970. 15/16. 72–98.

Macdonald, S. The Progress of the Early Threshing Machine. In *Agricultural History Review.* 1975. Vol. 23/1. 63–77.

Marshall, J. N. Old Kiln at Kilwhinleck. In *Trans. of the Buteshire Natural History Society.* 1935. XI. 84–87.

Maxwell, S. A Horizontal Water Mill Paddle from Dalswinton. In *Trans. of the Dumfries and Galloway Natural History and Antiquarian Society.* 1956. XXXIII. 185–196.

Maxwell, W. J. Old Corn Kilns at Barclosh. In *Trans. of the Dumfries and Galloway Antiquarian Society.* 1887–90. No. 6. 58–59.

Milligan, I. D. Corn Kilns in Bute. In *Trans. of the Buteshire Natural History Society.* 1963. XV. 53–59.

Tindall, F. P. *East Lothian Water Mills.* 1970.

Whitaker, I. Two Hebridean Corn-Kilns. In *Gwerin.* 1957. I/4. 161–170.

Williamson, K. Horizontal Water-mills of the Faeroe Islands. In *Antiquity.* 1946. XX. 83–91.

SHIELINGS

Adam, R. J. *John Home's Survey of Assynt* (Scottish History Society. 1960).

Campbell, D. Highland Shielings in the Olden Time, In *Trans. of the Inverness Scientific Society and Field Club*. 1895–99. V.

Carmichael, A. Grazing and Agrestic Customs of the Outer Hebrides. In *Report of H.M. Commissioners of Enquiry into the Condition of the Crofts and Cottars in the Highlands and Islands of Scotland*. 1884. 451–482.

Gaffney, V. Summer Shielings. In *Scottish Historical Review*. 1959. XXXVIII. 20–35.

Gaffney, V. *The Lordship of Strathaven* (Third Spalding Club). 1960.

Haldane, A. R. B. *The Drove Roads of Scotland*. 1952.

Henderson, R. A Deal in Cattle 200 Years Ago, and Reid, R. C. Some Letters of Thomas Bell, Drover. 1746. In *Trans. Dumfries and Galloway Natural History and Antiquarian Society*. 1942. XXII. 172–181.

Mackellar, Mrs. M. The Sheiling: Its Traditions and Songs. In *Trans. of the Gaelic Society of Inverness*. 1887–8. XIV.

MacSween, M. Transhumance in North Skye. In *Scottish Geographical Magazine*. 1959. Vol. 75. 75–88.

MacSween, M. and Gailey, A. Some Shielings in North Skye. In *Scottish Studies*. 1961. Vol. 5. 77–84.

Miller, R. Land Use by Summer Shielings. In *Scottish Studies*. 1967. Vol. 11. 193–221.

Ramm, H. G., McDowall, R. W., and Mercer, E. *Shielings and Bastles* (R.C.A.H.M. (Eng.)). 1970.

Stewart, A. *A Highland Parish or the History of Fortingall*. Glasgow 1928. Ch. XII.

Thomas, F. W. L. Notice of Beehive Houses in Harris and Lewis. In *Proc. Society of Antiquaries of Scotland*. 1857–60. III. 127–144.

Thomas, F. W. L. On the Primitive Dwellings and Hypogea of the Outer Hebrides. In *Ib*. 1866–8. VII. 153–195.

Whitaker, I. Some Traditional Techniques in Modern Scottish Farming. In *Scottish Studies*. 1959. Vol. 3.

FOOD

Barker, T. C., McKenzie, J. C., and Yudkin, J. *Our Changing Fare*. London 1966.

Burnett, J. *Plenty and Want. A Social History of Diet in England from 1815 to the Present Day*. 1968.

Cheke, V. *The Story of Cheese-making in Britain*. 1959.

Drummond, J. C. and Wilbraham, A. *The Englishman's Food*. 1957.

Farm Labourer's Food. *The Scottish Farmer and Horticulturist*. 21 Sept. 1864. 142.

Fenton, A. Hafer- und Gerstenmehl als Hauptgegenstand der schottischen Nahrungsforschung. In *Ethnologia Scandinavica*. 1971. 149–157.

Fenton, A. The Place of Oatmeal in the Diet of Farm Servants in the Eighteenth and Nineteenth Centuries, in Szabadfálvy and Ujváry, ed. *Studia Ethnographica et Folkloristica in Honorem Béla Gunda*. Debrecen 1971.

Fenton, A. Craig-Fishing in the Northern Isles of Scotland. In *Scottish Studies*. 1973. Vol. 17. 71–80.

Fenton, A. Pork in the Rural Diet of Scotland. In Escher, W., Gantner, T., and Trumpy, H., ed. *Festschrift für Robert Wildhaber*. 1973.

Fenton, A. Sowens. In *Folk Life*. 1974. Vol. 12. 41—47.

Ferguson, T. *The Dawn of Scottish Social Welfare*. 1948. Ch. II.

Ferguson, T. *Scottish Social Welfare 1864–1914*. 1959. Ch. V.

Grant, I. F. *Highland Folk Ways*. 1961. Ch. XIV.

Hamilton, H. *History of the Homeland*. 1947. Ch. III.

Hartley. D. *Food in England*. 1954.

Hutchison, R. Report on the Dietaries of Scotch Rural Labourers. In *Trans. of the Highland and Agricultural Society of Scotland*. 1869. II (Sec. 4).

Keith, Rev. Dr. S. On the Comparative Quantities and Values of the Different Kinds of Food used among the Common People in Scotland. In Sinclair, Sir J. *Appendix to the General Report of the Agricultural State . . . of Scotland*. 1914. II. 435–438.

Lochhead, M. *The Scots Household in the Eighteenth Century*. 1948.

Lucas, A. T. Irish Food before the Potato. In *Gwerin*. 1960. III. 8–43.

Lythe, S. G. E. *The Economy of Scotland in its European Setting 1550–1625*. 1960. Ch. I.

Plant, M. *The Domestic Life of Scotland*. 1952. Ch. V.

Sayce, R. U. Food in the Highland Zone of Britain in the Eighteenth Century. In *Folk-Liv*. 1948–9. XII–XIII. 199–207.

BUILDINGS

Clouston, J. S. R. Old Orkney Houses. In *Proc. Orkney Antiquarian Society*. 1922–3. I. 11–19; 1923–4. II. 7–14.

Crawford, I. A. Contributions to a History of Domestic Settlement in North Uist. In *Scottish Studies*. 1965. Vol. 9. 34–63.

Curwen, E. C. The Hebrides: A Cultural Backwater. In *Antiquity*. 1939. XII. 261–289.

Dunbar, J. G. Some Cruck-framed Buildings in the Aberfeldy District of Perthshire. In *Proc. Society of Antiquaries of Scotland*. 1956–7. XC. 81–92.

Dunbar, J. G. Auchindrain: A Mid-Argyll Township. In *Folk Life*. 1965. Vol. 3. 61–67.

Fairhurst, H. Scottish Clachans. In *Scottish Geographical Magazine*. 1960. Vol. 76. 67–76.

Fairhurst, H. and Dunbar, J. G. The Study of Deserted Medieval Settlements in Scotland. In Beresford, M. and Hurst, J. G., *Deserted Medieval Villages*. 1971. 229–244.

Fenton, A. Das Bauernhaus auf Orkney und Shetland. In *Deutsches Jahrbuch für Volkskunde*. 1967. 13/1. 50–68.

Fenton. A. Alternating Turf and Stone – An Obsolete Building Practice. In *Folk Life*. 1968. Vol. 6. 94–103.

Fenton, A. Clay Building and Clay Thatch in Scotland. In *Ulster Folklife*. 1970. 28–51.

Gailey, A. The Peasant Houses of the South-West Highlands of Scotland: Distribution, Parallels and Evolution. In *Gwerin*. 1962. III. 1–16.

Hay, G. The Cruck-Building at Corrimony. In *Scottish Studies*. 1973. Vol. 17. 127–133.

Matthew, R. H. and Nuttgens, P. J. Two Scottish Villages: A Planning Study. In *Scottish Studies*. 1959. Vol. 3. 113–142 (Ormiston, Ratho).

Maxwell, I. *Functional Architecture. Hopetoun Estate*. 1974 (typescript, 2 vols., copy in Scottish Country Life Section of the National Museum).

Roussell, A. *Norse Building Customs in the Scottish Isles*. 1934.

Sinclair, C. *Thatched Houses of the Old Highlands*. 1953.

Stell, G. Two Cruck-framed Buildings in Dumfriesshire. In *Trans. Dumfries and Galloway Antiquarian Society*. 1972. XLIX. 39–48.

Walton, J. Cruck-Framed Buildings in Scotland. In *Gwerin*. 1957. I. 109–122.

Whittington, G. The Imprint of Former Occupations and the Improver Movement on House Types in Fife. In *Folk Life*. 1967. Vol. 5. 52–57.

TRANSPORT

Fenton, A. Transport with Pack-Horse and Slide-Car in Scotland. In Fenton, A., Podolák, J., and Rasmussen, H., *Land Transport in Europe*. 1974. 121–171.

Fox, Sir C. Sledges. Carts and Waggons. In *Antiquity*. 1931. V. 185–199.

Jenkins, J. G. Two-Wheeled Carts. In *Gwerin*. 1959. II. 112–175.

Herring, I. The Scottish Cart in Ireland and its Contemporaries, *circa* 1800. In *Ulster Journal of Archaeology*. 1964. VII. 42–46.

Simpson, E. J. Farm Carts and Waggons of the Orkney Islands. In *Scottish Studies*. 1963. Vol. 7/2. 154–169.

Thompson, G. B. *Primitive Land Transport of Ulster*. Belfast Museum. 1958.

The Farming Community

Alexander, W. *Johnny Gibb of Gushetneuk*. 1871 (a study of the functioning of a North-East farming community).

Carter, I. *Illegitimacy Rates and Farm Service in North-East Scotland* (typescript, British Association 1974).

Carter, I. *Class and Culture among Farm Servants in the North-East of Scotland 1840–1914* (typescript, 1974).

Duncan, J. F. *Agriculture and The Community*. 1921.

Franklin, S. H. *The European Peasantry*. 1969.

Gully, W. S. *The Peasantry of the Border* (1842). 1973.

Gray, M. Scottish Emigration: The Social Impact of Agrarian Change in the Rural Lowlands, 1775–1875. In *Perspectives in American History*. 1973. VII. 95–174.

Kyd, J. G. *Scotland's Population Statistics*. 1952.

MacDonald, D. F. *Scotland's Shifting Population*. 1957.

Robertson, B. W. The Border Farm Worker 1871–1971: Industrial Attitudes and Behaviour. In *Journal of Agricultural Labour Science*. 1973. Vol. 2/2. 65–93.

Saunders, L. J. *Scottish Democracy, 1815–1840*. 1950.

Smith, J. H. *Joe Duncan. The Scottish Farm Servants and British Agriculture*. 1973.

Somerville, A. *Autobiography of a Working Man*. 1848.

Index